中國古典家具與生活環境

世襄題

ACKNOWLEDGEMENTS

Sincere thanks go to the many individuals who have assisted in the preparation and realisation of this book, and also to those who have generously shared their knowledge and expertise. Special thanks for the kind support of Dr. Kenson Kwok, Director, and the staff of the Asian Civilisations Museum, Singapore, for looking after and exhibiting the Kai-Yin Lo Collection of classical Chinese furniture. Immense thanks go to the authors of this book for their learned and illuminating essays. Particular thanks to Catherine Maudsley for editing the book and compiling the index, and Jack Lee for proof-reading the Chinese text. Also thanks to Yimmy Law and Josephine Li for their support.

鳴 謝

謹向所有協助籌備和出版這本書，及以其所知所專慷慨賜教的人士致以誠摯謝意，尤其感激新加坡亞洲文明博物館館長郭勤遜博士及其工作人員，安排展出和照顧羅啟妍中國古典家具藏品。並向撰寫鴻文的各位學者和專家、協助編輯工作和編纂索引的毛岱康女士、校訂中文內容的李世莊先生，以及羅文艷蘭女士、李琳小姐衷心銘謝。

Associate editor : Catherine Maudsley
Translation : Brenda Li, Art Text, Lijun Chadima, Donald Brix
Co-ordinator of Chinese Text : Jack Lee
Photography : C. C. Liu, Michel Porro
Design : Rosanne Chan
Production : CA Design, Hong Kong

副編輯：毛岱康
翻譯：李惠玲、藝文出版公司、林莉君、蒲思棠
中文校訂：李世莊
攝影：廖祖昌、Michel Porro
設計：陳麗香
製作：雅緻設計印刷有限公司

ISBN 1-878529-44-7

中國古典家具與生活環境
CLASSICAL AND VERNACULAR CHINESE FURNITURE IN THE LIVING ENVIRONMENT

羅啟妍收藏精選

Examples from the Kai-Yin Lo Collection

羅啟妍收藏精選

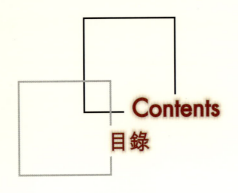

Contents
目錄

Message
Wang Shixiang

As early as the Southern Song dynasty, Chinese furniture was known as *jiasheng* and *dongshi* (see *Dongjing menghua lu* and *Mengliang lu*). *Jiasheng* means household implements, and is a term still used in the Wu dialect. *Dongshi* refers to "movable objects" in contrast to those that are "fixed" such as houses, main halls, and gardens. Although of differing sizes and ease of portability, these "movable objects" are all used to meet the needs of daily living. In addition, their design, structure, arrangement and usage represent the temperament and predilections of the owner. The term "living environment" is actually a framework encompassing furniture, architecture and gardens, long recognised to be inter-related and indivisible. Previously, studies have only focused on these aspects in isolation and have not examined the subject as an organic whole.

Now, in this book Kai-Yin Lo has assembled a series of essays focusing on these subjects in a concerted attempt to probe and examine their links and pattern to arrive at a new level of awareness of the living environment. Such pioneering work is indeed a significant feat in concept and a worthwhile contribution to scholarship. I am pleased to have been asked to write this short preface, and welcome your valuable opinions on my brief and tentative comments.

Spring, 1998, Beijing

而成相互關連密不可分早為世人所共識惟
歷來著述每言家具言建築言庭園獨少
合而論之者頃啟妍女士徵集有關家具建
築生活環境之作襄輯成集旨在開拓綜
合研究探索輔成規律藉收美化生活之效
誠藝林之創舉學苑之新猷可喜之至屬撰
小序爰抒鄙見如右博雅君子幸有以教我
戊寅新春暢安王世襄撰並書

小序

家具在南宋時已有家生動使之稱，見東京夢華錄夢梁錄。

家生者家中生活用具之謂，吳語沿用至今。

動使者可移動使用之謂，有別於固定不動，

之居室軒堂庭園，其間雖有大小之殊，動

定之異，為人使用則一，且其設計修造布置，

經營又無不見使用者之意志情趣，今日所

謂之生活環境，實由家具建築庭園組合

Foreword
前言
Kenson Kwok
郭 勤 遜

There has been tremendous interest in collecting Chinese furniture in recent years, and museums in Asia as well as the West have responded with permanent displays and temporary exhibitions on the subject.

When it became clear that a group of Chinese furniture of the best vintage from the collection formed by Kai-Yin Lo could be available for loan to the Asian Civilisations Museum, we jumped at the opportunity. A number of generous loans has enabled us to devote an entire gallery in the Chinese wing of our museum to Chinese furniture.

Furniture more than any other category of museum exhibit – with the possible exception of costume – gives a direct and tangible insight into how people lived. It is a basic prop and accessory of daily life. Moreover, and in common with other societies that have a strong furniture tradition, the Chinese also expressed status and rank through the placement and design of furniture.

In alliance with its utility, the sheer beauty of Chinese furniture is another reason for our giving it such prominence in our museum. The design of Chinese furniture ranges from the startlingly minimalist through to the elegantly ornate. The woods used in its construction are carefully chosen, particularly when the piece of furniture is intended to be unlacquered. Over time and with use, the colour, wear and patination of a well-preserved piece of Chinese furniture further increase its aesthetic appeal.

近年收藏中國家具蔚然成風，亞洲和西方的博物館紛紛以此題材，舉辦永久或定期的展覽。

亞洲文明博物館在獲悉羅啟妍女士願意借出她私人珍藏的中國家具展出時，為此雀躍不已。而誠蒙數位藏家慷慨借出藏品，本館中華文物部足以專廳展出這些珍貴的中國家具。

家具是日常生活的必需品和陳設。在博物館眾多類型的藏品中，除了服飾或堪比擬外，家具是最能直接窺探前人的生活。跟其他家具文化有高度發展的社會一樣，中國人也習慣透過家具的設計和擺設來顯示其身份和地位。

中國家具除了實用外，我們更重視它優美的製作：設計簡鍊的典雅脫俗，精雕細琢的富麗堂皇，可謂各有美態；使用的木料全經嚴格挑選，不髹漆的家具在選材方面尤為講究。假若保養得宜，縱使經歷多個世紀的使用，留在家具上的色彩和磨損痕跡反而增添它的韻味。

Furniture Gallery, Asian Civilisations Museum, Singapore
新加坡亞洲文明博物館家具館

Every piece in Kai-Yin Lo's collection has been selected with care. Her well-known sense of proportion and design, and interest in line and form, have been called into play. Scholarly concerns have also determined her choice, and some pieces are unique or of extreme rarity.

The stars of the collection are undoubtedly the classic Ming-style pieces in *huanghuali* and other desirable hardwoods. Exotic hardwoods such as *huanghuali* and *zitan* have always been expensive in China, and furniture made out of these woods was destined for wealthy households. Furniture in the less exalted softwoods made for the less affluent also finds a place in the collection. The fact that some of the latter have a distinct regional flavour further broadens the interest and scope of the collection. An in-depth examination of these various categories of furniture and their role in the household is addressed by the essays in this book.

The added value of the Kai-Yin Lo Collection is therefore the way in which it is contributing towards research. As the collection is still growing and developing, it should continue to be the source of new insights and discoveries. The loan of a part of the collection to the Asian Civilisations Museum has allowed us a privileged role in this exciting process.

November 20, 1997, Singapore

羅啟妍女士所藏家具每一件都是經過精挑細選，充份表現她在設計上敏銳的觸覺，對線條、造型、比例的興趣。此外，在挑選藏品時，她亦著眼其學術上的意義；而她部份的藏品不但極為罕見，有些更是獨一無二。

羅氏藏品中最觸目的是以黃花梨和其他優質硬木製成的明式家具。黃花梨和紫檀都是非常貴重的硬木，享用這些家具的家庭非富則貴。藏品中亦有些較大眾化的軟木家具，縱非富戶人家亦可負擔得來，其中部份帶有鮮明的地方色彩，更添藏品的趣味和意義。本目錄附數篇文章，專比較和深入研究這些不同種類的家具藏品及其在家居的角色，以加深我們對這題材的認識。

羅氏藏品的另一可貴處是在學術研究方面的貢獻。羅啟妍女士的藏品現正不斷建立，在未來日子裡定能為我們帶來更多的啟迪和發現。亞洲文明博物館有幸展出羅女士部份藏品，實在是得沾其惠。

1997年11月20日於新加坡

A corner in the Furniture Gallery, Asian Civilisations Museum, Singapore
新加坡亞洲文明博物館家具館一角

Foreword
前言
Tian Jiaqing
田 家 青

Kai-Yin Lo is an internationally recognised jewellery designer but she is less well-known as a collector of classical and vernacular Chinese furniture. It is not surprising that she brings the same consummate taste and developed aesthetic judgement to designing jewellery as she does to collecting Ming and Qing furniture. Although her collection of furniture is not very large, it amply reflects her commitment to acquire pieces of exceptional quality and superior craftsmanship. More unusual than her taste in furniture, though, is her in-depth understanding of the works in her collection. In her quest to understand the furniture's historical and social context, she brings a refreshing point of view to the collecting and study of classical Chinese furniture.

The most successful pieces of Ming and Qing furniture represent the combination of the artist-craftsman's sensitive vision with extraordinary inspiration, traits which are not always apparent to the untrained eye. As a designer and collector, however, Kai-Yin Lo possesses the ability to appreciate such subtleties. Thus, in the following paragraphs, I would like to discuss what I consider the three most exceptional pieces in her collection, not only as outstanding examples of furniture, but also as reflections of connoisseurship.

FOLDING *HUANGHUALI* LOW TABLE WITH WAIST PANELS AND CABRIOLE LEGS

The craftsmanship of this *kang* table (Plate 18) is exceptionally refined. The long table top is composed of two square pieces joined together by metal hinges which facilitate the folding of the table. The construction of these hinges is itself quite sophisticated and reflects considerable foresight on the part of the craftsman. The frame members and table top are secured through the use of battens underneath connected by tenon-and-mitre joints, strengthening the table while stabilising it. The apron and grooved waist form a single piece, while the cabriole legs with hoof feet move on wooden hinges secured by metal pegs. When folding the legs under the table, they were originally anchored in place by chains. Thus, from the viewpoint of artistic

羅啟妍女士是世界著名的珠寶設計師,她的明清家具收藏與鑒賞就像她在珠寶設計方面獨樹一幟,有其獨到之處。憑藉處積多年對藝術的理解和感受,羅女士站在較高的層次去審視、把握和評價所見到的一切。她收藏的明清家具數量雖不很多,卻體現了較高的藝術品味和少而精的收藏原則。更可貴的是,羅女士對每件藏品有獨特見解,反映出一種與眾不同的鑒賞角度。明清家具件件富有個性。成功藝術收藏家要具備敏銳的洞察力、超凡的開拓精神。羅女士的家具收藏個性鮮明,從中可以體味到她珠寶設計的創意、神韻和精粹。在此謹就印象最深的三件藏品談談觀感,以期與讀者共賞。

黃花梨三彎腿有束腰折疊式炕桌

此炕桌(圖版18)形制極為精巧。長方形桌面由兩塊攢邊打槽的四方形面板組成,兩塊面板之間以金屬合頁連接,便於折疊。合頁結構奇巧、製作考究。桌面下的兩根穿帶與大邊之間採用透榫結構,增加了桌面強度。牙子與束腰一木連作,腿足在牙子下斷開分成兩段,亦由金屬件連接,接疊時借以將腿足平臥進桌面下。無論從藝術的素質,還是設計、結構方面看,這是一件匠心獨運,不可多得的家具精品。

quality, design, and construction, this table stands out as an exceptional piece of craftsmanship rarely found.

In the past few years, through the increasing efforts of collectors and scholars, we have come to learn that a large proportion of the classical Chinese furniture that survives today is composed of pieces that are either collapsible, foldable, or portable in some way. Some people have even argued that among the types of Ming furniture, one category should be created for these numerous "portable" works. The importance of this type of furniture is evident from the large variety made, including folding chairs, tables, and large platforms. Recently, even large collapsible couch-beds have been discovered. Further examination of such pieces reveals that they can be roughly divided in terms of those that fold in half and those that do not. Although the main purpose in creating folding furniture is to reduce the size and area of the piece in order to save space and make movement more convenient, the actual construction requires exceptional foresight and study on the part of the craftsman. Form and function are thus both important considerations in the design and production. The *kang* table in the Kai-Yin Lo collection is a superlative example of this type of ingenuity and design.

This table is similar in terms of shape and construction to a six-legged *ta* daybed made of *huanghuali* wood in the Beijing Palace Museum which was discovered years ago by the famed furniture scholar, Wang Shixiang, who urged the museum to acquire the piece from a private collection. When the legs are secured underneath the table top with a fastener, the *ta* daybed folds evenly in half, and when the fastener is removed from the joint, the legs fold into the recess under the table top. Judging from these similarities, I believe that their date of production must have been at approximately the same time – that is, from the late sixteenth to the early seventeenth century.

Of all the folding and collapsible types of furniture that survive today, this *kang* table in the collection of Kai-Yin Lo is probably one of the most refined in design, material, and construction. The exceptional state of preservation makes it even more valuable to scholars and connoisseurs alike.

近年來，隨著研究和收藏的深入，我們發現在傳統中國家具中，可以拆裝、折疊、便於旅行攜帶的家具佔有相當比重。故此有人認為在對明式家具分類時，應再分出"可攜帶"家具一類。在已發現的可拆裝、折疊的家具中，不僅有椅凳、桌案，甚至有床榻。最近還見到了可以拆裝、折疊的大架子床。從形式上看，這類家具可分為對半折疊和非對半折疊兩類。對半折疊的家具折疊之後，體積縮小不少，但結構較為複雜。羅女士所藏炕桌即屬於這種類型。

此件家具在形式、結構上，與北京故宮博物院的一件黃花梨六足榻近似。該榻是早年經王世襄先生發現，建議故宮從民間收入的。榻的大邊也是可以居中對折，腿足以穿釘固定，拔出穿釘，可將腿足臥進榻內。兩件家具的製作年代大致相同，約造於十六世紀末至十七世紀初。

在為數眾多的各式可折疊家具中，羅女士珍藏的這件炕桌無論在造型、用料還是結構的機巧上都相當精彩，而且保存完好，頗具研究價值。

HUANGHUALI DAYBED WITH *LINGZHI* MOTIFS AND CABRIOLE LEGS

This masterpiece of a daybed (Plate 2) was originally in the collection of the Museum of Classical Chinese Furniture in Renaissance, California. Judging from the few examples of daybeds that have survived to this day, they appear to have been made less frequently than couch-beds during the Ming and Qing dynasties. Scholars valued this type of furniture for its classical style, but its design was probably considered too old-fashioned to have been widely popular. Of all the Ming and Qing daybeds that I have seen over my career, only three of them have left an impression on me. The first is a large daybed in a private American collection. It is marked by its archaic design and use of large pieces of wood. The second is a foldable *huanghuali* daybed with waist panels and six legs. This piece, illustrated in this author's *Classic Chinese Furniture of the Qing Dynasty* (no. 94), is unusual for its ability to fold even though large pieces of timber are used. And, finally, the third one is this piece in the Kai-Yin Lo Collection. Its design is perfectly worked out as the outlines are both flowing and elegant. Lively *lingzhi* are carved at the middle of the aprons (as well as near the corners), adding a simple yet refined touch.

At this point, I would like to pause briefly to answer a question that is often posed to me by friends – How exactly does one distinguish between a daybed and a couch-bed? At present, the most common way of dividing these two types of beds is based on form – the couch-bed has railings along three of its sides while the daybed does not. However, in the Ming dynasty, we read Wen Zhenheng's description of the daybed in his *Zhangwu zhi* [Treatise of Superfluous Things] as having "low support railings on three sides. One in the back and on both sides, this has become the set form of the daybed." With these two apparently conflicting views, how are we to say which one is right? To make matters even more complicated, in many places in China, the term *luohan ta* (monk's bed) is still used for furniture. So exactly how is this matter to be solved?

Actually, I believe the problem here centres on the classification of the daybed and couch-bed, rather than on the objects themselves. Nowadays, we quite commonly group these beds

黃花梨三彎腿有束腰靈芝紋榻

此榻（圖版2）原為美國加州中國古典家具博物館（Museum of Classical Chinese Furniture, Renaissance, California）所藏的珍貴家具之一。傳世實物証明，明清時期的榻少於羅漢床。其原因可能是榻的形式過於古老，只有少數不受時尚變遷之影響，懷古緬舊的文人使用。在我所見到的明清時期的榻中，有三件印象較深。一件是四面平式大榻（美國私人收藏），特點是造型古拙、用料厚重。第二件是黃花梨有束腰六足折疊榻（見《清代家具》第94件），它的特點是體態碩大雄壯且可折疊。第三件就是此榻，造型完美，線條自然流暢，在壺門的轉角處和分心處雕有靈芝紋，別緻而富有個性。

話說至此，想解釋一個朋友提到的相關問題—到底怎樣區分榻和羅漢床？當今其中一種流行的區分方法是羅漢床有圍子，榻則沒有圍子。而明代文震亨在《長物志》中對榻的描述則是："三面靠背，後背與兩旁等，此榻之定式也。"這兩種截然相反的說法，到底誰對誰錯？不少地區還有"羅漢榻"一稱，又如何解釋呢？這裡問題的著眼點是在於對床和榻的分類。當今我們熟悉的將羅漢床和榻同歸於床榻類，形制上以

together under the category of platform beds (*chuang ta*). However, the definition of a *chuang* couch-bed as having railings (while the *ta* daybed does not) originates from descriptions in the Ming dynasty carpenter's manual, *Lu Ban jing*. This over-simplified distinction between the two was adopted and perpetuated by twentieth century scholars and collectors of Ming and Qing furniture. I believe, moreover, these two types can be more accurately distinguished on the basis of function and context.

In antiquity, the *chuang* couch-bed was used as a piece of furniture on which to recline, as distinct from the *ta* daybed, which was used for sitting. Furthermore, in even earlier periods, we know that the *ta* daybed did not have railings and was both smaller and shorter than a *chuang* couch-bed. It was only over the centuries that the *ta* daybed was gradually raised, widened, and lengthened, approaching the dimensions of, and eventually becoming, the daybed that we know from the Ming and Qing dynasties. Yet despite the similarity in shape between these two types, the definition of a daybed and couch-bed is still more-or-less established on the basis of their function. For instance, a *chuang* bed with railings, when placed in the context of a bedroom, would naturally be used for reclining, and thus be known as a *chuang* couch-bed. However, put the same *chuang* bed in a studio, for example, and it becomes a *ta* daybed. In ancient times, the *ta* daybed was an important piece of furniture in the studio, and a large "bed" would often serve as the centre of daily activities for the scholar. Often there was room on the bed for placing books, scrolls, paintings, musical instruments, game boards, or writing instruments. Scholars could use a bed for sitting, leaning, or reclining, thereby serving as a convenient and ideal setting for meditation, reading books, and appreciating art, or for philosophical conversation and playing board games with friends.

Descriptions of such elegant scenes are often found in ancient texts, and have also been depicted in paintings and woodblock prints through the ages. Even archaeological evidence has been discovered to support these descriptions. More then ten years ago, for example, a tomb dating from the Five Dynasties (907–60 AD) was excavated in Jiangsu province. Inside, archaeologists found four wooden *ta* beds almost two metres in length, and on the beds were placed musical instruments (such as a *pipa*), writing instruments, and lacquerware. Thus, we can almost imagine this bed from the Kai-Yin Lo collection as the setting for these elegant activities.

有圍子為床、無圍子為榻的分類方法，是源於明清時期硬木家具業（俗稱魯班館）的説法。如此分類簡明易辨，已當今明清家具學術研究與收藏界認同。而若以使用功能區分，自古以來，床是臥具，榻是座具，兩者不為同類。而且，在較早時期，榻是無圍子的，尺寸比床要小、要矮。隨著歷史的發展演變，榻變高了、寬了、長了，形制上越來越接近於床，甚至相同了。但是，即使形制相同了，是床還是榻也可視其使用場合而定。例如，一件有圍子的床，放在臥室就寢而用，稱為羅漢床；將其抬出放入起居室就稱其為榻了。古時，榻是起居室中的重要家具，人們往往將其作為日間活動中心。榻上可隨意擺放書籍、書畫、樂器、棋枰、文玩等。人們在榻上或坐或倚，習靜參禪，讀書賞畫，或與友談玄、對弈，既方便又愜意。此種情景不僅在古籍中可找到文字記載，在歷代繪畫和版畫中也可見到。十多年前，江蘇省發掘的一座五代墓中，有近兩米長的木榻四張，榻上分別陳放琵琶等樂器以及諸多文具、漆器，是古時使用榻之一實証。

JICHIMU PINGTOU'AN TABLE WITH MITRED BRIDLE JOINTS

This piece of furniture (Plate 21) was once used at the imperial court in the mid-Qing dynasty. Made from *jichimu*, it has been worked to look like *zitan* wood in a process known as "*zitan* finishing." "*Zitan* finishing" was a technique practised by craftsmen during the Ming and Qing dynasties to imitate the qualities and appearance of *zitan* wood. This type of craftsmanship involved considerable knowledge and experience in dealing with *zitan* wood in order to produce these results. This "finishing", in terms of design, construction, the selection and use of materials, as well as the actual process itself, is quite unusual, and represents some of the most advanced and refined techniques of woodworking. The time and skill involved in this technique could only be reserved for furniture of exceptional quality or importance. This finishing process produces furniture with elegant and refined characteristics. So distinguishable is this process that craftsmen, collectors, or connoisseurs familiar with Ming and Qing furniture do not even need to look at the actual furniture itself, but can tell solely from photographs if a piece has been treated with the "*zitan* finishing" process.

To attain the "*zitan*" look, hardwoods other than *zitan*, and even softwood, were used to imitate it. Over the past few years, we have found that many examples of Qing softwood furniture from Shanxi province were treated with "*zitan* finishing." After all, Shanxi province in the Qing dynasty was one of the financial centres of China. Wealthy merchants, in their pursuit of a lavish lifestyle, sought to emulate the material life at the imperial court. This naturally included the imitation of court furniture. Although its design and finishing could be imitated, actual *zitan* wood was very difficult to acquire. The outcome was that wood of lesser quality was used to reproduce the qualities of *zitan* wood. Such are the origins of "*zitan* finished" softwood furniture. Of course, if a choice were available between using *zitan* or softwood to achieve the "*zitan* finish", the former was preferred for its distinctive properties. Thus, I find it sometimes difficult to compare these two types of furniture.

Jichimu, especially early examples with their lustrous qualities, was nonetheless highly valued for furniture making. It is for this reason that it was often selected for use by the Qing imperial

雞翅木插肩榫平頭案

這是一件清代中期的宮廷雞翅木家具（圖版21），是按"紫檀作工"製作而成的。"紫檀作工"本是明清時期的工匠順應紫檀的木性，逐漸摸索形成的一種專用於製作紫檀家具的工藝手法。這種"作工"從造型、結構、選料用料到製作工藝都十分獨特，屬最講究、最細膩的木器製作手法。精工施於美材，使得以這種"精工"製成的家具含有一種高貴的氣質。熟悉明清家具的工匠、收藏家或愛好者往往不需看實物，僅從照片就能認出某件家具是否為"紫檀作工"。

除了紫檀木採用"紫檀作工"外，亦有非紫檀的硬木甚至一些柴木採用這種作工的。近年來我們發現不少出自山西省的清代柴木家具，都是以"紫檀作工"製成的。清代時候，山西是中國的經濟中心之一，富商巨賈有仿效帝王追求排場的風氣，其中也包括對家具製作的仿效。然而，造型、作工雖可仿效，但紫檀木料難覓，只好賤料細作，於是就出現了"紫檀作工"的柴木家具。不過，這類家具終因其材質粗糙，有其形無其神，而無法與"紫檀作工"的紫檀家具同日而語。

雞翅木，尤其年代較早、質地潤美的老雞翅木，屬天賦美材，亦是清代宮廷家具的主要選材之一。實物証明，不少清代宮廷的雞翅木家具是按"紫檀作工"製作的。其金黃的色澤，如羽翼生動般的紋理與色澤凝

family. Evidence for this lies in the fact that many pieces of Qing imperial furniture were made from *jichimu* done in the "*zitan* finishing" process. The golden lustre of *jichimu* is characterised by a light feathery grain, whereas *zitan* wood has a deep, rich colour and a very fine grain. Both types of wood have their own distinctive characteristics. So impressive was the "*zitan* finishing" technique that when I once had the opportunity to see a *jichimu kang* table in a private collection, I found it to be almost identical in design, construction, and size to a *zitan kang* table on display in the Beijing Palace Museum.

Furthermore, the table in the Kai-Yin Lo Collection is closely related to a small *zitan* table with bridle joints and floral motifs illustrated in *Classic Chinese Furniture of the Qing Dynasty* (no. 80). Despite minor differences, such as the Kai-Yin Lo table having mitred bridle joints while the other does not, both are more-or-less the same. For example, the design and style of the pieces are the same, including the round knobs on the legs, which look like kneecaps. The sizes of the pieces also match perfectly and some of the techniques involved in making them are identical. This leads me to believe that both of them were made by Suzhou craftsmen working in the Palace Workshop at the Qing inner court. A small *pingtou'an* table with round legs published in Gustav Ecke's *Chinese Domestic Furniture* (plate 17, no. 35) provides another example of Ming-style furniture made in seventeenth century Suzhou that is very similar in design, style, and dimensions to the Kai-Yin Lo piece. Further examination of these two works also reveals how popular Ming-style furniture was adapted and patterned to meet the tastes and needs of the Qing court.

The *huanghuali* folding *kang* table and *huanghuali* waisted daybed in the Kai-Yin Lo collection amply illustrate the best of the beautiful lines and form of Ming-style furniture, and the *jichimu* occasional table is an extraordinary example of work executed by the Qing imperial court. These three pieces alone provide a greater understanding of the depth and range of Ming and Qing furniture. The Kai-Yin Lo Collection, however, also includes pieces of *tieli* wood furniture, simple and robust in style, as well as softwood furniture that reflects unique regional diversities. The two unifying characteristics of all these pieces are their high standard and individual style, each possessing its own "personality".

重、質地細密的紫檀木相比，另有一番風韻。我們曾見過一件私人收藏的雞翅木炕桌，造型、結構、尺寸都與故宮現在陳列的一張紫檀炕桌幾乎完全一樣。羅女士收藏的這件平頭案，明眼人會發現它與《清代家具》中收錄的第八十件紫檀夾頭榫雕花小平頭案相關。雖然一為夾頭榫、一為插肩榫，卻屬同一"家族"。此兩件家具不僅造型、風格相似（例如腿子中部起鼓，似人腿足的髕骨，工匠稱之為"骼離瓣兒"）、尺寸完全相同，而且一些工藝手法也完全一樣，相信兩者均是出於清代紫禁城內院造辦處中的蘇州工匠之手。Gustav Ecke所著*Chinese Domestic Furniture*一書中所錄用的圓腿小平頭案（圖版17，第35件）是一件蘇州地區製作的十七世紀明式家具，與羅女士的這件平頭案的造型、風格、尺寸也十分相近。對比兩者，可以看到民間製作的明式家具如何因應清代宮廷的品味和需要有所改變。

讀者透過此目錄可以看到羅女士收藏的明清家具範圍廣泛，其中有年代較早、造型優美的明式家具；有珍貴的清代宮廷家具；有風格古樸、醇厚的鐵力木家具；還有極具地方特色的民間家具。這些家具的共同特點，是富於個性、品位較高，充份體現出羅女士的收藏宗旨和在中國傳統家具方面的知識與理解，很值得熱愛傳統藝術和現代藝術的人士參考與學習。

Kai-Yin Lo, who studied Medieval English and European History at Cambridge and London Universities in England, has shown consistent concern for the preservation and study of both traditional and modern forms of Chinese culture. Her furniture collection reveals her interest in traditional Chinese art, and her efforts on behalf of contemporary Chinese painting are well-known. In 1992, Kai-Yin Lo demonstrated her concern for promoting awareness in this latter area by spearheading an exhibition for painter Wu Guanzhong at the British Museum. This was an important precedent as it was the first time the museum held a one-man show for a living artist. In 1995, she also played a key role in organising the first major international retrospective exhibition of twentieth century Chinese painting. After opening in Hong Kong, the exhibition toured leading museums world-wide. The accompanying symposium offered insight into the aesthetic and social context of modern Chinese painting, and Kai-Yin Lo's efforts have certainly aided the advances in appreciation and study of modern Chinese art.

To sum up, with the social and economic advances that take place year-by-year along the human path, moving towards a more progressive and sophisticated civilisation, more and more people are coming to appreciate matters of the spirit and the virtues of traditional cultures. The study and collecting of classical Chinese furniture from the Ming and Qing dynasties represents but one facet of what I see as this inexorable trend towards a new global awareness of culture. Thus, I find it most encouraging that an increasing number of people are coming to appreciate the cultural importance and artistic value of Ming and Qing furniture. I now see more and more people beginning on the long and rewarding road that begins as a passing interest, turns into a hobby, crystallises into connoisseurship and the formation of a collection, and is often fused with dedicated scholarship. This publication provides us with yet another building block to the understanding of Chinese furniture.

May 15, 1997, Beijing

羅啟妍女士曾先後在英國劍橋大學和倫敦大學修讀中世紀英國及歐洲歷史，對推動中國傳統和現代文化不遺餘力，她的家具收藏顯示了她在傳統中國藝術方面的興趣。一九九二年，吳冠中先生在大英博物館舉辦畫展，她便是發起人。此展覽開了該博物館為在世的藝術家舉辦個人畫展之先例。一九九五年，她籌辦了本世紀的一百位有代表性的中國繪畫大師的世界巡迴展覽，又舉行國際學術研討會，探討了中國現代藝術的背景和美學，羅女士積極的參予，正大大推動了對中國現代藝術的欣賞和研究。

隨著社會與經濟的發展，物質文明的提高，人們愈來愈來關注精神文明的提高與優秀傳統文化的宏揚。中國明清家具的收藏與研究，正是在這人類文明進步的必然趨勢中進入一個新的階段。愈來愈多人士認識到中國明清家具的文化內涵和藝術價值，走上了從興趣─愛好─收藏─鑒賞─研究的道路。

1997年5月15日於北京

This book started as an endeavour to record and illustrate my collection of classical hardwood furniture housed in the Asian Civilisations Museum in Singapore and elsewhere. As work progressed, so did clarity of purpose. This, I realised, should not be yet another catalogue describing the beauty, rarity and technical finesse of Chinese furniture in "esteemed" hard or dense woods. Instead, it should be a special opportunity to attempt an extended survey and inquiry into the corpus of Chinese furniture, the bulk of which comprise vernacular constructions in less valuable woods used by the greatest number of Chinese people throughout the country throughout history, known as *laobaixing*, the old hundred surnames. While much has been written about classical hardwood furniture of the late Ming and Qing period, vernacular furniture has so far received insufficient attention and study.

Armed with enthusiasm, I proceeded with this publication, the first time that classical and vernacular furniture are illustrated and discussed together. Visually, as my guiding criteria for collecting are proportions, flow of line and clarity of form, the vernacular pieces in the collection, with few exceptions given to rarity and inventiveness, hold their own in look, appeal and interest next to Ming-style furniture. Probing behind the facade of appearance, to understand the backgrounds, differences and common features of these two categories of furniture, requires comprehension of the social milieu and pattern of pre-modern China, with its rigidity of hierarchy, disciplines and traditions on the one hand and the diversity, distinctive cultures and characteristics of the regions on the other. Classical furniture was made for the social elite and the prosperous classes, entailing prescribed refinement in construction, finishing and decoration, using expensive hardwoods often imported from Southeast Asia, and conforming to aristocratic standards of elegance and craftsmanship. Vernacular furniture, while observing the outlines of traditional forms and styles, was not subject to the strict creeds of literati taste, and therefore could afford greater flamboyance, vigour and a freedom that led to variations on classic lines or adherence to earlier forms.

出版這本書的原意，是為本人藏於新加坡亞洲文明博物館及其他地方的中國古典硬木家具作一圖文記錄。但隨後想到不應只著重介紹各種貴重硬木家具的美態、巧工和珍貴處，而應該全面地研究和探討中國家具，把一般老百姓所用、大部份以較廉宜軟木製成的民間家具也包括在內。論述明末及清代硬木古典家具的著作不少，民間家具數量比古典家具多，但卻一直受到忽視和缺乏研究。

把古典和民間家具放在一起研究，是一個嶄新的嘗試。目標既定，遂滿懷熱誠地展開籌劃工作。本人收藏家具，一向重視線條、造型及形態的勻稱。藏品中的民間家具，除少數屬罕有和獨特外，其餘都以外型、觀感和意趣取勝，絕不比明式家具遜色。透過深入探索古典家具和民間家具之相異處及背景，證實社會環境和模式對二者有很大影響。古代社會一方面有嚴格的階級、律法和傳統限制，另一方面卻有豐富多姿、各具特色的地區文化。古典家具是士宦階級和富貴人家專用之物，所用名貴硬木多來自東南亞；其構造、製作及紋飾均有嚴格標準，以符合上層社會的高雅品味和對精湛造工的要求。民間家具雖亦跟隨傳統造型和式樣，但由於不受文士品味所規限，故此設計能夠更花巧，活潑和自由，可跟古典家具面貌各異，或保留較古老的造型。

Among the different regions of China, Shanxi and Fujian offer the most varied range of furniture styles, bearing marked local characteristics. In particular, I am drawn to Shanxi furniture in alternative woods where ancient forms are conserved and archaism is often fused with local features. Imagine the joy of finding an occasional table in rare Song style (Plate 20b) that is available and affordable! Other pre-Ming characteristics such as "four sides flush" (*simianping*) and "one leg, three spandrels" (*yitui sanya*) (Plate 24a, 24b) derived from traditional architectural structures are preserved well into the nineteenth century. Decoration depicting auspicious symbols indicate regional preferences and idiosyncrasies, and nowhere is it more apparent than in Shanxi. These images are also a common visual vocabulary throughout China, more readily understandable than writing, as most Chinese were illiterate.

Collecting can be an on-going learning process of self-improvement. It is at the same time humbling and stimulating to learn the way to learn. I have for sometime wanted to understand the role of furniture (*jiaju*). In Chinese, *jia* stands for both home, the dwelling and the family, and *ju* means tools – hence implements of the household. What were the functions of furniture? How were they used? What was the cosmological and social significance behind the prescribed arrangement of furniture in the house? What were the circumstances and rationale for which they were created and used, and what was the relation of the house with architecture? – these have been a few of my queries, and I am sure shared by others as well. Furniture, life in the household and architecture, primarily of the literati and official classes have been explored, researched and published separately. It is time to examine them as an organic whole or expression of living and lifestyle under the framework of the living environment.

The lack of records on vernacular dwellings account for the deficiency in textual information. However, the relaxation of travel restrictions since the 1980s within China facilitated greater possibilities of on-site visitations for researchers and enthusiasts, as well as a more open atmosphere for interchange of ideas. This has resulted in new studies of the village, the rural household and architecture, revealing glimpses of domestic lifestyle.

中國各地以山西和福建的家具最豐富多姿，地方色彩最鮮明。本人認為一些保存著古老造型而地方色彩濃厚的山西雜木家具尤其吸引。試想想，能擁有一件帶大弧度牙條起陽線、雲紋腿型的宋式夾頭桌，會是何等樂事（圖版20b）。直至十九世紀，一些山西家具仍帶有"四面平"、"三彎腿"及源於傳統建築的"一腿三牙"等古老型式（圖版24a，24b）。寓意吉祥的紋飾反映著當地人的喜好和特有個性，這特色在山西尤其鮮明。古代中國大部分人都不懂文字，這些純以視覺形象表達的圖案，有全國共通的涵義，更容易為一般老百姓所理解。

在蒐集的過程中，不斷的虛心求教和學習如何求知，使人自我改進。而本人一直都希望瞭解家具所扮演的角色。按傳統解釋，"家"指家居、家庭，"具"則指用具，"家具"即是指家居或家庭之用具。然而，家具究竟有何功能？如何使用？家具的擺設方式有何宇宙和社會意義？設計和製造家具的動機和理據、居室與建築的關係等等，都是我的疑問，相信很多人都有同感。過往的研究和著作慣把家具、家居生活和建築等分開來探討，而且以士宦階層為主。這部書則首次把這些課題全部置於生活環境這個大題目下，當作一個整體的生活方式來研究和探索。

鑑於缺乏民居記錄，實在難有文獻資料供進一步參攷。幸而自八十年代以來，中國內地的旅遊限制得到放寬，研究者和愛好家具的人士可到國內實地研究和考察。加上學術的交流和研討較前開放，遂興起有關農村、民居及建築等新課題，讓我們多了解家居生活方式。

The increasing availability of regional types of furniture brought to the antique market since 1990, unveiled styles, forms and carvings in miscellaneous woods hitherto unseen, or were the only isolated examples. This has enabled dealers, collectors and the interested to study, compare and come to some conclusions. A relatively unexplored subject is the wide range of woods, native to China, whose classifications have, so far, relied not so much on botanical knowledge, but on local or traditional references. The notion that the worthwhile woods were confined to *zitan*, *huanghuali*, and to a lesser extent, *jichimu*, continues to persist. Examining the common links and differences between classical and vernacular furniture, as well as the types of woods employed, some of which are indigenous to the locality, reveal artistic and cultural aspects of the region, thus throwing light on the social and economic developments of Chinese history and society.

Professor Wang Shixiang, the all-round scholar and pre-eminent authority on Chinese furniture, has been immensely encouraging by describing this book as a "pioneering work" and "a worthwhile contribution to scholarship" in his introduction. Wang's own pioneering research and studies, *Classic Chinese Furniture* (1986) and *Connoisseurship of Chinese Furniture* (1990), opened up new facets of the writings of Kates, Ecke, Ellsworth and others, further defined classical Ming-style furniture and stimulated interest that has since become world-wide. I sincerely hope that this publication will meet Wang Shixiang's expectations by acting as a catalyst for further explorations and comprehension, and that my collection of furniture will serve not only as examples to illustrate form, function and aesthetic value, but also play a part in enlarging our understanding and awareness of the living environment.

In this book, I am indeed fortunate to have obtained the valuable support of scholars, all experts in their fields, who have been patient and receptive to these new directions of inquiry. We have together, in many hours of discussions, reviewed and considered suitable approaches. Drawing on their reservoirs of knowledge and expertise based on textual analysis and fieldwork findings, they have contributed essays that provide new insights and interpretations. Tian Jiaqing, whose grasp of the fine points of Ming and Qing classical furniture is a combination of textual and "hands-on" experience, examines three outstanding pieces from my collection from

自一九九〇年以來，古董市場的地方家具不斷增加，部分雜木家具的風格、造型和雕飾為前所未見。這些與別不同的家具，成為古董商、藏家及愛好家具人士研究、比較和探索新知識的對象。中國家具所用的本土木材種類繁多，但有關研究卻比較少，而且大都並非從植物學入手，只是以當地或相傳的資料作依據。時至今日，有些人仍認為只有紫檀及黃花梨才是最值得珍視的木材，雞翅木次之。探討古典和民間家具風格和式樣的異同，以及其所用的土產木材，有助認識當地文化，進而瞭解中國歷史、社會民生以及經濟的發展。

博學多才的中國家具權威王世襄教授在其小序中稱這部書為"藝林之創舉、學苑之新猷"，實在是莫大的鼓勵。王教授之《明式家具珍賞》（1985）及《明式家具研究》（1989）為明式家具一詞下了定義，引起世人對中國家具的廣泛興趣。本人衷心冀盼這部書不負王教授所望，喚起更多人加入研究和探討，並希望本人的藏品除了為中國家具的造型、功能和美感提供實例外，同時也能增進人們對生活環境的認識和關注。

在籌劃這部書的過程中，本人有幸能得到多位學者和專家鼎力襄助，仔細而包容地探索這個新主題。為求切合主題，我們花了很多時間共同商討和修訂各個觀點。各人以其豐富學識，結合文獻資料和實地考察所得，彙集成文，讓我們對中國家具與整個生活環境有新的理解和認識。田家青對明清家具見解精闢，學術研究與實際經驗並重，就本人所藏的三件家具精品的特徵、功能和用途細加分析。柯惕思有關中國家具的

the point of view of function and context in their usage. Curtis Evarts, who has written extensively on many aspects of classical furniture, traces the historical development of furniture and furnishings from the grand to the modest, "from sumptuous palaces to courtyard dwellings." John Kwang-Ming Ang interprets vernacular furniture gathered from fieldwork investigations in the light of social, economic and artistic developments of the regions. Dr. Puay-peng Ho presents a holistic view of the living environment, which includes "the architecture of the house, the furniture and objects housed inside and the activities conducted in the house, through which the aspirations of the owner are expressed." This is probably the first time that these elements are discussed as an organic entity. Dr. Wang Qijun, a specialist in vernacular dwellings, defines the arrangement of furniture in the most important room of the house, underscoring the inherent functional, social and symbolic values. Professor Chen Zengbi, whose knowledge and expertise apply equally to classical and vernacular architecture and furniture, succinctly outlines the interiors of northern homes and explains how furniture was created and commissioned

I strongly believe that art must be made understandable and approachable. In order to be made vivid and relevant to the widest possible circle of people, encompassing both laymen and connoisseurs alike, scholarship, information, communication and appreciation need to go hand-in-hand. The lack of documentation of vernacular furniture and dwellings necessitates on-site observations. A new investigative approach must rely on it, in addition to traditional textual studies, to be able to reconstruct how people lived and expressed their deeply-held beliefs and aspirations. The underlying principle of this book and its essays, in their attempt to place furniture in the framework of its social and historical contexts, embodies such an approach, emerging as an illuminating, creative, and pleasurable exercise.

January 27, 1998, Hong Kong

著作廣泛，其文章深入探索家具和其擺設的歷史發展，由華麗至簡樸，由宮殿至民間院落，都一一論及。洪光明以實地考察所搜集得的民間家具為例，探討各地的社會、經濟和藝術發展。何培斌則闡述有關生活環境的整體觀念。"生活環境包括了房屋建築、室內的家具擺設和屋內進行的活動，及所表現屋主在生活上的期望。"這是首次集合這些元素作整體研究。王其鈞是研究民居的專家，以廳堂的家具擺設為題，剖釋其固有功能、社會及象徵意義。陳增弼教授對古典和民間建築與家具同樣有深入的研究，他的文章扼要地勾畫出北方民居的室內情景，並談及家具製造和訂製背境。

本人認為藝術一定要讓人容易理解和接受。學術研究、資料搜集、交流推廣及鑑賞等必須攜手進行才能夠將藝術變得更吸引和大眾化，讓門外漢和藝術愛好者同樣受惠。由於缺乏有關民間家具和家居的文獻資料，唯有利用實地考察，以新的探索形式，結合傳統的文獻研究，才可重建前人的生活方式，瞭解其風俗習慣、思想抱負。這部書的立場和其中的文章正好從這觀點出發，把家具置於其社會和歷史架構中去研究和探討，既具啟發性，又充滿創意和樂趣。

1998年1月27日於香港

Kai-Yin Lo with her first piece of Ming furniture.
Behind is Beijing artist Wang Huaiqing's painting "Half table, half chair".
羅啟妍與她第一件明式家具，後為北京藝術家王懷慶油畫《半桌半椅》。

Traditional Chinese Furniture -- From Sumptuous Palaces to Courtyard Dwellings

中國傳統家具——從華麗到簡樸

Curtis Evarts
柯惕思

Throughout the recent history of collecting Chinese furniture, objects of carved or inlaid lacquer were the earliest treasures. In the 1920s and 30s, Western expatriates were attracted to hardwood furniture of minimalist style, and with the later involvement of Chinese connoisseurs, the appreciation and knowledge of traditional "Ming-style" furniture significantly broadened. The reopening of China since the 1980s has also ushered in a furniture culture that is richly variegated in its materials, forms, and stylistic characteristics. The increasing presence of vernacular furniture and its widespread appeal has led to a reassessment of traditional Chinese furniture.

Furniture's forms and use, as well as the quality of materials and refinement of craftsmanship, all reflect economies and lifestyles of a wide ranging social spectrum – from the splendid palace furnishings bestowed upon a Son of Heaven to the rustic needs of the peasant family. This essay will explore traditional Chinese furniture through a review of its historical development within its social context.

A BRIEF HISTORY OF PRE-MING CHINESE FURNITURE

The history of Chinese furniture, and its gradual evolutionary process of not less than five thousand years to modern times, is a subject that has been well documented. Nonetheless, it will be briefly be reviewed here in part to re-establish its deeply rooted traditions, as well as to advance more recent findings. Evidence dating from nearly 7000 years ago has established that woodworking techniques were already relatively advanced at the time. At Hemadu, for example, mortise-and-tenon as well as tongue-and-groove joinery was discovered in the construction of Neolithic timber frame buildings; archaeologists also determined that these buildings were optimally sited in relation to the sun. No traces of Neolithic furniture have yet been found.

The earliest representations of tables and platforms appear in oracle bone pictographs and a few objects excavated from tombs dating from the Shang period (sixteenth-eleventh century

縱觀近代中國家具收藏的歷史，雕刻或有鑲嵌的漆製品是最早被收藏者所青睞的。在本世紀二、三十年代，僑居中國的西方人士對那些造型簡潔的硬木家具深感興趣，及後隨著中國鑑藏家的出現，大大的擴闊了對傳統「明式家具」的欣賞和學問。自八十年代中國重新開放，家具文化在質地、樣式和風格上，變得更為豐富多彩。民間家具的持續出現及廣泛分佈，令我們要對中國的傳統家具作出新的評價。

家具的樣式和用途，用材的質地和做工的考究程度，反映了上自天子，下到鄉村農夫的經濟狀況和其生活方式。本文就中國傳統家具的社會背景，考察它的歷史發展。

明代以前中國古代家具簡介

中國古代家具及其五千餘年的發展歷程有很完整的記錄。然而，在這裡仍有需要對其悠久的傳統和一些最新發現進行討論。有證據顯示中國早在七千多年前，木作技術已經相當進步。如河姆渡遺址的杆欄式建築上就採用了榫鉚技術，考古學家還證明這些建築是有意識安排在向陽的位置上。但暫時仍未有發現新石器時代的家具。

BC). Low tables, armrests, pillows, beds, chests, stands, and low screens excavated from Eastern Zhou (770–256 BC) tombs are representative of the types of furnishings used in the daily life of the aristocratic ruling class. The decorative styles of furniture excavated at sites corresponding to the ancient kingdom of Chu range from "elegant simplicity" to "richly ornate"; surfaces were patterned with vibrant, fluid designs in contrasting red and black lacquer; carving techniques, including incised, relief, and layered open-carved work, all rival the best Chinese carving throughout time.[1] Simultaneously, continued advances in the tradition of architectural woodworking are recorded in *Chuci*, where decorative patterns for doors and windows are noted.[2]

The furniture culture of the Han dynasty (206 BC–220 AD) continued to characterise a lifestyle at ground level, and records indicate that furniture of beautifully figured woods as well as that decorated with tortoiseshell or ivory were all highly prized.[3] Woven mats, used for sleeping as well as sitting, had also become a standard of measurement for rooms. Wall murals and stone engravings further illustrate the use of low couches, or platforms, elevating a master or special guest in a distinguished seat of honour. At that time, the sitting platform was called *ta* while the relatively longer platform used both for sitting and reclining was called *chuang*.[4] Separate low armrests and backrests provided additional comfort whether sitting on a platform or on the ground. Decorated screens were often placed behind the couch – besides their honorific and decorative use, the literal terminology "windscreen" (*pingfeng*) also implied a functional protection against drafts. Although clothing was the principal means of keeping warm, archaeological evidence indicates that portable braziers provided a localised hearth during the cold winters. Excavations of chests, decorated lacquer and woven cane, along with pottery models of strong-box storage units and clothes racks suggest that the aristocratic Han household was well furnished.[5]

Han tomb pottery models of dwellings, as well as stone engravings from this period, also convey some idea of the contemporary architecture. Relief carving on a tomb tile from Chengdu illustrates an entire compound surrounded by a wall with a gate on the presumed southern wall. The three-bay building across the farmyard/courtyard has no interior divisions; screens and

案和几最早的記載，見於商代（公元前十六世紀─公元前十一世紀）甲骨文和商代墓葬中的一些出土。而東周墓葬中出土的案、憑几、木枕、榻、箱以及架等家具，則反映了當時貴族日常生活的風貌。楚地出土的器物，顯示了楚式家具的裝飾從質樸簡潔到繁褥細緻兼而有之，表面流暢生動的紋樣及其紅黑的底色爭相輝映，雕刻技術包括陰刻、浮雕和鏤空等，均代表了這一時期的最高水準。[1]同時，《楚辭》亦提及到建築上的木作技術的進展，如其中就提到了一些用來裝飾門和窗的紋樣。[2]

漢代（公元前203年─公元220年）的家具文化繼承了席地而坐的生活方式，有文獻記載了那些造型優美，裝飾有龜甲或象牙的木質家具在當時備受推崇。[3]編席用於睡和坐，也成了當時居室的必備之物。漢代的壁畫和畫像石清楚地說明了榻或枰的功用，在其上主人和客人各有特定的坐次。在漢代，用來供人坐的家具稱為榻，較榻稍長，且既用於坐和臥的是床。[4]當人坐在榻或地上時，也在其肘部和背部放置較低的几，以便坐姿更為舒適。在床和榻的後面經常設置屏風。除了其尊貴和裝飾作用外，屏風也有一定的防禦功能。雖然當時主要是以保暖的，但在考古發掘中，也見到一些便攜式的溫手爐，以便在寒冷的冬天裡可以隨時隨地取暖。考古所見的箱、漆器、竹笥以及陶明器中的各種盛儲器和衣桿，均說明漢代貴族的家居生活是相當講究的。[5]

漢代墓葬出土的陶樓以及這一時期的畫像石，都反映了當時建築的特色。成都出土的一座漢墓中的畫像石上刻劃了一座完整的，被圓牆所包圍的莊園，僅在其南牆上開一門。儘管這座面闊三間的莊園並沒有表現出隔間、屏風和卷簾一類的東西，但

1 Teng: 54, Compare with examples illustrated
2 Chen Wanli: 157
3 Cui: 51
4 Cui: 52, 60
5 Pirazzoli: 52–62

1 Teng：54，和插圖相比較
2 陳萬里：157
3 崔：51
4 崔：52, 60
5 見英文注釋5。

curtains, however, would likely have been used to divide and enclose the open space to protect from drafts and sunlight. This basic plan continues to be used in rural areas in modern times.

During the Han dynasty, China's domain expanded to more distant regions. Foreign influences were popularised by the Han emperor Lingdi (reigned 168–88 AD) whose legendary fascination with the folding stool (huchuang) is often cited. These portable seats were used by the nomadic tribes in the north-western regions for mounting and dismounting horses. The popularity of this nomadic seat, along with the simultaneous eastward migration of a throne-like dais associated with Buddhism, is generally accredited with the shift in seating from mat to chair level.

Fig. 1   Master and Students. Detail, Buddhist cave sculpture from Cave #8, Yungang. Northern Wei (d. 470–93 AD).
圖1   佛和弟子（局部），北魏（470-493）雲崗石窟第八窟。

Buddhism flourished in China over the following centuries, and simultaneously, a greater variety of seats began to appear. Hourglass-shaped stools made of straw and basket work are repeatedly found in Buddhist cave sculpture during the Northern and Southern Dynasties (386–586 AD) period. A scene from a Northern Wei cave at Yungang (d. 470–93 AD) depicts a master seated upon a large central pedestal while his disciples sit on smaller stools. (Fig. 1) During this flourishing period of cultural exchange, the influence of Western architecture can also be traced along the Silk Route via Gandhara. The classical Greek pedestal, for example, may have been the inspiration for the xumi platform from where the master expounds his doctrine. This early platform may also reflect the origins of those still used for contemplative meditation over one thousand years later (see Plate 4).

The sphere of China's influence again extended to distant foreign lands while reunified under Tang dynastic rule (618–907 AD). Buddhist wall paintings at Dunhuang include an image of an armchair which closely resembles an actual Chinese-style armchair of the same period of lacquered zelkova now housed at the Imperial Treasury in Nara, Japan. By this time, raised seating around high tables had also become more common amongst aristocratic circles. Representations in Tang paintings often depict court ladies sitting upon carved and elaborately decorated stools. The popularisation of the raised box platform for seating is also reflected in many representations in paintings and wall murals – those arranged with awning-like canopies

它應該是有這些設施的，以便將整個莊園分成內外兩進，並可以遮擋陽光和起著防禦作用。時至今日，這種布局還見於農村。

漢代的疆域較今日更為遼闊。漢靈帝（168-188）時期一些來自域外的器具被大力推廣，如他對胡床的鍾愛就經常被提及。這種便攜式的坐具，原是西北游牧民族專為上馬和下馬而做的。胡床和隨著佛教東漸而來的御座狀榻的流行，通常被認為是從席地而坐向椅坐的轉變。

在隨後的若干世紀裡，佛教在中國一直很流行，與此同時，愈來愈多的坐具出現了。在南北朝時期（386-586）的佛教石窟中，草或藤編的沙漏狀墩隨處可見。在雲岡一個北魏時期的石窟中（約470-493），其主佛坐在石窟中央的巨大寶座上，而其弟子們則坐在較小的墩子上（圖1）。這一時期的文化交流十分繁榮，西方建築的影響經犍陀羅地區沿著絲綢之路東進。如佛主講經時所坐的須彌座，就很可能受到古希臘風格基座的影響。這些早期的雕塑，也揭示了那些流行於千餘年後禪椅的淵源（圖版4）。

唐代（618-907）統一天下之後，中國文化對外域的影響也波及很遠。見諸於敦煌佛教壁畫中的一件憑几，和日本正倉院收藏的一件同時期的中國風格的實用器十分相似。在這一時期，和高桌相配套的高椅在上層社會中已經很普遍。唐代的繪畫中的宮廷仕女們，也是經常坐在精心雕刻和裝飾的凳子上。根據唐代

appear to mark the advent of the canopy bed.

The raised seating mode of living had fully blossomed within aristocratic circles by the late Tang and Five Dynasties periods. The often-cited tenth century painting *Night Revels of Han Xizai* provides a glimpse of the contemporary furniture culture. Guests sit upon large U-shaped couch beds which are surrounded with decorative railings; men, some with feet pendant and others with legs crossed, sit on yokeback chairs draped with silk chair covers; courtesan musicians sit on large round stools; food and wine is served upon high recessed-leg tables; large standing screens are decorated with painted panels and provide space division; canopy beds are draped with brocades, and clothes racks stand adjacent, draped with bed covers and clothes. A group of Five Dynasties period full-sized daybeds of the "inserted shoulder joint" style (cf. Plates 19, 20) excavated from a princess's tomb in Jiangsu province[6] provide further evidence of the breadth of furniture design developed by this time.

Architecture and furnishings of the Northern and Southern Song (960–1279) dynasties are both considerably lighter and airier in structure than those of preceding times. This stylistic shift was likely due as much to severe timber shortages – necessitating more resourceful use of materials – as it was to the fully developed intellectual and artistic climate of the time. New techniques and tools arose which permitted the use of smaller components firmly secured to one another with ingenious systems of wooden joinery.

Paintings and excavated material reveal the Song dynasties' ever-widening range of furniture and materials. Liu Songnian's (1174–1224) painting of a scholarly gathering on a garden

Fig. 2a–e
a) Basin/brazier stand,
b) chair,
c) couch-bed,
d) table, and
e) clothes rack.
Reproduction of miniature tomb model excavated from the Jin dynasty tomb (d. 1189) of Yan Deyuan, near Huayan Temple. Datong.
圖2a–e
a,盆架；
b,椅子；
c,床；
d,桌子；
e,衣架。
均據大同華嚴寺附近金代閻德源墓（1189）所出的家具模型複製。

繪畫和壁畫中的有關描繪，這一時期還流行一種高型的箱式坐具，當它們和篷狀的帳子共用時，預示了帶帳床的產生。

這種高坐姿在晚唐和五代時期的上層社會中得到了充分的發展。畫於十世紀的《韓熙載夜宴圖》，是人們常引用的畫，它為我們提供了當時家具文化的大致情況。客人們都坐在一巨大的U-字形床上，床的四周有供裝飾的屏風。男士們垂足或交腳坐在鋪有絲墊的弓背椅上，而宮廷樂工們則坐在較大的圓墩上；酒食放置在一些高桌上，桌腳內收；而那些裝飾有彩繪嵌板的立屏則用作分隔空間。一件帶有幔帳的架子床上蓋有錦緞，床邊立有衣架，其上則搭有衣服和鋪蓋。在江蘇發現的一座五代時期的公主墓中，出土了一組實物大小的「插肩式」床（圖版19、20），是了解這一時期的家具種類重要的材料。[6]

兩宋時期的建築和家具的結構，較之前代更為輕巧流暢。這一變化趨勢很大程度上是歸結於木料的短缺，令到對材料的運用要更加精打細算，也因此造就了這一時期家具製作中追求意境和藝術的風氣。隨著新技術和新工具的出現，更小的構件製作使用，最終產生了精巧的細木作。

繪畫和考古中所見的材料表明兩宋時期（960–1279）家具及其質料的種類仍在不斷地增加。劉松年（1174–1224）在一幅描繪文人在花園聚會的畫中，表現了宋代家具製作中極為精緻的工藝。其中的藤環墩、漆雕凳、束腰鑲石案、高腰帶裝飾橫棖香几以及放置在一件小桌上的多格書櫃，均體現了高

6 Chen Zengbi: 24

6 陳增弼：24

Fig. 3 Folding chair and table. Detail from wall murals at Yanshan Temple (d. 1167), Fanshi. Jin Dynasty. After Chai 104.

圖3　折疊椅和桌子。據繁峙嚴山寺金代壁畫，據柴104。

terrace illustrates the considerable skills of Song furniture makers. A round stool of rattan, a stool of carved-and-lacquered wood, a waisted table inlaid with decorative stone panels, a high-waisted incense stand with delicate ornate stretchers, and a small table-top book cabinet of multi-panel construction all reflect sophisticated techniques.[7] Well-developed methods in the use of bamboo and root for armchairs of high-back construction are also finely detailed in a long handscroll (d. 1173–76) of Buddhist monks.[8] Similar renderings, as well as archaeological finds, reveal that tables, chairs, stools, and benches of the recessed-leg style had become widely used by various social strata. And while the more elegant form of waisted cornerleg furniture is connected primarily with the activities of the elite or those of ritualistic and ceremonial significance, the miniature wood model (d. 1189) of a more functional cabriole leg high waisted basin/brazier stand (Fig. 2a) suggests a gradual assimilation of this noble form into the more utilitarian furnishings of daily life.

Fig. 4 Carrying a stool. Detail from wall murals at Yanshan Temple (d. 1167), Fanshi. Jin Dynasty. After Chai 110

圖4　背凳。繁峙嚴山寺金代壁畫，據柴110。

This and others models – excavated near Datong, Shanxi province from a site of the former Jin Kingdom (1115–1234 AD) – may well represent other kinds of furniture used at the time (Figs. 2a–e). Other Jin period tables, screens, and beds are also found in wall murals (d. 1167) at Yanshan Temple, Fanshi, Shanxi province.[9] There, an early and firmly dated representation of a folding horseshoe armchair is found; moreover, its rather informal arrangement and casual use suggests a customary seating form. (Fig. 3) In another scene, handsome stools of *simianping* form serve as step stools for ladies to raise a pavilion's bamboo curtain in order to observe a ceremonial offering on the terrace outside; the *wanzi* lattice pattern of the balustrade as well as the open-carved panels of the basin stand suggest a common decorative theme used at that time. (Fig. 4)

Furniture illustrated in a Yuan dynasty album leaf painting of a leisurely scholarly gathering includes a previously unrecorded table form. (Fig. 5) It resembles a low waisted *kang* table

超的技藝。[7]而在一幅描繪高生僧的長卷軸（約1173–1176）中，則反映了多種形式帶高背的竹和根雕扶手椅。[8]類似的圖像以及考古發現都表明隱足的桌、椅、墩和凳愈來愈被社會各階層所接受。那些造型更為精緻的束腰角足家具，主要在重大的慶典場合使用，但這一件高束腰曲足盆架（1189）的木製模型（圖2a），則反映了這種貴族家具逐步轉變成日常用具。

Fig. 5 Scholarly Gathering. Album leaf painting. Yuan dynasty. Suzhou Museum. After Suzhou Bowuguan.

圖5　元代學士會聚圖冊頁。蘇州博物館藏。

這一件以及其它從山西大同一金代（1115–1234）遺址中出土的模型，大體反映了當時的家具種類（圖2a–e）。在山西繁峙嚴山寺的金代壁畫（1167）中，也可見當時的桌、屏風和床等家具。[9]在這裡還發現一件有明確年代，早期的折疊式馬蹄形扶手椅，同時，這件椅子相當隨意的放置和使用，表明了當時的習慣性坐姿（圖3）。其中的另一場景則描繪了亭閣內一群仕女正踢在輕巧的「四面平」凳子上掛竹簾，以便觀看亭外的典禮。欄桿上的格子和盆架上的鏤空開扇，代表了當時流行的裝飾手法（圖4）。

在一幅以文人消閑為題材的元代冊頁中，描繪了一種未見諸於記載的桌子（圖5）。它看起來有點象低矮的束腰炕桌，但又有

7 Lin: 28
8 Lin: 82, Handler 32–3
9 Chai: 123, 143, 145, 158

7 林：28
8 林：82, Handler 32–3
9 柴：123, 143, 145, 158

from which leg extensions appear to be fitted; each leg also appears to have a "giant's arm brace." Similar tables with removable legs, as well as those which only imitate the "knockdown" form, are found amongst extant examples of Ming and Qing period furniture (cf. Plates 21, 22).

TRADITIONAL CHINESE FURNITURE IN MING AND QING DYNASTY SOCIETY

Although there are few extant examples of pre-Ming Chinese furniture, excavated pieces and literary and pictorial records provide evidence of the origins and continuity of traditional forms. Throughout the Ming and Qing dynasties, these traditional forms continued – mature, while new forms and styles developed simultaneously. Moreover, significant quantities of furniture from these periods are preserved, although few pieces are dated or signed, and little is generally known of their provenance. By linking the objects themselves with the considerably greater body of literary and pictorial sources, as well as dated material from excavations, the social and cultural context of furniture can be better understood.

Fig. 6 Table excavated from the tomb of Zhu Tan (d. 1389). Shandong Provincial Museum, Jinan.
圖6 朱檀墓（1389）出土的桌子。山東省博物館。

EARLY MING FURNITURE

Prince Zhu Tan, tenth son of the first Ming emperor, died in 1389. A group of miniature wood furniture excavated from his tomb in Shandong province include a rare folding chair and a couch-bed of waisted form with cabriole legs, foot stretcher, and a five-panel railing.[10] Of eight full-sized red lacquer tables discovered, the most outstanding are ornately styled with open-carved spandrels, concave moulded legs, high humpback stretchers carved with florid decoration, and central panels of agate. (Fig. 6) These tables are generally regarded as the earliest known examples of "Ming furniture" and may even be earlier. Furthermore, their pleasing proportions, and perfected balance between elegant decoration and solidity of structure are all features prized in classical "Ming-style" furniture. The innovation of the raised stretcher, as well as the above noted "giant's arm braces," can both be seen as responses to the awkward placement of intermediate or ground stretchers which hindered sitting at tables with chairs.

較長的桌腿，而且每條桌腿還有一霸王棖。在現存的明清家具中，還可見類似但帶有可拆卸桌腿的桌子，也有一些不能拆卸桌腿的實例（比較圖版21、22）。

明清時期的傳統家具

雖然明代以前的傳世家具十分罕見，但出土器物以及相關的圖像資料，為了解一些傳統家具的淵源和發展提供了證據。縱觀明清時期，在傳統家具趨於成熟的同時，也出現了新的樣式和風格。此外，相當數量的明清家具完好地保留下來，儘管其中只有極少數的年代和來源是明確的。但如果把這些傳世品和那些相關的文字、圖像資料以及考古出土的年代確鑿的遺物聯繫起來，我們就能更好地了解家具的文化和社會背景。

早期明代家具

朱檀是明太祖第十子，卒於1389年。在山東朱檀墓中出土的一組微型木質家具，其中包括一件罕見的折疊椅、束腰曲足床、腳凳、五格巾架等。[10] 另外，朱檀墓中還出土了八件實物大小的桌子，最引人注目的是它們的裝飾，如透雕花牙、內斂的曲足，華麗的弓背棖子以及鑲嵌在桌面中央的大理石桌心等（圖6）。這些桌子一般被當作是最早的明式家具，甚至更早年代的家具。同時，這些桌子在精美裝飾和堅實結構上的完美統一，以及它們那些賞心悅目的構件，都堪稱為經典的「明式」家具。高型棖子以及上文所提及的霸王棖的使用，可以看成是對中低棖子的改良，因為後者對憑桌而坐造成極大的不便。

10 Shandong: 31, Addis: 65

10 山東：31, Addis 65

With the establishment of the new Imperial Palace in Beijing during the Yongle period (1402–23), Imperial Workshops were re-established; skilled craftsmen were recruited nation-wide and the finest materials were sought out and were also regularly sent as tribute from regions afar. Furnishings were continually required for the many new buildings as well as those which had been expanded or renovated. The Yongle emperor recruited renowned lacquer carvers to establish the Orchard Garden lacquer workshop,[11] from which later representative works may well include the celebrated carved altar table at the Victoria and Albert Museum, London,[12] as well as a square corner cabinet of flush panel construction with thick lacquer coating and dragons ornamenting the door panels at the Palace Museum, Beijing.[13] Both of these rare pieces – bearing Xuande period (1425–36) regnal marks – appear as unprecedented prototypes from which the compound wardrobe and altar coffer have survived into the twentieth century as classical Ming-style forms.

MING VERNACULAR FURNITURE

The Ming dynasty carpenter's manual *Lu Ban jing* is an important document for understanding the scope of Ming furniture as well as for penetrating into the woodworking cult of Lu Ban.[14] Although the earliest known edition is dated to the Wanli period, the text appears to be an assemblage of assorted materials dating from the early-to-middle Ming period (if not earlier) which is uniformly reprinted and bound with accompanying Wanli period illustrations. The preface suggests the work was compiled in conjunction with the general organisation of craftsmen at the new northern capital, Beijing.

The second chapter of three has entries for over fifty types of furniture. Amongst many standard forms already evident, other categories include a variety of canopy beds, knockdown tables (see Plate 21), tables with drawers, cosmetic cases, round tables, tapered cabinets, and medicine cabinets; however, a few categories that surely existed – folding stool, *kang* table, bookcase, balance stand, seal chest – are curiously absent. While generally comprehensive in scope, the pithy formulas of rather minimal content are elusive in interpretation. Nonetheless, it is clearly a reference for *wood* working craftsmen – no mention exists of bamboo, stone,

隨著永樂年間（1402-1423）北京新都的建立，宮廷作坊也重新設立；熟練的工匠從全國各地徵調到北京，最好的材料也從四處搜羅出來，作為貢納運送到北京。那些新建、擴建和重建的宮殿都需要新的家具。永樂皇帝把當時一些著名的雕漆工匠召集在一起，在皇城內設立了製作漆器的專門作坊—果園廠，[11] 以後在這裡生產了大量有代表性器物，其中很可能包括倫敦維多利亞及艾爾拔博物館中所收藏的精工雕琢的祭案，[12] 以及北京故宮博物館所藏的一件剔紅方角櫃，其門扇上裝飾有龍紋。[13] 這兩件帶有宣德年款（1425-1436）的稀有之器，可算是流傳至二十世紀的組合衣櫃和香案的明式原型。

明代的本土家具

明代的木工手冊《魯班經》是我們了解當時家具，以及透視木器業中崇拜魯班的重要文獻。[14] 儘管現在可見的是萬歷時期版本的《魯班經》，但這部著作看起來像是一部明代早中期有關資料的彙編（如果不是更早的話），只是到了萬歷時期又加入了插圖並一起刊行。在該書的序裡記載了當時北京的行會參予了此書的編撰工作。

《魯班經》全書共三章，其中在第二章的相關條目裡，記載了五十餘種家具，除了那些常見的標準器形外，還包括一些其它器類，如架子床、帶屜桌、奩、圓桌和藥箱等。但是，有一些當時確實存在的器類，如馬扎、炕桌、書箱以及悶戶櫥等卻未見記載。這部書從整體上看是較完整的，但也有極少的術語是沒有解釋的。但不管怎麼說，對於木匠而言，它是一部很

11 Beurdeley: 98–9
12 Clunas: 1988, 79
13 Wang Shixiang: 36, pl. 21
14 Ruitenbeek, Evarts: 33–44

11 見英文注釋11。
12 見英文注釋12。
13 王世襄：36, 圖版21
14 見英文注釋14。

porcelain furniture, hardware fittings, carved or plain lacquer, or finishes of any sort; neither is there mention of any precious hardwoods.

The furniture described is generally of a plain undecorated style. Besides a few standard mouldings, the few decorative motifs prescribed include "fanged swallowing heads" (*sichi tuntou*) (typically carved on the shoulders of table legs), *wanzi* pattern, relief carving of "scrolling grass" and "double scrolling lotus", and spandrels carved like the "sun, moon and coiled elephant trunk." That decorative motifs such as dragons, phoenixes, *lingzhi*, *ruyi*, and auspicious characters are entirely omitted offers further evidence that the text of the *Lu Ban jing* predates the late Ming period when the widespread popularity of such furniture decoration was commonly acknowledged.[15]

Although some correlation can be drawn between the luxurious furniture discussed above, the furniture described in the *Lu Ban jing* generally appears to be representative of common household furniture. Furthermore, little distinction is made between the agricultural implements – bellows, granaries, animal stables, and irrigation devices, wheel barrows, etc. – which are grouped in the same chapter. A carrying cage for chickens directly precedes the entry for a large standing screen; an irrigation wheel follows a tea tray. Craig Clunas has recently brought to light the self-sufficiency of the household/agricultural-garden estates of the early-to-mid Ming period wherein the gentry often engaged in some level of involvement with their orchards, fish ponds, and vegetable gardens – even Prince Zhu Quan (younger brother of Prince Zhu Tan), glorified the agronomic arts of cultivating trees, flowers, fruits and vegetables.[16] Perhaps in the context of these agrarian estates as well as the grouping of implements found in the *Lu Ban jing*, the term *jiaju*, commonly translated as "household furnishings," may have once embraced the more encompassing range of "implements of the agrarian household."

LATE MING: SOCIAL DYNAMICS AND FURNITURE

On the other hand, exalted Imperial custom and fashion penetrated deeply into society. The traditional Chinese social structure may be loosely defined as a class society which, following

清楚明瞭，專為木工而設的手冊 — 書中沒有言及竹、石、瓷質家具、金屬構件以及雕或平漆器等，也沒有提到任何貴重的硬木。

以上提到的家具總體上反映了明式家具簡練質樸的風格。除了一些標準的樣式外，另外僅見的裝飾體裁包括四螭吞頭（主要裝飾在桌腿的肩部）、彎子、浮雕卷草紋和成對的卷蓮紋，以及經常雕成太陽、月亮和象鼻狀的拱肩等。在書中未見到如龍、鳳、靈芝、如意和其它的吉祥用語等內容，這就進一步說明《魯班經》的成書要早於明代晚期，因為在這一時期上述裝飾體裁已經極為流行了。[15]

雖然和上述一些豪華家具存在著某些聯繫，但《魯班經》中所登錄的家具總體上還是當時普通的居家用具。另外，在其中的一章裡還涉及少量的農業工具，如風箱、谷倉、牲口圈、灌溉用具和獨輪車等。其中一只雞籠被直接放在有關立屏的條目之前，而一架水車又被安排在茶盤之後。克魯納斯（Craig Clunas）最近發表文章，探討明代早中期農村家庭自給自足的生活方式。在這裡不同的家庭在不同程度上經營著他們自己的果園、魚塘和菜園——甚至像朱權（朱檀之弟）也欽羨諸如種樹、養花、栽培水果和蔬菜這樣的農藝工作。[16]也許從農村這一角度以及《魯班經》中所記錄的各種工具而言，家具一詞可以理解為「家庭用具」，它可能包含了比「農居用具」更為廣泛的內涵。

15 Wen: *juan* 6, 2a, Wen Zhenheng notes with disapproval most of these vulgar decorative motifs.
16 Clunas: 1996a: 16–59

15 文震亨：卷6, 2a，文震亨對這些粗鄙的裝飾圖案極為反感
16 見英文注釋16。

30

the eminent status of the inner and outer circles of the Imperial family, was divided into four classes of descending rank: military and scholar-officials, peasants, artisans, and merchants. Actually, these categorical divisions do not reflect the much broader diversity of the Chinese population, nor the interplay between them; moreover, clear cut divisions in the furniture associated with them did not exist. Nevertheless, various sumptuary regulations – ranging from the use of personal ornament to the size and architectural style of housing – had provided a means of differentiating rank and class in Chinese society. The status of an individual was thus well represented by outward show.

Candidates for the scholar official class were traditionally schooled according to Confucian principles, and endured a rigorous period of study and examinations in the Classics previous to qualifying for such status. Their manifestations of upright moral character and frugal discipline were to serve as role models for a society whose dynastic cycles recurrently fell into decay because of corruption, moral decadence and luxurious consumption. The exemplary scholar-official led a frugal, unpretentious life, and made little outward show of extravagance or luxury. In terms of furniture design, perhaps the simple, minimally decorated style of the miniature furniture excavated from the tomb of two late Ming minor officials, Pan Yunzheng[17] and Wang Xijie[18] would have reflected the idealised reserve and integrity of this class. Much of the *huanghuali* furniture of the understated classical style falls into this category (cf. Plates 9, 26, 27).

Extravagance and conspicuous consumption were seen as antithetical to the sober Confucian ideology and threatened to destabilise social order. Thus, it was perhaps that the luxurious possessions and properties of Shen Wansan, an extremely rich man from Suzhou during the early Ming period,[19] as well as the extraordinary holdings of Grand Secretary Yan Song (1480–1565),[20] were not only confiscated, but also published as objects of scorn. These detailed inventories reveal that benches, chairs, beds, tables, cupboards, and screens of carved lacquer, lacquer inlaid with mother of pearl, or decorated with panels of marble were all available to those of sufficient means. The all but complete disappearance of such elaborate, yet more fragile works should not be overlooked in the history of traditional Ming furniture.

明代晚期：社會變遷和家具

從另一角度來講，那些尊貴的宮廷習俗和時尚也滲入社會。中國傳統社會結構屬於階級社會，在宮廷成員的尊崇地位之下，可以依次分為四個等級：文武官員、農民、匠人和商人。但事實上，這些群體的劃分並沒有反映出中國人口的多樣性，也未能反映出他們之間的聯繫，導致在家具上的截然分化也是不存在的。但不可否認的是一些帶有等級觀念的制度——從個人的裝飾用具到房屋建築的尺寸——還是用作區別不同等級的標記。一個人的社會地位，可以通過某些外在的東西清楚地表現出來。

文官傳統上是接受儒家教育，要經年苦讀和考試才可得官職。他們高尚的品行和廉潔的作風，是為了給當時因腐敗、道德淪喪和窮奢極欲而日益沒落的社會作出榜樣。一些模範官員倡導了一種儉樸、謙遜的生活方式，拒絕任何外在的驕逸或奢華。在家具的使用上，也許從這一時期潘[17]、王[18]兩位小官員墓中出土的家具模型，可以反映這一階層人士的自我約束和廉正作風。很多帶有典型次等級風格的黃花梨家具，也屬於此一類型（比較圖版9、26、27）。

奢華鋪張的消費與傳統儒家思想是背道而馳，同時也威脅了社會秩序的穩定。所以，明代早期奢華的蘇州鉅富沈萬三[19]和權相嚴嵩（1480–1565）[20]不僅被沒收家產，還被當成譏諷的對象。在這些詳盡的抄家目錄中，凳子、椅子、床、桌子、茶几、雕漆屏風、鑲螺鈿漆器或嵌大理石漆器均被當作奢侈品。這些精緻的器物雖然已經失傳了，但在談論明代家具史時，不應該把它們忽視。

17 Berliner: 76
18 Suzhou shi bowuguan
19 David: 148–9
20 Clunas 1996: 23–5

17 見英文注釋17。
18 蘇州市博物館
19 見英文注釋19。
20 見英文注釋20。

The ultimate role model was the Emperor. Although previous emperors had exerted relative restraint with regard to court expenditures, historians generally note the Wanli period (1573–1620) court for its extravagance as well as a turning point for the decline of the dynasty. The Wanli palace was lavishly furnished with lacquer and hardwood furniture.

Although precious tropical hardwoods had been used for furniture since ancient times, the widespread appearance of hardwood furniture in the late sixteenth century was partially due to lifting a ban on maritime trade in 1567 which permitted Chinese cargo ships to frequent ports throughout Southeast Asia from where hardwood timber was exported. Corresponding records from the Wanli period indicate that ivory, *huali*, *baitan*, *zitan*, ebony, *jichimu* were all being used to make furniture for the palace.[21] That there are no known hardwood pieces with regnal marks in light of the number of extant lacquer objects with Wanli marks must point to a separate tradition of lacquer specialists whose finishing work was distinct from wood-working furniture makers.

Hardwood furniture from the late Ming period synthesised traditional designs into sleek minimalist forms, hence earning it the name "classical Chinese furniture." The polished, translucent surfaces of hardwoods were rich with vibrant and abstract imagery that delighted the eye, as did other prized natural materials like jade. With these incredibly strong woods, craftsmen were able to achieve elegant designs without sacrificing the integrity of the structure. These densely grained hardwoods also held exceptionally sharp, crisp lines to their moulded edges.[22] And when their surfaces were embellished with carved decoration, the result often rivalled that of carved lacquer. Moreover, it was much less expensive than lacquer, more durable, resilient, and resistant to decay which were certainly all additional factors contributing to its widespread popularity.

By the late Ming period, weak centralised control led to the unregulated spread of entrepreneurship, particularly in the coastal regions. This newly-rich merchant class became ardent consumers of art, including furniture. At the same time, social norms were slowly breaking down. Whether through corruption which ran deep within the ranks of government, or

皇帝是重要的人物。明代早期的一些皇帝，在節約宮廷開銷方面發揮了一定的作用，歷史學家也基本上把萬歷年間（1573–1620）的腐化，看成是這明朝趨於衰落的轉折點。萬歷時期的宮殿，均大量地使用漆器和硬木家具。

雖然那些珍貴的熱帶硬木在很早以前就用來製作家具，但十六世紀後期硬木家具的廣泛使用是和1567年重開海禁，中國海船可以頻繁往來東南亞各地運輸硬木木料有關的。萬歷年間的一些相關材料，記載了象牙、花梨、白檀、紫檀、烏木、雞翅木都被用來製作宮廷家具。[21] 但迄今未見一件硬木家具上有某些漆器上所見的萬歷年款，説明當時漆匠和木匠各有其不同的傳統。

晚明時期硬木家具強調傳統設計中光亮精巧的造型，後來被譽為「中國經典家具」。硬木家具打磨得光滑透亮的表面，具有一種輕微顫動、抽象的感覺，看上去非常賞心悦目，因此也有人將它和玉相比擬。就是這些極為堅硬的木料，工匠們能夠在不損害整體結構的情況下，為這些家具裝飾很精細的圖案。不可思議的是，這些紋理極為緻密的硬木家具，還經常在其邊緣刻劃有尖細的線條。[22] 但這些家具表面有陰刻裝飾時，其效果通常比雕漆好。況且，它們比漆器便宜得多，也更耐用、更有彈性、更耐碰磕，這一切都使得硬木家具廣泛流傳。

明朝末年，中央權力的衰落使得商業畸形發展，這情況在沿海地區尤甚。暴富的商人成了工藝品的急切消費者，其中也包括了家具。與此同時，社會上道德標準也在逐漸喪失。且不管是因為各級政府的

21 Liu: *juan* 16, 15b
22 cf. Plate 13

21 劉若愚：卷16, 15b
22 比較圖版 13

because of the depleted reserves in the Imperial Treasuries which eventually led to policy changes permitting the sale of official degrees, even merchants were able to gain access or purchase official rank through their wealth; and further status gained in the creation of large estates with little regard to traditional sumptuary regulations.

Such is the caricature of the illiterate, wealthy merchant Ximen Qing, the main character from the infamous late Ming novel *Jin Ping Mei*, whose extravagantly furnished courtyard estate reflected immoderate behaviour and ostentatious living – a lifestyle that could only be deemed vulgar by the standards of contemporary proponents of sophisticated cultivation. In noting the sudden fashion for scholar's studios furnished with hardwood furniture in the homes of the illiterate *nouveau-riche*, a late Ming official wryly commented, "...but what books they study is open to question!" [23]

As the central governing authority floundered in the waning years of the dynasty, the Tianqi emperor (1621–27) himself appears to found some distraction from official responsibilities with a personal fascination for furniture-making; meanwhile, his unbridled court eunuchs were said to have vied with one another in the elegance and lavish expense of their furnishings. [24]

These apparent conflicting social dynamics may well have stimulated the *Treatise on Superfluous Things* [*Zhangwu zhi*], a publication on connoisseurship compiled/written near the end of the Wanli period (c. 1615–20) by Wen Zhenheng. [25] Although much of the text is extracted from at least two earlier works by Gao Lian [26] and Tu Long, [27] Wen Zhenheng's additional remarks often reflect a highly critical attitude towards the more recent decadent cultural trends which had developed. [28] These aside, *Zhangwu zhi* yet reveals a snapshot of the furniture culture within this dynamic of social change. In two of twelve chapters, [29] furniture – including various types of platforms and beds, stools, chairs, various types of tables, cabinets, bookcases, armrests and foot stools – are all sufficiently discussed to reveal in-depth details about style and decoration, materials, construction, and use.

極度腐敗,還是皇室財政的急劇枯竭,導致了賣官政策的出現,商人最終是有了用錢謀取官位的途徑,而依靠巨額財富謀取地位者,也不再會在意個人消費的限制。

在《金瓶梅》這部名聲不太好的晚明小說中,主角西門慶就是這樣一個被諷刺的對象:他的裝飾奢華的居處,反映的是他荒淫無度的生活,而這種生活方式在當時受過教育的人看來是粗鄙不堪的。當時一位官員見到一些沒有教養的暴發戶,開始流行在書房裡陳列硬木家具時,只好通過譏諷這些人不讀書聊以自慰。[23]

正當中央政權苟延殘喘的時候,天啟皇帝(1621-1627)自己卻荒落政事,而對木工製作產生了濃厚興趣。同時,他那些驕揚跋扈的宦官們,也被攛嗖起來,互相攀比著購買昂貴的奢華家具。[24]

當時的社會潮流,很大程度上促使了文震亨在萬曆末年(約1615-1620)編著《長物志》。[25] 雖然這部書中的很多內容是從高濂 [26] 和屠隆 [27] 等人的著作中徵引而來,但在文震亨自己的有關論述中,反映了他對當時每況愈下的文化氛圍持極度的批判態度。[28] 除此之外,《長物志》還勾畫了在當時社會變遷下的家具文化。全書共十二章,[29] 在其中的兩章裡對相關家具如各種形製的床、凳子、椅子、桌子、箱、書櫥、扶手椅和腳凳的風格、裝飾、用料、結構和用途等均作了詳盡的描述。

23 Wang Shixiang: I:17
24 Wang Shixiang: I:16
25 Wen Zhenheng
26 Gao Lian, *Eight Discourses on the Art of Living* (published 1592)
27 Tu Long, *Desultory Remarks on the Furnishings the Abode of a Retired Scholar* (published 1606)
28 Clunas 1991, Clunas 1996a, In these two works – *Superfluous Things* and *Fruitful Sites* – Craig Clunas has penetrated deeply into these shifting socio-economic issues as well as attitudes and motivations of the late Ming elite.
29 Berliner: 85–8, See for a translation of the Placement section of this text.

23 王世襄:I:17
24 王世襄:I:16
25 文震亨
26 高濂:《遵生八箋》,1592年刊印
27 屠隆。在其著作中散見有關退休官員家中家具陳設
28 Clunas 1991, Clunas 1996a, 在這兩部著作中伯important深入分析了晚明時期社會、經濟的變遷以及當時人的生活態度和思想變化。
29 見英文注釋29。

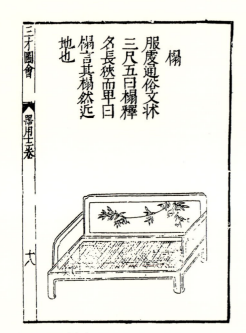

Fig. 7   Couch-bed
(Ta). Late Ming
(d.1607) woodcut
illustration to the
encyclopedia San Cai
Tu Hui. After Wang Ji
1332.
圖7   榻。晚明
(1607) 百科全書
《三才圖會》中木刻插
圖，據王圻1332。

Thus we learn that the lacquered *chuang* – incised and filled with designs of bamboo and trees – such as that illustrated only a decade earlier in the popular encyclopaedia *San Cai Tu Hui* (Fig. 7) – were highly prized. We also learn that the elite preferred the more antique-styled beds with legs supported with a floor stretcher, or the early box style platform.[30] He also tells us that the folding *chuang* was convenient to use on a boat. And in one line, Wen states "of recent are those carved like bamboo from cypress wood which are quite elegant and suitable for the woman's chamber or the centre of a small study." (ibid.)

Although the popularity of wood furniture abstractly styled or carved like bamboo furniture appears with more frequent reference during the early part of the Qing dynasty, these remarks offer possibly the earliest hint of this fashion – moreover, it is perhaps with some irony that it is a fashion which he himself has apparently promoted. Nevertheless, such vogue likely found its height during the Yongzheng and Qianlong periods when the imitation of materials and finishes was practised throughout the decorative arts and reached the height of technical achievement.

In discussing stools, Wen also gives us an early reference to the flush-sided construction terminology – *simianping* – a form that can now be dated from the Yanshan murals to the Jin dynasty;[31] he also infers that simple wood folding stools were used by the *literati* when roaming about in the mountains or travelling on a boat.[32]

Wen also guides the reader about the construction of altar tables (*tianran ji*), "....the end flanges must not be too sharp, but smooth and rounded, which is the antique pattern." Regarding their decorative end panels, "....use pieces of thick wide timber like that of the top, hollow them out and carve them lightly with designs such as cloud scrolls and *ruyi* heads. They must not be carved with such vulgar patterns and dragons, phoenixes, flowers, and grass." This comment is especially interesting in light of the fact that there is no mention of such decoration in the *Lu Ban jing*, and this clearly signifies the prevalence of such decoration at that time. He also tells us,

由此我們知道當時那些刻有竹木圖案漆床獲譽甚高，這些圖案也見諸於比《長物志》成書早十年的一部百科全書性質的著作《三才圖會》中（圖7）。我們也由此獲知當時的文人們更喜歡那種「下座不虛」的古式床，或者說早期箱式的榻。[30] 作者甚至還告知我們折疊式的交床，是為了便於在船上使用。在其中的一處，文震亨還強調在當時人看來那種「柏木琢，細如竹者，甚精，宜閨閣及小齋中」。（同上）

在清代早期的著述中，常提到這種風格抽象，看似竹製的木質家具的流行，但文氏的有關描述應當是最早的記載。另外，文震亨的記載多少也帶有一些自嘲的意味，因為他本人就是這一流行的積極推動者。無論如何，這一潮流最終在雍正和乾隆年間達到了新高潮，因為此時的家具在用料、樣式和裝飾手法上，均開始仿古，在技術成就上達到了新的高度。

在談論凳子時，文震亨還為我們提供了「四面平」這個用來表示各面平齊的術語，這種形制現在可以追溯到嚴山寺的金代壁畫。[31]他還指出在文人們在遊山玩水時，也使用那種簡單的小馬扎。[32]

文震亨同時也向讀者介紹了天然几的結構，例如按照古製天然几的飛角處不能太尖利，而應該較平圓；而在裝飾下部擋板時，應該使用較寬厚的木板，並略雕出卷雲紋或如意頭，不能裝飾粗

30 Wen: *juan* 6, 1ab
31 Wen: *juan* 6, 3a
32 Wen: *juan* 6, 3b

30 文震亨：卷6, 1ab
31 文震亨：卷6, 3a
32 文震亨：卷6, 3b

"The long, narrow ones of recent make are abominable." [33]

Wen also offers an explanation for the form of the book cabinets in Plate 31: "Books should not be placed upon the bottom shelf because of the proximity to moisture from the floor. This is the reason that the opening at the base should have a little additional height, or should be placed upon on stand." [34] And regarding the foot stool with rollers, "...massaging the feet excites the vital energies (*jingqi*) to bubble forth like a fountain." [35]

He cites the use of *huali*, *zitan*, *wumu*, and *nanmu* as furniture making materials. Stools of Sichuan cypress inlaid with *wumu* were especially elegant. [36] Nonetheless, lacquered furniture or that inlaid with mother of pearl was clearly the most highly prized – especially Song and Yuan lacquer. On the other hand, he also tells us that old lacquer square tables take on a nice weathered look when placed in an outdoor pavilion [37] which accounts for their rarity today.

Wen also notes the use of bamboo beds, bookcases, stools, and foot stools. He states that a meditation chair should be made of *tiantai* cane. [38] Although marble is commonly associated with Qing furniture, Wen also favourably notes several types for use in *chuang* railings, [39] chairs splats, [40] as wells as screen panels. [41]

Wen Zhenheng was the great-grandson of perhaps the most famous of all Ming *literati*-scholars, Wen Zhengming. To what extent his written words reached out – influence others is not clear, nevertheless, Wen's penetrating insights further our understanding taste in late Ming times.

THE REFINEMENT AND ELABORATION OF QING FURNITURE

After the fall of the ineffective and corrupted late Ming ruling house in 1644, and under benevolent early Qing Manchu rule, China once again flourished. While furniture-makers generally held to classic patterns, a tendency towards formality and refinement emerges during the subsequent Kangxi (1662–1722), Yongzheng (1723–35) and Qianlong (1735–95)

鄙的紋樣或者龍鳳、花草等。值得注意的是文氏的説法並未見於《魯班經》中,這就清楚地表明了這些紋樣的來源。文震亨還認為天然几的形製以「近時所製狹而長者最可厭。」[33]

在文氏的著作中他還談到如圖版31所示的書櫥,他認為:「下格不可置書,以近地早濕故也。足亦當稍高,小者可置几上。」[34] 而關於帶滾軸的腳凳,文氏説:「以腳踹軸滾動往來,蓋湧泉穴精氣所生以運動。」[35]

文震亨還談及花梨、紫檀、烏木和楠木在家具製作上的用途,而用四川柏木製成並鑲嵌有烏木的凳子尤為精緻。[36] 但不管怎麼説,上漆或嵌有螺鈿的家具在當時受到的稱譽最高,尤其是宋元的漆器。另外,文氏説如果把那種古老的漆方桌置於室外的涼亭時,它會呈現出一種悦目的舊色,但當時已經非常罕見了。[37]

文震亨還提到了竹床、書箱、凳子和腳凳的功用。他強調説禪椅應該用天臺藤製作。[38] 雖然在清代家具中才較多地使用了大理石,但文震亨還是提到大理石用作床檔 [39]、椅背擋板 [40] 和屏心 [41] 的例子。

文震亨是明代最著名的文人文徵明的曾孫。雖然文震亨的這些著述對當時人們的影響如何還不可確知,但他敏鋭的洞察力,無疑大大加深了我們對晚明社會風貌的了解。

改良和精細的清代家具

明室腐敗,在1644年滅亡。清初較為緩和的統治,使中國重新走向繁榮。在家具製作保存舊有傳統的同時,康熙(1662-1722)、雍正(1723-1735)和乾隆(1735-1795)年

33 Wen: *juan* 6, 2a
34 Wen: *juan* 6, 4a
35 Wen: *juan* 6, 5a
36 Wen: *juan* 6, 3b
37 Wen: *juan* 10, 3a
38 Wen: *juan* 6, 2a
39 Wen: *juan* 6, 1b
40 Wen: *juan* 6, 3a
41 Wen: *juan* 6, 5a

33 文震亨:卷6, 2a
34 文震亨:卷6, 4a
35 文震亨:卷6, 5a
36 文震亨:卷6, 3b
37 文震亨:卷6, 3a
38 文震亨:卷6, 2a
39 文震亨:卷6, 1b
40 文震亨:卷6, 3a
41 文震亨:卷6, 5a

periods. A set of twelve scroll paintings dating to early part of the eighteenth century illustrate elegant ladies within the inner private quarters at the Yuanmingyuan Palace[42] where furnishings of natural wood, lacquer, speckled bamboo, root, cane, and porcelain furniture are all realistically portrayed; although of traditional form, they appear modernised against the backdrop of late Ming works, updated with subtle refined qualities and innovative variations, yet lacking the animated line and robust figure of their predecessors.

Records from the Yongzheng Imperial Workshops specify the recruiting of furniture-makers from Guangdong and the Suzhou region, two areas renowned for their superb craftsmanship. At that time furniture was being produced in many materials – lacquer, painted wood, and in numerous woods including *huali*, *zitan*, *jichimu*, *nanmu*, *yumu*, *songmu*, *duanmu*, *shanmu*, *baimu*, *huangyangmu*, as well as their various combinations. Decoration of cloisonné, glass, jade, silver and gold inlaid fittings, etc. were also contributed to the furniture creations by other workshop disciplines at that time.[43] The refined workmanship and archaistic style of the Kai-Yin Lo Collection *jichimu* table (Plate 20) suggest that it may well have been produced at the Imperial Workshops during this period.

A major point in the evolution of the decorative arts is marked by the Qianlong reign. Like others before him, Qianlong highly venerated the knowledge of the ancients and, with dominating influence in the Imperial Workshops, effected archaistic tendencies to communicate this devotion. Qianlong was a lover of the decorative arts, and became personally involved with design and craftsmanship in numerous disciplines ranging from archaic jade carving to *zitan* furniture design. A fancy for Guangdong-style furniture, *zitan* and refined archaic (*fanggu*) motifs are all reflected in what has become known as Qianlong style furniture. Qianlong's expeditions into Burma near the end of the eighteenth century also reinvigorated the trade route to the south-west resulting in large supplies of highly-figured marble coming out of the nearby Dali region in Yunnan province which subsequently became widely fashionable as decorative inlays for furniture.

Concern for low inventories of *nanmu* and *zitan*, which had already been noted during the Yongzheng reign, prompted a monopolisation of sources during Qianlong reign. By the end of

間出現了一股趨於格式化但很精細的潮流。十八世紀初的雍正十二妃圖描繪了這些妃子及其各自在圓明園內的臥房，[42]其中布置有天然樹木、漆器、斑竹、根雕、藤製品和瓷器等。雖然從傳統上說這些家具較晚明時期更為時髦，在製作質量上更為精細，在工藝技術上也更富有變化，但它們缺乏晚明家具活潑的線條和堅實的造型。

在雍正年間的造辦處檔案中分別登錄來自廣東和蘇州的木匠，他們均以其高超的手藝而著名。這一時期家具原料來源十分廣泛，諸如漆器、彩木以及花梨、紫檀、雞翅木、楠木、榆木、松木、椴木、杉木、柏木、黃楊木等均可見，或者將它們配合使用。同時，這一時期的家具還由其它匠作的工匠們裝飾鑲嵌琺瑯、玻璃、玉器和金銀等。[43]圖版20所示的工藝精良、古意盎然的雞翅木桌子，就很可能是由這一時期的宮廷匠作製作的。

乾隆年間，家具的裝飾藝術發生了較大的變化。乾隆皇帝像他之前的多位皇帝一樣，也崇尚仿古，在他的直接影響下，造辦處也盛行仿古。乾隆還是個裝飾藝術愛好者，甚至親自參予仿古玉器和紫檀家具的設計和製作。對廣式作法、紫檀和精細仿古圖案的追求，被稱為典型的乾隆式家具。十八世紀末清王朝在緬甸的擴張，重新開拓了西南貿易通道，便利雲南大理地區所產紋路清晰的大理石料大量向外輸出，並最終使得在家具上鑲嵌大理石的做法變得非常流行。

早在雍正年間就已經提到楠木和紫檀的缺乏，乾隆朝時其來源更是被壟斷。到了十八世紀末，宮廷的紫檀供應是如此緊張，以至在乾隆晚期和嘉慶時期製作家具時，只能使用剖開的紫檀料

42 Tian: 23-6
43 Zhu: 1&2

42 田家青：23-6
43 朱：1和2

the eighteenth century, Imperial supplies of *zitan* were so depleted that during the late Qianlong and Jiaqing periods, it became necessary to construct furniture with laminated materials, or with veneers over softwood cores. The deeply pigmented colour of prized *zitan* was found in an inferior material of similar characteristics, *hongmu*, and was also simulated with coatings of deep reddish-black semi-transparent lacquer (see Plate 12).

Jesuit missionaries, who gradually established respect at court for their knowledge of Western science and techniques, often presented members of the Imperial court with gifts of Western decorative art, and also introduced European baroque architecture to Palace designers. After the Opium War in 1840, Western influences were even more prevalent. An eclectic mixture of Chinese and Western decorative styles and motifs can be witnessed in furnishings from this period, especially in the larger cities and coastal regions where there was more frequent contact. In remote inland areas such as Shanxi, such influence was hardly noticed until recent times; moreover, Song, Yuan, and Ming styles continued to be reproduced. Deteriorating economic conditions and a severely weakened political structure in the nineteenth century contributed to a general decline in quality amongst the decorative art produced at that time.

FURNISHING SUMPTUOUS PALACES TO COURTYARD DWELLINGS

The appearance, materials and role of Chinese furniture varied tremendously in a society that was both hierarchical and diversified. It found its place in both sacred and secular settings and in dwellings of the exalted and lowly. The precedent set by the Imperial model filtered downward through to the homes of scholar officials and government functionaries, and all were concerned to a greater or lesser degree with the axially oriented courtyard architecture and its influence on furniture placement.

PALACES

The Imperial Palaces were organised around a series of southerly facing central halls. These lavish structures were each furnished with an elaborately carved throne raised upon a central

或者將其黏貼在軟木芯上。因為紫檀那種倍受稱道的顏色，也見於紅木這種較低廉的木料上，所以紅木通常被漆上一層紅黑半透明的油漆以模仿紫檀家具（圖版12）。

西方傳教士們依靠他們的科學知識和技術，逐漸在清廷裡贏得了尊重。他們經常為宮廷用具提供西方的裝飾藝術手法，也為宮廷設計者們帶來了歐洲巴洛克式建築風格。1840年鴉片戰爭後，西方的影響更為流行。這一時期的家具清楚地揭示了那些中西結合的裝飾樣式和體裁非常流行，尤其是在中西接觸更為頻繁的大城市和沿海地區。而在內地如山西，這些影響即使在近代也還很少見；同時，宋、元、明時期的風格還在繼續被採用。十九世紀日益惡化的經濟狀況和嚴重削落的政治體制，導致了這一時期家具裝飾藝術水平的整體下降。

奢華宮殿和院式家居的家具裝飾

中國古代家具的樣式、質料和地位在一個階級分化、多元化的社會裡急劇地變化。在宗教和世俗的陳設中、在豪華府第和寒門陋室裡，都有家具的地位。而上自宮廷內府，下到文職官員家中，以及衙門裡的家具陳設，都或多或少地和傳統的沿中軸線排列的建築布局有關。

宮殿

皇城內的宮殿，包括一系列各以一座面南宮殿為中心的建築群。在這些主殿的中央高臺上，都設有一件精雕細琢的御座，其後立著一件大屏風。兩旁則依次對稱擺設著工藝精良的桌子和架子，以供陳列禮儀用

dais with a decorative screen placed behind. To either side were placed symmetrically ordered arrangements of exquisitely crafted tables and stands set out with ritual implements. Along the walls on either side, long tables were arranged with decorative objects and cabinets of monumental proportion were filled with ceremonial objects. This grandeur of space complimented with exquisitely refined furnishings was intended to reflect the Emperor's mandate from Heaven.

Dwellings facing courtyards to the east and west, as well as additional courtyards further removed, provided gradient layers of hierarchically based housing for court officials, eunuchs, wives, and concubines, etc. Although these residential quarters were reduced in size to human scale, they were elegantly furnished with works made in or acquired through the Palace Workshops. Typical quarters were divided into three rooms. The main central room was generally furnished with a long altar table standing against the back wall with a formal arrangement of small tables, couches, chairs set in front. To the left was a bedroom which had a built-in *kang* platform or bed set at the back wall, along with appropriately placed clothes cupboards, clothes racks, basin stands, and so on. The room to the right may have been more loosely arranged as a study or work space, with items such as tables, shelves, and chairs. Here, the elegant ladies' quarters of Yuanmingyuan mentioned above come to mind.

The Imperial monarchy also supported an extended family whose nobility reached throughout China. At the beginning of the Ming dynasty, for example, Hongwu's twenty-four sons, although deprived of power, received endowments that included sumptuous estates furnished with servants and guards. By the Wanli period, the descendants who had inherited nobility of rank had grown in number to over twenty-thousand, and needless to say, their multiple salaries added significantly to the financial burden the Imperial Treasuries. Nevertheless, their palatial estates followed the Imperial model, and were undoubtedly appointed with copious quantities of luxurious furnishings.

COURTYARD ESTATES AND DWELLINGS

The walled courtyard compound was a standard living space of modular plan found throughout

具。沿著兩側牆擺放的長案上，放置有裝飾用品以及裝滿慶典用具的大箱子。這一充滿精緻家具的宏大場面是為了顯示君權神授。

大內東西兩側的建築以及其它一些偏殿按照等級高低以供宮內官員、大監和嬪妃居住。儘管這些居處的面積大小由其主人地位而決定，令陳設有宮廷造辦處製作或從造辦處要來的家具。最典型的房子有三間屋，中間主室內後牆前通常擺上一條長香案，香案前再按照一定的規則擺上小桌子、長椅和成套的椅子。臥室居左，在其後牆下設下炕臺或置床一張，以及與此相應的衣櫥、衣架和盆架等。右邊的房間大都用作書房或工作間，其中陳設書案、將寶格和椅子等物件。這裡我們自然會想起上文中所提到的圓明園內那些雅緻的閨房。

皇室的至高無上，確保了其家族成員在全國範圍內貴族地位。例如在明朝建立伊始，明太祖的二十四個兒子儘管被剝奪了政治權利，但都被賜予了大量裝修豪華的宮室和相應的衛士。到了萬曆時期，有權繼承爵位的皇室子弟超過了兩萬人。毫無疑問，這些人的巨額俸祿，大大增加了內庫的財政負擔。他們依照皇宮樣式建造的華麗宮室，無疑需要大量的豪華家具來裝飾。

院式家居

封閉式院落是中國家居的標準形式，它也是從中軸線宮殿布局衍生而來的。那些官宦和有錢人家，經常是居住於一座有一間或多間正房的院落裡，正房周圍及其後面的房子，則供家中其他成員和僕人居住。正

China, and was also derived from the axially-oriented palace model. Officials and those of sufficient wealth frequently lived in large compounds with one or more central halls, to which quarters adjacent and behind provided housing for the extended family and servants. The main hall, study, various bedrooms, and sometimes even a separate temple, which itself followed the layout of the Imperial model, were all common elements within the courtyard plan, and each was typically arranged with a variety of furnishings.

The large central hall (*tingtang*) was multi-functional, and traditionally served both ritual and secular purposes. Whether simple or grand and lavishly decorated, this room often has its long "altar-like" table placed against the back wall (or an intermediate screen wall) where ancestral tablets, images of Buddhist and Daoist deities, and various ceremonial vessels were arranged. A large decorative painting was usually hung above the table. Periodic to regular offerings of food and incense were set out to acknowledge patrilineal descent and communal links. The main hall was also a place for entertaining visitors, and required seating and table arrangements to be prepared for the occasion. (Fig.8)

Fig. 8 "Qingfu ruhe." Woodblock print illustration to *Shengyu xiangjie* [Explanatory Images of the Imperial Edicts], Kangxi period (1662–1722).
圖8 《聖諭像解》木刻插圖．康熙年間 (1662–1722)。

In larger residences, the kitchen was not central to the household; moreover, it being staffed by servants, meals were delivered in food boxes and served wherever the master or the mistress of the household might fancy – in the bedroom, the study, or perhaps under a flowering tree in the garden. On the other hand, in a modest courtyard dwelling, the kitchen hearth was a central element in the home. The square table – formally situated in front of the long "altar-like" side table as in the temple tradition – was brought forward at meal time into the central part of the room where chairs, stools, and benches were gathered around for seats.

房、書房和多間臥室都屬於這種院落式家居布局中最基本的單位，有時甚至仿照宮廷布局那樣，還有一處單獨的祭堂，而所有這些房間裡都擺設有相應的家具。

中央較大的廳堂通常是多功能的，既可以舉辦典禮儀式，也可進行日常活動。不管其裝飾簡單還是複雜，在正房的後牆（或者是房子中間的一堵隔牆）下都陳放著一張香案，其上經常有祖宗的靈牌、佛教或道家神靈塑像和各種禮儀用具。在香案的上方則經常掛上一幅巨大的裝飾性圖畫。供品和香火按時獻上，以示父子相承以及其它家族關係。因為正房也是用來接待客人的場所，所以要求桌椅布置停當，以便來客時使用（圖8）。

在一些大戶人家裡，不用操心廚務，廚下的事情由僕人們來做，食物也是裝在食盒裡，然後送到主人或主婦吩咐的地方，如臥室、書房或者花園裡某株正在開花的樹下。但另一方面，在一個溫暖的家庭中，廚房又是家居生活的中心之。香案前的方桌在吃飯時需前移到房間的中央，而椅子、凳子和長凳則圍在其周圍供使用。

The idealised Chinese interior is more closely associated with the traditional study. (Fig. 9) This room reflects the Confucian ideal of a highly educated class of moral and virtuous officials versed in the classics, and in the four traditional arts of calligraphy, painting, poetry and music. Ideally, the studio was simply, yet elegantly furnished. A large painting table served as a desk and was central to the studio. A footrest was often placed below the table in front of the master's chair. Those with massaging rollers stimulated the circulation and excited the internal state for creative production. Cabinets were filled with books, scroll paintings, and treasured writing utensils. A couch, or daybed, placed along a wall provided a place for quiet relaxation, as well as a platform to entertain a friend while playing enchanting music on the *qin*.

In northern China, with its cold winters, raised and heated hollow brick platforms (*kang*) were constructed along an interior wall where individuals would sleep at night and could also sit comfortably during the day. The *kang* was thus commonly furnished with low furniture that was made especially for use while sitting on its matted surface.

The bedroom quarters of the master of the house can be inferred from traditional scenes in paintings and book illustrations (Fig. 10), and also corresponds to a late Ming formula:

Place the bed (*ta*) facing south. The half of the room behind the bed where people do not go should be used for such things as a brazier, clothes rack, washbasin, dressing case, and reading lamp. In front of the bed, place only a small table with nothing on it, two small square stools, and a small cupboard for incense, medicine, and delightful curiosities. The room should be refined, elegant, and not too cluttered. If too ornate, it will be like a ladies' room and unsuitable for a recluse sleeping in the clouds and dreaming of the moon.[44]

Fig. 9 *"Tong qi lian zhi"* (Harmonizing Energy with Nature). Woodblock print illustration to Shengyu xiangjie (Explanatory Images of the Imperial Edicts), Kangxi period (1662–1722).
圖9 《聖諭像解》 木刻插圖，康熙年間 (1662–1722)。

Fig. 10 Bedroom. Woodcut print illustration to *Xixiang ji*, late Ming period.
圖10 臥室。據晚明木刻本《西廂記》插圖。

Fig. 11 Bedroom. Woodcut print illustration to *Yuchai ji*, late Ming period.
圖11 臥室。 據晚明木刻本 《西廂記》插圖。

書房是最為理想化的中國室內布局（圖9）。這間書房反映了一位熟讀四書五經、精通詩書琴畫、有道德、有修養官員的儒家理想。這間書房雖然簡單，但家具陳設卻很精緻。書房中間放著一張很大的畫桌，同時兼作書案。在桌子下面、主人的椅子前經常放置一件腳凳。那種帶有按摩滾軸的腳凳，可以促進血液循環，激發主人的內在創造力。箱子裡則裝滿了書、卷軸和珍貴的書寫用具。一條長椅或者是榻放在牆邊以供歇息，另有一案用來鼓琴悅友。

在中國北方，由於冬天寒冷，室內建有可以加熱的炕，既方便夜裡睡覺，白天也可以舒適地坐在上面。與此同時，尤當坐在炕上時，炕上需要一些較低家具。

從一些古畫和書中的插圖，可知主人的臥室布置（圖10）。晚明時期的情況大低如此：「面南設臥榻一榻，後別留半室人所不至以置薰籠、衣架、盥器、廁菡、書燈之屬。榻前僅置一小几、不設一物、小方杌二、小櫥一，以置藥、玩器。室中精潔雅素，一涉絢麗便如閨閣中，非幽人眠雲夢月所宜矣。」[44]

文震亨《長物志》中的這一段文字和其它有關段落裡，提到了女性臥室內適當的家具布置，也觸及了中國傳統社會中男女間的差別，以及由此造成對家具和裝飾風格上的影響。在那些大院落裡有很多分隔開的房間，供男女家庭成員們居住。女性房間裡陳放的家具很多是嫁妝（圖11）。除了較為典型的女性風格外，這些家具通常大量裝飾一些傳統的寓意圖案，如鴛鴦、麒麟和吉祥花卉等，這些圖案都是希望新娘能懷上男孩以續香火，同時也為將來祈求平安和富貴。

44 Wen *juan*: 10, 2b, 3a
44 文震亨：卷10, 2b, 3a

This and other passages from Wen Zhenheng's *Treatise on Superfluous Things* which note the suitability of specific furniture design for the ladies' apartments, touch upon the gender gap characteristic within traditional Chinese society – and moreover, its relationship to furniture and decorative style. Within large courtyard residences, separate quarters existed for male and female members. The furniture arranged in the ladies' quarters was generally provided as part of a dowry. (Fig. 11) Besides its effeminate style, such furniture was often ornately decorated with traditional rebuses – mandarin ducks, *qilin*, auspicious flowers, and so on – which sent wishes for the newlywed bride to bear male children with the implied promise of sustaining the family lineage and providing security and wealth for the future.

Fig. 12 Outdoor sleeping on a hot summer evening. Woodcut from the novel *Jin Ping Mei*. Chongzhen period (1628–1644)
圖12　夏夜露宿。木刻本《金瓶梅》，崇禎年間 (1628–1644)。

The interior space of the courtyard house is less defined by individual rooms than it is by its surrounding walls. Whether inside or outside the walls, in both the temperate seasons and temperate regions, outside areas were also used as an extension of the interior living spaces. Decorative screens, tables, and chairs were commonly moved into the garden according to the occasion. Of more enduring materials were tables of stone and porcelain stools. During a hot summer evening, a mosquito gauze-lined enclosure set up on the terrace and appropriately furnished with a daybed, incense stand, stool, and side table would have served as a comfortable sleeping quarters. (Fig. 12)

Thus, while derived from the formal Imperial Palace, the "traditional Chinese living space" was also flexible, with furnishings arranged in accordance to the occasion as well as with the season. Nevertheless, even in informal arrangements, the phenomenon of relative hierarchy, due respect, and status were all manifest in subtlest detail. Whether through the intentional placement of guests seated at a table, a footrest placed in front of one of several seats, or a servant's feelings of inappropriateness at sitting together with her mistress on a bed, elements of social etiquette were pervasive.

Writings on Chinese furniture frequently concern themselves with furniture's aesthetic merit and technical achievements. In fact, the origin and development of furniture within its social context is equally important. Embracing traditional and regional decorative styles from richly ornate to rustically crude, and constructed from myriad of materials, the story of "traditional Chinese furniture" has only begun to be written.

這些各自分隔的房間對院落內部空間的限制，遠不如院牆的作用那樣明顯。不管是在牆內還是牆外，在適當的季節和適當的地點，室外也可以當作室內生活空間的延伸。在適當的情況下，屏風、桌子和椅子都可以搬到花園裡，較多的是耐用的石桌和瓷質的凳子。在炎熱的夏夜，在高處設一頂紗布蚊帳、配以一榻、一香几、一凳和一桌，就構成了一處舒適的歇宿場所（圖12）。

因此，儘管中國傳統的家居空間來源於宮廷樣式，但它的家具陳設是可以隨著季節一類因素的變化而變化的。不管怎樣，即使在非正式的場合下，等級觀念和地位的尊卑也是通過一些細節清楚地體現出來。諸如客人們在桌前的坐次、腳凳該放在哪一條椅子前、僕人不能和其主婦一道坐在床上這樣一類生活禮儀，在當時是人人皆知的。

中國家具的研究經常被局限在一些較小的專題上，而對於中國傳統家具的研究，只是這一廣泛研究領域中的一小部分。從平民百姓到王孫公子，從暴富的商人到世代相承的書香門第，家具都是他們日常生活中的一部分。在傳統和地域上，從豪華裝修的室邸到質樸的鄉居，在裝飾風格都有差異，只有了解這些差異，以及其極為廣泛的原料來源，我們才談得上開始討論中國傳統家具。

BIBLIOGRAPHY
徵引書目

Addis, J. M. *Chinese Ceramics from Datable Tombs*. London and New York: Sotheby Parke Bernet, 1978.

Berliner, Nancy. *Beyond the Screen; Chinese Furniture of the Sixteenth and Seventeenth Centuries*. Boston: Museum of Fine Arts, Boston, 1996.

Beurdeley, Michel. *Chinese Furniture*. Tokyo, New York and San Francisco: Kodansha International, 1979.

Chai Zejun, Zhang Chouliang (ed.). *Fanshi Yanshansi*. [Yanshan Temple, Fanshi]Beijing: Wenwu chubanshe, 1990.
【柴澤俊、張丑良編：《繁峙嚴山寺》，文物出版社，北京，1990。】

Chen Wanli. *Zhongguo chuantong jianzhu* [Chinese Traditional Architecture]. Hong Kong: Wanli shuduan, Zhongguo Jianzhu gongye chubanshe: 1991.
【陳萬里：《中國傳統建築》，香港萬里書店，中國建築工業出版社聯合出版，香港，1991。】

Chen Zengbi. "A One-Thousand-Year-Old Daybed." *Journal of the Classical Chinese Furniture Society* Autumn 1994: 24-8.
【陳增弼：《一件一千年歷史的榻》，見《中國古典家具協會會刊》4:4（1994年秋季號）：24-8。】

Clunas, Craig. (1988) *Chinese Furniture*. London: Bamboo Publishing Ltd, 1988.

Clunas, Craig. (1991) *Superfluous Things; Material Culture and Social Status in Early Modern China*. Urbana and Chicago: University of Illinois Press, 1991.

Clunas, Craig. (1996) "Furnishing the Self in Early Modern China." Catalogue essay in *Beyond the Screen; Chinese Furniture of the Sixteenth and Seventeenth Centuries*. Boston: Museum of Fine Arts, Boston. 1996: 21-53.

Clunas, Craig. (1996a) *Fruitful Sites; Garden Culture in Ming Dynasty China*. Durham: Duke University Press, 1996.

Cui Yongxue. *Zhongguo jiaju shi zuoju pian* [The History of Chinese Furniture Seating Furniture]. Taipei: Mingwen shuju, 1987.
【崔詠雪：《中國家具史‧坐具編》，臺北明文書局，1987年。】

David, Sir Percival. *Chinese Connoisseurship; the Ko Ku Yao Lun, the Essential Criteria of Antiquities*. London: Faber and Faber, 1971.

Evarts, Curtis. (Win 93) The Classic of Lu Ban and Classical Chinese Furniture *Journal of the Classical Chinese Furniture Society*. Winter 1993. 33-44.】

Gao Lian. *Zunsheng bajian*. [Eight Discourses on the Art of Living]. Ming text, National Central Library, Taipei.
【高濂：《遵生八箋》，明刻本，臺北國立圖書館。】

Guo Xi. *Linjuan gaozhi* [The Lofty Message of Forests and Streams]. Yishu congbian ed., vol. 10, no. 67. Taipei: World Publishing Co., 1967.
【郭熙：《林泉高致》，藝術叢編本，卷10，第67，臺北世界書局，1967。】

Handler, Sarah. "A Ming Meditating Chair in Bauhaus Light." *Journal of the Classical Chinese Furniture Society*. Winter, 1992: 26-38.

Lin, Lina. *Special Exhibition of Furniture in Paintings.* Taipei: National Palace Museum, 1996.
【林麗娜：《家具繪畫特展》，臺北國立故宮博物館，1996。】

Liu Ruoyi. *Zhuozhong zhi.* Baibu congshu jicheng. Printed by Yiwen yinshuguan.
【劉若愚：《酌中志》，百部叢書集成，藝文印書館印行。】

Pirazzoli-t'Serstevens, Michele. "Chinese Furniture in the Han Dynasty (206 B.C.–A.D. 220)." *Journal of the Classical Chinese Furniture Society.* Summer, 1991: 52–62.

Ruitenbeek, Klaas. *Carpentry and Building in Late Imperial China; A Study of the Fifteenth-Century Carpenters Manual Lu Ban jing.* Leiden: E. J Brill, 1993.

Shandong Provincial Museum. "Fajue Ming Zhu Tan Mu Jishi" [A Record of the Discovery of the Ming Tomb of Zhu Tan]. *Wenwu,* 1972, 5:25
【山東省博物館："發掘明朱檀墓紀實"，《文物》，1972年5期：25。】

Suzhou bowuguan huaji. Beijing: Wenwu chubanshe, 1981.
【《蘇州博物館畫集》，北京，文物出版社，1981年。】

Suzhou Municipal Museum. "Suzhou huqiu Wang Xijue mu qingli jilue." *Wenwu,* 1975,3: 51–6.
【蘇州市博物館："蘇州虎丘王錫爵墓清理記略"，《文物》，1975年3期：51–6。】

Teng Rensheng. *Lacquer Wares of the Chu Kingdom.* Trans. by Vivian Hung Wai-yuen and Zena Cheung. Hong Kong: The Woods Publishing Company, 1992.

Tian Jiaqing. *Classic Chinese Furniture of the Qing Dynasty.* London and Hong Kong: Philip Wilson Publishers and Joint Publishing Company Limited, 1996.
【田家青：《清代家具》，Philip Wilson出版社和聯合出版公司出版，倫敦和香港，1996。】

Tu Long. *Qiju qiwn jian.* Meishu congshu 2:9 Jiangsu, 1986.
【屠隆：《起居器物箋》，美術叢書2:9，江蘇，1986年。】

Waley, Arthur. *Introduction to the Study of Chinese Painting.* London: Ernest Benn, 1923.

Wang Qi. *San Cai Tu Hui* [Pictorial Encyclopaedia of Heaven, Earth and Man], 1609. 3 vols. Shanghai: Shanghai guji chubanshe, 1985.
【王圻：《三才圖會》三冊，上海古籍出版社，1985。】

Wang Shixiang. *Connoisseurship of Chinese Furniture.* 2 vols. Hong Kong: Joint Publishing (HK) Co., Ltd., 1990.
【王世襄：《中國家具鑒賞》兩冊，香港聯合出版公司，1990。】

Wen Zhenheng. *Zhangwu zhi* [Treatise on Superfluous Things]. Compiled 1615–20. *Yishu congbian 29.257.*
【文震亨：《長物志》，1615–1620年編成，藝術叢書29.257。】

Zhu Jiajin 1. "Yongzheng nian de jiaju zhizao kao" [A Study of the Yongzheng Imperial Furniture Workshops, Part 1]. *Gugong bowuyuan yuankan* 1985, 3: 104–11.
【朱家溍："雍正年的家具製作考"，《故宮博物院院刊》，1995年3期：104–11。】

Zhu Jiajin 2. "Yongzheng nian de jiaju zhizao kao (xu)" [A Study of the Yongzheng Imperial Furniture Workshops, Part 2]. *Gugong bowuyuan yuankan* 1985,4: 79–87.
【朱家溍："雍正年的家具製作考"，《故宮博物院院刊》，1995年4期：79–87。】

The Seventeenth Century House – The Dialectic of The Living Environment

十七世紀的宅第—
生活環境的辯證關係

Puay-peng Ho
何培斌

A house is more than a functional entity. It is also the embodiment of the aesthetic taste of its owner in the way the building is constructed, decorated, and furnished. As such, the house is a marker of social class, according Bourdieu.[1] In philosophical discourse, the house is also used as a thinking language for making cosmological outlooks.[2] Thus, included in the idea of a house are functional, social and symbolic values. This is also true of a Chinese house. A comprehensive understanding of a Chinese house needs to include all three values. In this way, we will be able to look at the living environment in totality, in the way it is created and used, in the way the choice of decoration and furnishing reveals social classifications, and in its role in projecting the symbolics of the culture. This living environment would include the architecture of the house, the furniture and objects housed inside and the activities conducted in the house, through which the aspirations of the owner are expressed. In this article, I will attempt a glimpse of the house of the seventeenth century China through some extant examples, examining them side by side with texts of the period. This will be a limited reading of the subject and it will not provide a comprehensive view of the domestic architecture of that period. However, it is hoped that studying within the context of the buildings and the texts will result in a better understanding of the meaning of the living environment of the time. It will also underscore the approach that this living environment includes both the building and the furniture together as a holistic entity, rather than separately and fragmentarily.

Seventeenth century China is characterised as a tumultuous period in Chinese history, marked by uncertainty, warfare, pendulum swings of the economy, tightly controlled rule by the "barbarian", and the withdrawal of the literati from the government. However, as demonstrated superbly by Craig Clunas, the early seventeenth century saw the rise and maintenance of Jiangnan region as the richest part of China, and a consumerism that was unhindered by the sorry state of the last days of the Ming empire.[3] In the early Qing period, with the increasing

房屋是一個功能實體，通過其建築形式、裝飾及家具陳設，可顯出屋主的品味。如Bourdieu所論，房屋本身就是社會階級的標誌。[1] 在哲學的論述裡，房屋亦是表達宇宙觀的思想語言。[2] 因此，房屋的概念是包含了功能價值、社會價值和象徵意義，而這些概念亦適用於中國房屋。故要全面了解中國房屋，便要從這三方面入手，這樣才能整體地研究中國人的生活環境，了解房屋如何建造和使用，裝飾和家具如何顯露不同的社會階層，以及它突顯文化象徵的角色。生活環境包括了房屋建築、室內的家具擺設和屋內進行的活動，及所表現屋主在生活上的期望。本文嘗試以一些現存的十七世紀中國房屋為例，加上同時期的文章，對當時的房屋作出分析。由於此題目可供研究的材料有限，本文並非要提供當時宅第的全貌，而希望在研究建築形式和有關文章時，可加深理解當時的生活環境。此外，生活環境這個詞彙是綜合了建築、家具和裝飾，是一個整體而非分割的概念。

十七世紀的中國是一個混亂時期，戰禍連連、經濟動盪，加上外族的高壓統治，文人辭官的情況十分普遍。然而，如Craig Clunas指出江南一帶在十七世紀開始成為中國最富庶的地區，明末的動亂未影響該地區的消費能力。[3] 清初政

---

1 Simply put, Pierre Bourdieu suggests that the function of taste in society is to the make distinct the classification of social subjects. In as much as art is a free choice for the members of society, it fulfils a function of legitimating social differences. Bourdieu 1979:6-7.

2 This is particularly used by Heidegger as a metaphor for being. That language is the house of being, in whose gathering and sheltering let the being reveal itself. In Laozi, the house is a metaphor for the usefulness of emptiness: "And it is on these spaces where there is nothing that the usefulness of the house depends." Chapter XI, trans. by Arthur Waley.

3 Clunas 1991:161-2.

1 Pierre Bourdieu 指出品味具有社會功能，能夠劃分社會不同的階層。在藝術上各人有自由選擇的權利，藝術於是把社會階級的差別正規化了。Bourdieu 1979：6-7。

2 海德格特別用此來比喻存在。而這語言便是存在的房屋，人聚集、居住在屋內，便可揭示自我。《老子》則用房屋比喻「無用之用」、「鑿戶窗以為室，當其無，有室之用。」（第十一章）

3 參見Clunas 1991：161-2。

political and social stability came a strong economy with rich and powerful merchants of Jiangnan and Shanxi areas as the main players. Evidence from the material culture of the time points to the fine taste of connoisseurs in patronising the highest form of art and excellent craftsmanship. This is in contrast to literati who refused to participate in the imperial examination system, thereby alienating themselves from the government. There are two reasons for this attitude: the blatant corruption and bloody power struggles in late Ming politic and the indignity of serving the foreign "pretenders to the throne" in early Qing times. These literati sought after eremiticism and promoted simplicity and frugality in the art of living.

In this historical context, I will examine a corpus of texts of the seventeenth century and the houses of Jiangnan region and Shanxi province of the same period to construct the idea of a house of the time. The main texts were written by Gao Lian, Wen Zhenheng, Ji Cheng and Li Yu. These are supplemented by contemporaneous anecdotal writings. The earliest of the four texts is contained in *Zunsheng bajian*, [Eight Notes on Respectful Living],[4] published in 1591 by Gao Lian, a rich merchant who lived in Hangzhou with a cultural taste expressed in his vast collection of works of art.[5] The work contained advice and practical hints for elegant living as an aid to self-cultivation. Many of these recommendations are elaborated upon in the work of Wen Zhenheng (1585–1645). The great-grandson of the famous painter Wen Zhengming (1470–1559), Zhenheng had the benefit of being born into a family steeped in the literati tradition of connoisseurship and of great taste. Wen Zhenheng had never attained success in the imperial examinations, but that had not precluded his reputation as a man of taste. His work on the art of elegant living, *Zhangwu zhi* [The Treatise on Superfluous Things] was probably completed around 1615–20 in Suzhou, a city where he spent most of his life.[6] The highest ideal in connoisseurship during the late Ming may be glimpsed from this full and meticulous account of a true literatus. Ji Cheng (1582–?) described himself as a painter and garden designer of note. A native of Jiangsu, he probably started out as a craftsman skilled at

治及民生漸趨安定，經濟日益繁盛，江南及山西地區有財勢的商人操控了經濟，當時的物質文化可看到鑑賞家選購最好的藝術品和追求極盡完美的手藝，顯示他們優雅的品味。這情況與拒絕科舉試的文人形成了強烈的對比：明末貪污嚴重、權力鬥爭、結黨舞私，導致官場風腥血雨，加上清初文人不恥為外族效命，自絕於官場，過著歸隱的生活，提倡節儉優雅的生活藝術。

筆者將就此歷史背景，解讀十七世紀的著作，以及明末清初江南和山西的民居，建構當時宅第的概念。本文主要集中研究高濂、文震亨、計成和李漁編著的文章，並輔以其它雜記。高濂是一名富商，家住杭州。他的《遵生八牋》[4]寫於1591年，是四個著述中時代最早的，而他廣泛的藝術收藏，顯露了他的文化品味，[5]此書載有他對優雅生活和提高個人品味的實用意見。文震亨（1585-1645）的書中亦詳述這方面的見解。文氏生於一個文人傳統的家庭，乃名畫家文徵明（1470-1559）的曾孫，自少便受到藝術的浸淫。雖然文震亨從未考取科舉，但無礙建立他個人的品味。文大半生居於蘇州，其著作《長物志》是有關典雅的生活藝術，於1615年至1620年間寫於蘇州。[6]在這本既全面又嚴謹的著作裡，可見明末至善臻美的鑑賞品味。計成（1582-?）原籍江蘇，自命為畫家和園林設計家，他可能是以疊石起家，後來以建造園林為

4 Translated as the *Eight Discourses in the Art of Living* by Craig Clunas, which deviates from the author's intention. In the preface to the book, Gao Lian expresses that the book is intended to show the way of the cultivation of one's life by taking it seriously. This is because one's life is given by the parents, and to respect one's life is to respect one's parents. The way to respect one's life involves the cultivation of one's mind in the classics, the cultivation of one's body in taking care of it in the four seasons, and the cultivating of one's spirit in the house one dwells and the things one uses. See a summary of the content of the work in Clunas 1991: 18.

5 See a discussion of his life and works in Clunas 1991:14-20.

6 See Clunas 1991 for a detailed account of the life of Wen Zhenheng and a discussion of the dating of the work. Clunas also conducts a detailed analysis of the work in the light of Ming material culture.

4 Craig Clunas將書名譯為*Eight Discourses in the Art of living*，實不符合作者的原意。高濂在書內的序言中表明此書的主旨是要說明人要認真對待自己的身體，才是培養身體的方法。由於身體髮膚受諸父母，尊重自己的生命便是尊重父母；尊重生命的方法須從經典中培養心性；四季均要善其身，以育其體；從所居之處及所用之物中陶冶性情。內容概要見Clunas 1991：18。

5 有關高濂生平詳述及著作的討論，參見Clunas 1991：14-20。

6 有關文震亨生平詳述及著作年份的討論，參見Clunas 1991。Clunas亦從明代物質文化的角度，對這些著作作出詳細的闡釋。

piling stones in gardens and earned his living from garden-making commissions.[7] He is known by the book *Yuan ye* [The Making of Gardens], published in 1631.[8] Although the book focuses primarily on garden making, it also includes a section on house and building construction. The last of the four main works discussed in this article was written by Li Yu (1611–80), a resident of Nanjing and an accomplished dramatist, theorist, writer, and publisher. Li is a complex character who earned a living by composing essays and eulogies for rich and powerful clients. His work, *Xianqing ouji* [Occasional Records of Leisurely Sentiment], published in 1671, contains his idiosyncratic and eccentric views on drama, garden design, houses and other aspects of good living.[9] All four works taken together represent a segment of Ming society in the seventeenth century, that of the literati world seen through people of various backgrounds. Such study would afford us a deep understanding of the perception of what is proper, beautiful and in good taste by these heterogeneous grouping of authors.

Unlike monumental architecture where there is usually a good record of its building history from first construction to subsequent renovation or rebuilding, vernacular buildings lack proper accounts of their history. On top of this deficiency in textual history, a house is subjected to the vicissitudes of time including neglect in its repair. Houses change hands frequently and each owner would modify and add or completely rebuild the previous building. Thus there are very few houses in China which one can safely attribute to the late Ming period. Apart from scarcity and uncertain provenance, the other difficulty in discussing houses of the seventeenth century is that the extant buildings are mainly owned by rich and wealthy families who could afford to keep their houses in good repair. It is therefore difficult to delineate a balanced picture of houses of the rich and the common, of the vulgar and the literati. Nevertheless, there are a few houses of the seventeenth century that will be used in this article for illustration. They are mainly from the merchant class and probably exemplified the taste of their masters. The buildings selected for discussion are the mansions of Dingcun, near Xiangfen, southern Shanxi province; Zhouzhuang, near Shanghai; and Dongyang and Longmen towns in Zhejiang province.

業。[7] 計成以《園冶》一書聞名於世，[8] 該書在1631年刊印，主要集中討論營造園林，但也涉及房屋設計和建造。李漁早期定居南京，是一位才情橫溢的劇作家、理論家、作家及出版商。他生平複雜，為權貴寫作，歌功頌德。所著《閑情偶記》寫於1671年，載有對戲劇、園林、居室和優雅生活的獨特見解，[9] 是本文中主要討論的四本著作中年代最近的。縱觀此四部著作，從不同背景透視當時的文人世界。透過這些研究，可加深我們對生活藝術中何謂合宜、美觀和高雅品味的了解。

關於十七世紀宅第的歷史資料並不完整，它不像一些宏偉的建築，留下有關的營造、重修和使用的資料。更甚於此的是這些宅第都是經過時間的磨難、荒廢易手、修葺改建，原來的風貌已蕩然無存。況者，能保留下來的建築，多屬王謝世家，他們有能力保養修葺房子，而平民百姓的房子，倖存無幾。因此，本文並未能提供當時貧富階層、文人俗子房子的全貌。今天，尚有少量十七、十八世紀的房子可作為本文的例子，它們多半是由商人興建，完全代表了商人階層的品味。本文所舉的例子，位於山西南部襄汾附近的丁村、近上海的周莊及浙江的東陽

7 The building of a garden involved the laying out of the garden by either a professional garden designer or an amateur literatus knowledgeable in garden design. This person would also be closely involved in the construction of the garden and the piling of stones to form artificial mountains – the most important activity in the process. To use the word "design" may not be appropriate in the context of the creation of a Chinese garden, as it connotes an activity covering only a part of the process described above. In a preface to *Yuan ye*, Ji Cheng's friend used the term *zaoyuan*, that is garden making, to describe garden building. (Ji: 31) Ji Cheng himself described the person who is in charge of the activity as a *jiang*, a craftsman. (Ji: 41) In the modern preface of Kan Duo, Ji Cheng is said to have applied painting techniques in the piling of stones, and Kan claimed that Ji Cheng was not a vulgar craftsman. (Ji: 18) See also his brief biography in Craig Clunas, *Fruitful Sites: Garden Culture in Ming Dynasty China*, London: Reaktion Books, 1996: 174.

8 See the annotated edition in *Yuan ye*, 1981 and Hardie's translation in *The Craft of Gardens*, New Haven and London: Yale University Press, 1988.

9 Some passages are translated in Lin Yutang. *The Importance of Living*. London: William Heinemann Ltd., 1938.

7 造園需由專業園林設計家或精通園林設計的雅士悉心布置，他們亦會積極參與建園的過程，其中對疊石為山尤為重視。營建中國園林時採用「設計」一詞或不甚合宜，因這意味著上述過程的一部份。在《園冶》的序言中，計成的朋友以「造園」一詞描述營造園林。《園冶》：31）而計成本人則稱負責建園者為「匠」。（《園冶》：41）闞鐸在序言中稱計成「並非俗工，其攝山由繪事而來」。（《園冶》：18）有關資料可見Craig Clunas, *Fruitful Sites: Garden Culture in Ming Dynasty China*, London: Reaktion Books, 1996：174，計成的簡傳。

8 參見《園冶》1981年註釋本。

9 林語堂在*The Importance of Living*, London: William Heinemann Ltd., 1938中亦有翻譯部份篇章。

Located near the bank of the Fen River, the group of mansions in Dingcun dates from 1593 with later additions. The merchants from this area were well known throughout the seventeenth and eighteenth centuries. In the Jiangnan region, around the fertile land of the Suzhou area and in central Zhejiang province, are found many mansions of the late Ming period. They were built by retired officials, merchants and recluses from well-known families. Many of these mansions are preserved in groups within the village setting.

FUNCTIONAL VALUE

While it is too simplistic to look at a house by just examining its functional value, it is nevertheless essential to note that most importantly, the house has to fulfil the function of providing a shelter for its inhabitants. This practical aspect of a house can be studied through its setting, form, construction and the building elements. To begin with, for Li Yu, the house's functional appropriateness takes precedence over its beauty.

Whether a house is refined or rugged, it is most treasured if it can serve as a shelter for wind and rain. Very often one finds houses with painted columns and carved beams, ornate towers and jade balustrades, but these are good for entertaining the eyes, and cannot even provide cover from rain. (Li: 147)

Much of the other advice he gave on the house, such as the construction of its ceiling, and its floor and the way to sweep it is taken from a practical point of view. Thus practicality of the house is utmost in the mind of Li Yu.

Most houses found in China are grouped in clusters located in villages and towns, very seldom do they exist independently on their own. The clusters of houses usually face a certain direction, south in the case of urban houses, and south or any other auspicious direction in rural houses. The orientation is both practical and magical. Southerly orientation provides the house with the best use of the sun's path for light and warmth. This is taken by Li Yu as a matter of fact. (Li: 145) There are also cases, such as in Zhouzhuang, where the orientation of a house depends on the course of the river or street, for ease of transportation and commerce. On the other

和龍門。丁村位臨汾河,該地的商人在十七、十八世紀聲名顯赫,最早的宅院可追溯至1593年。蘇州及浙東一帶土地肥沃,存有許多明末清初的房子,多由退休官員、商人和出自名門的隱士興建,仍保存原有的村落布置和院落結構。

房屋的功能價值

研究民居只著重其功能價值,未免過份簡化,但要注意的是房屋最重要的是提供一個棲息之所。透過布局、形式、營建和建築的基本元素,可探討房屋的實用功能。李漁認為房屋最重要是能恰當地滿足功能上的要求,外型美觀與否只屬次要:

「居宅無論精粗,較以能避風雨為貴。有畫棟雕樑,瓊樓玉欄,而止可娛睛,不堪坐雨者。」(《閑情偶寄》卷四:147)

他對房屋提出的其他見解,如置頂格、甃地(天花、地台)或灑掃,均以實用角度出發,可見李漁認定房屋的實用功能是最為重要。

中國大部份房屋都是集結在鄉村或城鎮,有特定的整體布局,絕少個別獨立興建。鄉間的建築多面向同一方位,較常見的是朝向南面或其它吉位,這些取向既有實用價值又富神秘感。房屋向南可充份利用陽光照明及取暖,李漁視此為正確的作法。(《閑情偶寄》卷四:145)其他例子如周莊房屋的方向,是視乎河道或街道位置而定,房子盡量朝街向河以便交通、商貿往來。另一方面,村莊亦講究地理風水,以保佑家宅

hand, geomantic reading of the land form surrounding a village would suggest an auspicious orientation to ensure the prosperity of the inhabitants. The approach to a house is usually directly off the street or river. Both Wen and Li agreed that the house should not be accessed in a straightforward manner. Li went further in saying that: "the path has to allow quick access and be convenient, but it is also intriguing if it is zigzag and indirect. Thus if the path has been purposely made to meander for the sake of interest, a separate door should be open [to the house] in order to allow the servants to approach the house quickly when needed. The door can be closed when not needed. In this way, both the elegant and the vulgar are satisfied and both rationality and interest are taken care of." (Li: 146) Such provision seems to be found in Dingcun houses where the entrance to the cluster of houses is through a zigzag path, and entries to individual cloisters are through courtyards of other houses, or internal streets.

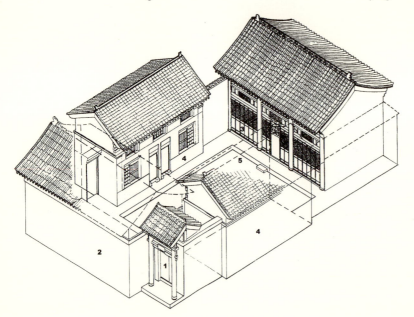

Fig. 1   An axonometric drawing of house no. 3, dated to 1593, in Dingcun.
圖1   山西丁村第三院的平面圖（1593年）。

1 Entrance gate 大門
2 Southern parlour 倒座房
3 Main parlour 正房
4 Side rooms 東西廂
5 Courtyard 庭院

The form of a traditional Chinese house is rectangular and introverted. A house is made up of buildings and courtyards, usually organised in succession along an axis. On the outside is an external wall with a minimum of openings. Ming houses of Dingcun are of the two-layered type, consisting of a front building, a rear hall and two side chambers all forming a rectangle enclosing a courtyard. (Fig. 1) The entrance to the house is through a door located to the side of the simple complex. In the Suzhou area, houses are usually made up of three layers, an entrance building, a hall, and a two-or-three-storeyed building to the back. This results in the buildings along the central axis progressing in height. Li Yu too suggested that a house should be constructed with varying heights, so that the buildings to the rear would be higher than those to the front. If the ground does not permit such an arrangement, the rear building should be made in two storeys, so as to achieve the visual interest. Such picturesqueness can also be

丁財兩旺。通往房屋的路徑大多離大街和河道不遠，而文震亨和李漁均同意通往房屋的路徑不宜直達屋子。李漁更指出：

「徑莫便於捷，而又莫妙于迂。凡有故作迂途，以取別致者，必另開耳門一扇，以便家人之奔走，急則開之，緩則閉之，斯雅俗俱利，而理致兼收矣。」（《閑情偶寄》卷四：146）

丁村的房屋入口處設有之字形小路，往個別院子需穿過其他屋的庭院或內街，與上述形式近似。

傳統中國房屋的外形是長方形和內向的，由房子和庭院組成，一般沿著一條縱軸排列，外圍建有一道外牆，牆身的開口減至最少。山西丁村的明代房屋有兩進，包括前廳、後廳和兩個廂房，圍著庭院形成一個長方形（圖1），出入口則位於結構簡單的房子側面。蘇州一帶的房屋多是三進，其中有門廳、大廳和一座兩三層高的後院。房舍沿著縱軸高矮錯落，正如李漁所提倡：

「房舍忌似平原，須有高下之勢，不獨園圃為然，居宅亦應如是。前卑後高，理之常也。然地不如是，而強欲如是，亦病其拘。總有因地制宜之法：高者造屋，卑者建樓，一法也。」（《閑情偶寄》卷四：146）

found in the mountains that are in nature, according to Li. (Li: 146) Here, Li was probably influenced by the concept of "adopting the ground to the design" of Ji Cheng, an important concept in garden design. (Ji: 41)[10] The number of buildings and layers would very much depend on the wealth of the family. The size of a house varies, the earliest house in Dingcun, house no. 3 which has only one courtyard, measures 29 x 18 metres. House no. 1 dated to 1745, one of the largest in the village with two courtyards, measures 46 x 14 metres. The Shen mansion in Zhouzhuang was rebuilt in 1742 over the Ming dynasty house of the family, the richest in the area. It has four courtyards and measures around 80 x 18 metres. The Zhang mansion of the late Ming dynasty with four courtyards measures around 70 x 20 metres.

As in extant examples of seventeenth century houses, most authors accept that the buildings in a residential complex would be rectangular. Wen explicitly warned against building in the shape of the letter "I" as this form resembles a magistrate's office, probably representing vulgar taste in the view of the author. (Wen: 36) Between these buildings are two courtyards. Flanking the side of the courtyards are more buildings. These buildings are simply subdivided for receiving guests, for living and sleeping. The allocation of rooms was determined by gender and one's position in the family. The central hall is the most honoured and lived in by the parents. The side chambers are for male members of the family, and the rear tower for the female members. This arrangement indicates a strict social hierarchy based on the Confucian concept of proper positioning of individuals within the society.

The size of these buildings and the decorative details were also determined by the social hierarchy, as regulated in the state law of the Ming dynasty. The law pertaining to buildings, contained in *Ming Huidian* [The Administrative Law of the Ming dynasty], was chiefly compiled in 1393. The size of the main hall in a mansion is described by the number of bays in the frontal elevation, a bay being the space between two structural columns. It is determined by the wooden construction of the houses, and usually measured around four metres in the Ming dynasty. It is stipulated that no houses should have halls more than nine bays in size, being reserved for the Emperor only. A duke or a marquis was allowed to have front and rear halls of

李漁此見解應是受計成「因地制宜」的園林設計概念影響。(《園冶》卷一：41) [10] 房子的數目和層數，極大部份取決於家宅是否富裕。房屋的大小各有不同，丁村最早期的房屋中，三號房子僅有一個庭院，深廿九米，闊十八米。一號房子建於1745年，是村內其中一座最大的樓房，有兩個庭院，深四十六米，闊十四米。周莊的沈廳以明代房屋為基址，於1742年重建，屋主是當地最富裕的商人，其屋有四個庭院，深八十米，闊十八米。而明末的張廳也有四個庭院，約深七十米，闊二十米。

大部份作者認同民居群裡的房屋是長方形的，這與大部份十七世紀的房屋相近。就房屋的外形，文震亨清楚指出「前後堂相承，忌工字體，亦以近官廨也」(《長物志》卷一：36)，認為工字形過於俗氣。各進之間有一個庭院，旁邊建有廂房，這些建築物簡單地細分成各個房間，作款客、住宿之用。房間的分配是由性別、家族地位而定。中堂至為尊貴，供雙親居住，廂房由家中男丁居住，女性則住在後樓。從以上房間的分配，反映了儒家思想中強調的長幼尊卑的觀念。

明代的律法規定宅第的大小和家具的布置，是按社會階級來決定。1393年頒行的《明會典》中，刊載了有關房屋的規格。房屋中廳堂的大小以間數來形容，一間即是前立面木結構兩柱之間的空間，在明代一般是四米左右為標準。除了天子外，所有房屋規定不得大於九間。公侯的前廳後堂可建為七間或五間，一品及二品官則可建五間，門屋則為三間。三品至五品官的廳堂亦可建成五間，只是進深較淺。至於六品至九品官員，

10 *Yindi zhiyi* is Ji Cheng's main concept in garden design which is essentially the placement of garden elements according to natural topography, rather than forcing one's way against the contours and land form. See a discussion in Stanislaus Fung and Mark Jackson's paper "Four Key Terms in the History of Chinese Gardens" in Puay-peng Ho ed.: *Issues in Methodology: Proceedings of the International Conference on Chinese Architectural History*. Hong Kong, The Chinese University of Hong Kong, 1995: 21–34.

10 「因地制宜」是計成園林設計的主要概念。園林要素的配置，須因應天然地形，而非強行改變地勢和地形。參見Puay-peng Ho, ed., *Issues in Methodology: Proceedings of the international conference on Chinese architectural history*, Hong Kong: CUHK, 1995：21–42 中對Stanislaus Fung及Mark Jackson論文 "Four key terms in the history of Chinese gardens" 之討論。

seven or five bays. Officials of the first and second grades were allowed halls of five bays, and an entrance building of three bays. The same sizes were also permitted for officials of the third to the fifth grade, except that the depth of their halls would be smaller. For officials of the sixth to the ninth grade, the halls could not be larger than three bays, and the entrance building only one bay wide. For ordinary people, the houses were to be no more than three bays wide, such as the late Ming dynasty hall in Longmen town, Zhejiang province. (Fig. 2) In a later amendment, officials of the first and second grades were also allowed to have a seven-bay hall. Following this law, most buildings of Dingcun and Zhouzhuang mansions are three bays in width. The inside of the buildings is divided into three spaces and the divisions are aligned with the structural line. The divisional wall may be in the form of a solid brick wall, a pounded-earth wall or

Fig. 2   A main hall in a residence in Longmen town, Zhejiang province, late Ming dynasty. The hall is three *jian* wide, which is the maximum size allowed by the law.
圖2   浙江省龍門鎮一晚明宅第的三進大廳，是當時律法允許下面積最大的廳堂。

wooden shelves and cabinets. In the case of southern houses, it is more common to see shelves and cabinets used to divide the building, providing an opportunity to have added surfaces in the room for rich ornamentation.

External walls are usually constructed with pounded earth in northern China, and bricks in southern China, such as in Zhouzhuang. In Dingcun, a mixture of pounded earth and brick is used for the construction of the external wall. Whether in pounded earth or bricks, these walls are simply and solidly constructed providing protection and privacy for the house. Li Yu also provided the advice on the way an external wall should be constructed: "The best way of construction is by piling up of rocks, which should not be restricted in size and shape. ... If it is done properly, it would seem natural even though made by human hands. ... As for the earthen wall, it suits both the rich and the poor, as it exudes the charms of elegance and simplicity." (Li: 168) The idea of "man-made but as if natural" is again taken from Ji Cheng, a key concept of

廳堂不得大於三間，門屋不得闊於一間，平民百姓的房子則不得大於三間，如這所龍門鎮的明代宅堂。(圖2) 後來，一、二品官的廳堂亦可建成七間。按此律法，丁村、周莊、龍門、東陽大部份房舍均為三間闊。這些房子沿著結構線分隔成三間，牆以磚塊或夯土築成，或以木板壁分隔。南方的房屋較常以格門、碧紗櫥、博古架等作分隔，可增添房屋的空間。

中國北方的房屋，外牆或用夯土建成，南方如周莊的用磚塊砌成，丁村的則兩者兼用。不論是用哪種材料，外牆建造都是簡單穩固，以保護房屋及私人空間不受干擾。李漁認為外牆應是以此方法建造：

「莫妙於亂石疊成，不限大小方圓之定格，壘之者人工，而石則造物生成之本質也… 於泥牆土壁，貧富皆宜，極有蕭疏雅淡之致」
(《閑情偶寄》卷四：168)

his garden design. (Ji: 71) The building structure is commonly the post-and-lintel type constructed in wood. The method of construction was well developed by the time of the late Ming and manuals, such as the *Lu Ban jing* [The Classic of Master Carpenter Lu Ban], were available to the trade. Writing from the angle of a builder, Ji Cheng also included detailed and practical descriptions of various building structures. (Ji: 85–98)

The roof form and external decoration of the houses were also controlled by the Ming administrative law. As a rule, no buildings other than imperial ones could have double eaves, stepped brackets, or painted ceilings. All buildings would have simple pitched roofs covered with grey clay tiles. Brackets were only allowed on buildings of officials above the second grade, while decorative roof animals were allowed for officials above the fifth grade. The colour of the timber elements in these buildings was also regulated according to rank. Apart from the structure, the other elements found in a house that may express status are the doors and windows. The main door leaves are constructed of a solid timber plank socketed into the stone base on the ground and timber lintel on top. The stone bases are joined to a threshold. In Shanxi houses, the door base is usually rectangular and richly carved. (Fig.3) In large mansions of Suzhou, a large stone drum may be seen added to the top of the stone base. The door leaves are usually left plain except for a pair of door knockers, usually made of copper. Wen Zhenheng was very specific in the design of the door, which should be: "constructed with timber in a horizontal strip and laid over diagonally with bamboo stems." The use of bamboo stems reflects his literati taste. However, this author has not seen an extant example of this form of construction. Wen continued to specify the use of the solid stone threshold to match with the solid timber door, and that the door knockers should be in the form of a butterfly, an animal face, a heavenly chicken or a *taotie* mask. (Wen: 20) Most bronze door knockers in extant houses are in the form of an animal face, as allowed in the administrative law.

他沿用了計成「雖由人作，宛自天開」（《園冶》卷一：44）園林設計的概念。至於營建結構方面，一般為穿斗式的木結構。明末，建築方法已發展得頗為完善，如《魯班經》等書已廣泛流傳。計成從建築的角度，在著作中也詳細地描述各種樑架結構。（《園冶》卷一：85–98）

房屋的屋頂和外牆裝飾亦受明代律法監管，除皇宮外，其他房舍一律不得建重簷、重栱或繪畫藻井。所有房舍只許是簡單的斜屋頂上蓋灰瓦，僅二品以上之官可建斗栱，五品以上方可作瓦獸裝飾，木料的顏色亦根據官階高低有所規定。除房屋結構外，門窗的形式也可顯露身份地位。正門門扉採用實心木板製造，上有門楣，下有石枕，與石檻相連。山西房屋的石枕一般是長方形，佈滿雕刻（圖3）；而蘇州的大宅還加上一個石鏤鼓。門扉上除了裝有一對銅製門環外，並無其他裝飾。文震亨對門的設計描述得非常仔細：「用木為格，以湘妃竹橫斜釘之」。（《長物志》卷一：20）竹反映了文人的氣質，但在現存的房屋中，筆者尚未發現以此法建築的例子。文另詳述了用石門檻配襯實心木板門，門環應是蝴蝶或獸面、天雞或饕餮等形狀。（《長物志》卷一：20）現存的房屋所安裝的銅門環，均是獸面形狀，以符合當時的律法。

Fig. 3   Door bases of the main door of a house in Dingcun. It is decorated with floral, literati motifs.
圖3   丁村一所房屋的門枕石，上有花鳥、文房圖案。

The wall facing the courtyard in the houses can be rather opaque with only a door and two windows set into the wall, such as in the case of Shanxi houses. (Fig.4) It can also be more open with a row of doors and windows, such as in Jiangnan houses. (Fig.5) This is explained by the differences in the climate of the two regions, the northern house needs more protection against the elements, while the southern house needs more openings in the wall to provide good ventilation in the wet weather. This difference results in the feeling that Jiangnan houses are more decorative and intricate. Windows are protected with a lattice, whose simple design consists of

Fig. 4   The courtyard of house no. 2, dated to 1612. The walls are solidly built with pounded earth on a brick base. Openings are kept to a minimum. The eaves are short.
圖4   第二院的內庭（1612年），牆身結構穩固，在磚牆腳上夯土建成。門窗數量減至最少，屋簷則較短。

fine vertical timber members intersecting with horizontal members. (Fig.6) Layers of paper are pasted on the inside of the windows for protection against the elements and for privacy. This construction can still be found in Shanxi houses while in Jiangnan houses the lattice design is much more varied and delicate. (Fig.7) Three authors, except Gao Lian, wrote about the design of the lattice window. While Wen specified the lattice design and colour, Ji provided many patterns. And Li was more interested in the practical aspects:

The windows have to be transparent and allow brightness [to enter the interior], while the balustrade should be refined. However, these are secondary requirements. The most important requirement is that they are solidly built. Only when the window and balustrade fulfil the criterion of being securely built that one would consider if they are finely or crudely made. ... There are only two principles in the design of these elements: they should be simple and not complicated, they should also look natural rather than man-made. ... When the window and the balustrade are overly carved, their structural integrity suffers. (Li: 152)

屋內面向庭院的牆，可以像山西的房屋般，密封得只有一扇門和兩扇窗（圖4），也可以像江南房子般開揚，有一排門窗。（圖5）這些建築上的分別，在於兩地氣候的差異：北方天氣較為惡劣，房屋需要更多保護；南方天氣潮濕，門窗多可令室內空氣更流通。兩地房屋的差別亦會令人覺得江南的較為細緻，有較多裝飾。窗以窗櫺（窗花）作保護，窗櫺的設計簡單，以木條縱橫相疊而成。（圖6）窗內貼有數層紙張，以防禦天氣，窗櫺的設計就更式式具備，精巧細緻。（圖7）除了高濂外，三位作者均提到窗櫺的設計。文震亨集中描述窗的設計和顏色（《長物志》卷一：23）；計成則詳列風窗戶牖的設計（《園冶》卷一：106-128）；而李漁對窗櫺的實用性較有興趣：

「窗櫺以明透為先，欄杆以玲瓏為主，然此皆屬第二義；其首重者，止在一字之堅，堅而後論工拙。…較其大綱，則有二語：宜簡不宜繁，宜自然不宜雕斫。… 然頭眼過密，筍撤太多，又與雕鏤無異，仍是戒其體也。」（《閑情偶寄》卷四：152）

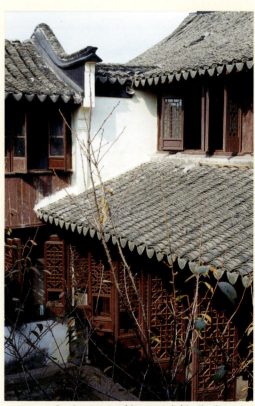

Fig. 5   A corner of the courtyard of the Shen house, Zhouzhuang. The wall facing the courtyard in this example is almost entirely covered with lattice windows.
圖5   從周莊沈廳庭院一角可見朝向庭院的窗櫺。

The idea of simplicity may be found in most Ming windows, however, towards the end of the seventeenth century, ornate window design began to appear, relating more to the economic prosperity of the Kangxi era, which was expressed in the preferred taste for lavishness.

Inside the house, the form of furniture and its placement are likewise determined by the social hierarchy and function of each room. Wen and Li include a list of furniture for the different rooms of the house in their books. And most authors had their own idea of how a studio, the most important room in the house of the literati, ought to be furnished.

SOCIAL VALUE

Taste has been taken to be an indicator of aesthetic judgement as well as a marker of social class structure.[11] The study of taste in house and furniture design would centre on how consumer choices in objects, furniture and building decoration were influenced by aesthetic inclination and its projected social value. While many of

Fig. 6 Lattice windows in house no. 1, Dingcun. Here two lattice designs are used for a window, creating an interesting juxtaposition of compact and loose lattice.
圖6 丁村第一院的窗櫺，一扇窗沿用了兩款窗櫺設計，揉合了一疏一密的效果。

the houses of the past are now devoid of furniture and decoration of the period, such as the houses used in this article as examples, we are helped by the seventeenth century texts. It is in the matter of internal decoration and placement of furniture that the authors differed the most. This is evidence of how their social station influenced their taste, expressed in the dialectic of elegance and vulgarity.

Wen Zhenheng was extremely forthright in what an elegant hall should be like: broad and open, refined and pleasing. (Wen: 27) Ji Cheng's definition of a hall is similar, one facing the

雖然明末宅屋的窗戶以簡單輕快的線條為主，但到了十七世紀末，精細繁瑣的窗櫺設計開始出現，這現象與康熙時代經濟蓬勃、窮奢極侈的社會風氣不無關係。

家具的形式及在房舍內擺設的位置，同樣是根據社會階級和房間的用途來決定。文震亨和李漁均列出一系列屋內不同房間陳設的家具。對於如何布置文人認為最重要的房間－書房，大部份作者均有獨特的見解。

Fig. 7 Lattice design of an early Qing dynasty house in Zhouzhuang. The timber members in the latticework are much finer and the pattern more decorative than the Shanxi example.
圖7 清初周莊房屋的窗櫺設計，選用的木條較山西房屋的更為幼細，亦有較多圖案。

宅第的社會價值

品味不單反映個人的審美標準，同時也是社會階級的標誌。[11] 研究房屋及家具設計的品味，是要集中探討美學上的取向，以及它包含的社會價值如何影響營造、布置和裝飾。正如上述，雖然那時期老房子的家具和裝飾現已不存，我們仍可從十七世紀的文獻中略知一二。室內裝飾和家具布置正正是各作者最大分別之處，證明了社會地位如何影響他們的品味。透過雅俗的辯證，他們的品味便表露無遺。

文震亨認為高雅的廳堂應是宏敞精麗（《長物志》卷一：27）；計成也認為堂者當為向陽並

11 Bourdier 1979: 2.

11 見英文注釋11。

sun. (Ji: 75) Existing Ming halls in Zhejiang province, such as the Shuyong Hall in the well-preserved mansion of the Lu family in Dongyang, fit the description. (Fig.8) It is three bays in width, with no internal subdivision. The construction is of a mixture of post-and-beam type in the centre to allow for a spacious interior, and post-and-lintel type for the end wall to save on materials. The side facing the courtyard is entirely open to allow unobstructed access to the courtyard, and to provide the major source of light for the interior. Decorative timber elements are placed around the structural members of the hall, and all are richly painted. In the case of the Shuyong Hall, no false ceiling is used which means that the roof structure is exposed and utilised as a decorative surface. (Fig.9) In order to achieve elegance in the living environment, Wen advised against the use of a ceiling, the provision of a partition down the middle of the room (dividing into two halves), covering the wall with paper, and painting the wooden structural members with motifs and patterns. He also said that *wan* motif (a reversed swastika) is never to be used, nor bird and flower design at the bottom of a wall.[12] No one should write or paint on a paper-pasted wall. (Wen: 36) However, for a bedroom, Wen allowed the use of movable floor tiles and ceiling, as the room needed to be dry. (Wen: 354) Those who decorated the house as he suggested is termed an "elegant gentleman", while those who did not is a "vulgar commoner".

Accordingly, Li Yu, who advocated the use of a ceiling in a room and painting on the papered wall, is very vulgar indeed. Li even went so far as to suggest the combination of painting with actual twig cages to keep singing birds on the wall, thus forming a natural picture with the full

Fig. 8 Shuyong Hall, ca. 1462, Lu Mansion, Dongyang town, Zhejiang province. This is a simple three-bay hall with the front fully open to the courtyard. The hall is probably used for entertaining guests and for festive gatherings.
圖8　浙江省東陽城盧宅肅陽堂內貌（約1462年），屬簡單的三間式，前端面臨庭院，多作宴會賓客和敘會之用。

高大開敞。（《園冶》卷一：75）現存東陽的盧宅明代廳堂如肅穆堂符合以上的描述（圖8）。這堂闊三間，內無間隔，中為抬樑式結構，使堂內的空間更為寬敞；山牆則用穿斗式結構，藉此省卻材料。面向庭院的一面全無牆物身，供觀賞及通往庭院，也是室內主要的光源。頂上無天花，雕飾彩繪便集中在木結構的構件上。以肅陽堂為例，其頂部不設假天花，外露的結構於是便成為了裝飾表層。（圖9）為求達至優雅的生活環境，文震亨也不主張用天花，或稱「承塵」。他亦反對在小室中用中隔，卍字圖案，牆角畫上雀鳥或花等圖案及紙糊的牆身。[12]（《長物志》卷一：36）然而，為了實際需要，文震亨也不反對使用他認為俗氣的裝飾：「地屏天花雖俗，然臥室取乾燥，用之亦可，第不可彩畫及油漆耳。」（《長物志》卷十：354）如此，只有依照文的意見裝飾，才算得上是文雅之士，否則的只是凡夫俗子。

李漁則主張屋內用天花，牆壁上糊紙圖畫，這又是否俗不可耐呢？他更進一步建議在廳壁上實畫著色花樹，並以樹枝織成鳥籠，使雀鳥能在牆上唱歌，構成一幅視聽俱備的自然

12 This is consistent with Wen's disgust for the *wan* motif. See also pp. 25, 30. He regarded this motif as only suitable for a girl's room, and the reason for not using it is that it is not ancient nor elegant.

12 這與文震亨討厭卍字圖案相符。參見頁25及30。他認為這種圖案只適合女子的房間，而不使用的原因是這圖案既不古，亦不雅。

sight and sound effect.[13] Is his lowly position in society a factor in such taste? As for the wall of a studio, Li advised against the use of paint, which would render the room very vulgar, in keeping with Wen's advice. According to both Li and Wen, the best is to whitewash the wall of the studio. The next best solution is to paste the wall with paper, which will render the wall, beam and window surrounds all one colour. On the wall would be pasted calligraphy and painting, but Li's advice was that these should be sparsely pasted. To create interesting features on the wall, Li suggested covering the wall with two layers of different colour paper, with patterns on the top layer. It is said that this would create the beautiful appearance of crackled ge wares (one of the five imperial kilns of the Song dynasty) on the wall.[14] Li's idea of elegance and a fine living environment is thus rather different from Wen Zhenheng and Gao Lian, both of whom wanted the studio to be kept really simple, with only a painting or an ancient qin (a lute) hung from the wall.

Fig. 9   The interior of Shuyong Hall. Flamboyant decorations can be found on the surface of timber structural members.
圖9   肅陽堂內貌。木材結構表面可見火焰式裝飾。

Although all authors use the complementary opposite of elegance and vulgarity in classifying taste in house and furniture design, it has been demonstrated that their ideas of taste were not homogenous. Gao Lian described a pavilion constructed with four rustic tree trunks as having an elegant appearance and is deemed appropriate for pure appreciation. (Gao: 7.33b) A layered or circular roof for a pavilion was described as elegant, but a hexagonal double-eaved roof is said by Gao to be quite vulgar. (ibid.) To Li Yu, a house is valued for its refinement, elegance and interest, rather than for its embellishment, cleverness and colourfulness. (Li: 145) Ji Cheng also described house details in terms of elegance, a rectangular stone door base, for example, is said to be ancient, simple and elegant, while adding a stone drum on it, seen commonly in Jiangnan houses, is said to be unnecessary. Colourful painting and ornate carvings on wooden structural members are said to be extremely vulgar and inappropriate. (Ji: 71)

圖畫。[13] 這種品味是否顯示他較低的社會地位呢？至於書房牆壁，則忌用油漆：

「書房之壁，最宜瀟灑。欲其瀟灑，切忌油漆。油漆二物，俗物也，前人不得已而用之，非好為是沾沾者。門戶窗櫺之必油漆，蔽風雨也；廳柱楄楹之必須油漆，防點污也。若夫書室之內，人跡罕至，陰雨弗浸，無此二患而亦蹈此轍，是無刻不在桐腥漆氣之中。」（《閑情偶寄》卷四：170）

這與文震亨的見解不謀而合。按照李漁和文震亨的意見，最佳方法是在書房壁上白堊石灰，其次是在壁上糊紙。然而，李漁進一步提議室內全糊上紙，使四週的牆壁、樑和窗都同一顏色，並貼上詩詞圖畫，但不應排得過份緊密。要在牆上加添特色，李漁提議糊上兩層不同顏色的紙，上層的可有花紋。他認為這樣可在牆上造出哥窰冰碎紋的圖案。[14] 文震亨和高濂則認為書房要保持簡潔，牆壁只掛一幅圖畫或一張古琴便可，與李漁優雅家居環境的概念是有明顯的出入。

雖然當時所有作者都以雅俗對立關係，去品評房屋和家具陳設，但他們的品味並非完全一致。高濂描述用茹皮棕皮覆亭柱，為淳樸雅觀，最宜「清賞」。（《遵生八牋》卷七：33b）高濂也說單簷圓頂的亭為雅，六角重簷為俗。（同上）李漁則認為：「房屋貴精不貴麗，貴新奇大雅，不貴纖巧爛漫」。（《閑情偶寄》卷四：145）計成亦從雅俗的角度，討論房屋的設計：「升栱不讓雕鸞，門枕胡為鏤鼓，時遵雅樸，古摘端方。畫

13 See pp. 169–70. This method of decorating the walls of the hall in the house is said by Li as an innovative method so that his interest in bird can be satisfied. He also suggested for parrot, one does not even need a cage, just a short tree branch projecting from the wall for the parrot to rest on is sufficient to satisfy his requirements of keeping a live bird in the hall and at the same time merged it with the wall painting. This provision must be very vulgar indeed to Wen Zhenheng.

14 The crackled pattern of ge ware and broken-ice pattern seem much like by many authors.

13 參見頁169至170。據李漁說，此裝飾廳壁的方法令人耳目一新，亦可滿足他對養鳥的興趣。他亦指出飼養鸚鵡不須用雀籠，只須在牆上伸出一枝短樹枝，讓鸚鵡立足，已可滿足他在廳中飼養雀鳥的要求，同時亦可與壁畫合而為一。此方法文震亨必定視為非常庸俗。

14 哥窰冰裂紋看來受許多作者喜愛。

Among the four authors, Wen Zhenheng has provided the fullest discussion on what constitutes an elegant or vulgar design:

The method of positioning varies between a complicated layout and a simple layout, cold season is also different from hot season. Lofty halls or spacious pavilions, crooked rooms or hidden chambers – there is an appropriate way of laying out the furniture in each [type of room]. Even for objects such as books, tripods and vases, they are to be properly positioned so as to be like that shown in painting. In the paintings of Ni Zan, only a stool and a *ta* bed are seen amongst lofty *wutong* trees and aged rocks. This has aroused people's desire to want to see his fine character, which will make our spirit and bone as cold [or detached] as [Ni Zan]. That is why the house of a person of charm would exude an interest of lofty elegance, with all vulgarity avoided. Now, if the front of the hall was used to keep chickens and rear pigs, while at the rear the owner boasted about [the activity] of watering flowering plants and washing rocks, would it not be better to allow the table to be covered with dust and the four walls left very empty, at least, this will give a sense of sparseness and quietude. (Wen: 347)

Some examples of elegant and vulgar details for achieving the lofty milieu are described: For a ceremonial screen in a hall, it would be elegant to use *nanmu* with exposed grain, and vulgar when painted in gold. (Wen: 26) For a building, it is good to have two storeys, and most vulgar to have three.[15] (Wen: 34) It is also elegant to have a timber balustrade painted red surrounding the platform of a building. (Wen: 35, Fig.10) In construction, fine brick paving is elegant, using palm trunk as gutter is very elegant, diagonal struts in a structural system are not. (Wen: 37) Most importantly, in the house, it is better to feel ancient and not modern, better to be plain than clever, better to be frugal than vulgar, and sparseness, elegance and purity are all naturally born and cannot be forced, said Wen Zhenheng. (ibid.) Some of these criteria for elegance are also suggested by other author's works.

Fig. 10 A corner of Shen house, Zhouzhuang. The balustrade around the courtyard is simply decorated. It is probably considered elegant in the eyes of the seventeenth century critics.
圖10　周莊沈廳一角，院內的欄杆裝飾簡單，以十七世紀的標準必視之為雅。

In the same vein, many construction methods and details in furniture design are described by Wen Zhenheng as pure and elegant. Wen dismissed much of the furniture design of the time as overly concerned with carving and decorative quality, made, according to him, for the

彩雖佳，木色加之青綠，雕鏤易俗，花空嵌以仙禽」。(《園冶》卷一：71)

四位作者中，文震亨花最多篇幅討論何謂雅俗：

「位置之法，繁簡不同，寒暑各異，高堂廣榭，曲房奧室，各有所宜，即如圖書鼎彝之屬，亦須安設有所，方如圖畫。雲林清秘，高梧古石中，僅一几一榻，令人想見其風緻，真令神骨俱冷。故士所居，入門便有一種高雅絕俗之趣。若使堂前養雞牧豕，而後庭侈言澆花洗石，政不如凝塵滿案，環堵四壁，猶有一種蕭寂氣味耳。」(《長物志》卷十：347)

文震亨透過以下一些有關雅俗的例子，詳述了如何方可達至高雅境界："照壁若要華而復雅，得用豆瓣楠等木為之，灑金描畫為俗。"(《長物志》卷一：26)"樓閣兩層為佳，三層最俗。"[15]（同上：34）"台用粗木造，作朱欄亦屬雅。"（同上：35，圖10）"牆壁用細磚屬雅，以栟櫚為承溜則極雅，樑上用叉手則不甚雅。"（同上：37）在總結雅俗的作法時，文震亨認為最重要的是「隨方制象，各有所宜，寧古無時，寧樸無巧，寧儉無俗，至於蕭疏雅潔又本生，非強作解事者所得輕議矣。」(同上)

entertainment of vulgar eyes. (Wen: 225) Thus, a *ta* bed placed in a studio must have an ancient elegance. (ibid.) A low table with carved cloud and *ruyi* patterns is considered elegant, whereas, dragon and phoenix motifs are said to be vulgar, and long and narrow shapes the most detestable. (Wen: 231) In terms of shape, an octagonal Eight Immortals' table is not deemed a piece of elegant furniture. (Wen: 234) In terms of decoration, Wen described *ta* beds inlaid with Dali marble, with polished black and red lacquer incised and filled in with bamboo and tree painting, or with new mother-of-pearl, as not elegant. Likewise, a folding chair with gold paint is extremely vulgar, (Wen: 237) the wan motif and continuous geometric motif on the railing of a bed are vulgar too. (Wen: 241) Thus material, shape, construction, colour, motif, and pattern are the basis for distinguishing elegance from vulgarity for Wen Zhenheng. The long list of what is elegant and vulgar from Wen's text on both house and furniture design only underscores his interest in trumpeting his social class, being born of an illustrious literati family. In contrast, Li Yu, who did not have the pedigree of Wen Zhenheng, had a slightly different outlook. He disagreed with the common saying of the time that: "to change vulgarity to elegance is as difficult as turning metal to gold, only one with the ability as vast as the hill or forest may achieve the transformation". Instead, he felt that someone who is wise, who has an inquisitive mind and great intelligence would achieve that change. (Li: 185-6) This can also be seen as the way for Li to cross the class barriers and claim to possess the literati elegance, as seen in his innovative ideas. However, he was careful not to call these details elegant. Contrasting Wen Zhenheng to Li Yu allows us a further insight into the discourse of the dialectic of elegance and vulgarity as a social classification device.

SYMBOLIC VALUE

The highest ideal of a house is to serve as a bridge allowing the inhabitants to reach and be one with nature. This is the symbolic value of the house in the Chinese context. Joseph Needham recognised that when he said that in China "man cannot be thought of apart from Nature", and that in domestic buildings, "there was embodied throughout the ages a feeling for cosmic pattern and the symbolism of the directions, the seasons, winds and constellations." (Needham: 60-1) The house with its exterior setting and interior furnishing was designed to

其他作者的著作中亦有提及這種雅潔的標準。文震亨認為不少家具的建造、裝飾和陳設都是很清雅，但也批評了當時許多過份雕鏤的裝飾，覺得只是娛俗人之目。《長物志》卷六：225）如此，書房的几榻必須古雅。（同上）几台雕上雲頭和如意圖案，更添雅緻，但切忌雕上龍鳳圖案，而窄長的几桌更是可厭。（同上：231）就形狀而言，八仙桌並非雅緻的家具。（同上：234）裝飾方面，文震亨描述榻背鑲有大理石，或上朱黑漆，中刻竹樹，又或鑲滿新螺鈿，均非雅緻。此外，塗金的摺凳簡直俗不堪用。（同上：237）床邊刻有卍字回紋亦屬俗氣。（同上：241）對文震亨而言，用料、形式、結構、顏色、花紋和圖案是分辨雅俗的基準。他在文中詳列房屋和家具雅俗的定義，清楚顯示出他是出身士大夫家庭。相反，李漁出身的背景與文不同，對雅俗的看法亦不盡相同。他並不同意「變俗為雅，猶之點鐵成金，惟具山林經濟者能此」。反之，李認為只要聰明、有好奇心和智巧，便能變俗為雅。《閑情偶寄》卷四：185-6）李漁此觀念亦可從他嘗試打破階級障礙，宣稱自己有雅士風韻中清淅可見。他的作品充滿新穎獨特的意念，但他並沒有意思將這些新意稱為雅。在比較文震亨和李漁時，可讓我們深入理解雅俗辯証是分別社會階級的方法。

房屋的象徵意義

房屋的最高理念是讓居者接近大自然，與自然合一，是中國傳統裡房屋的其中一個象徵意義。Joseph Needham認為在中國「人不能脫離大自然」，同時亦了解房屋「在悠久歷史中，孕含著一種宇宙規律的感覺，也是方向、季候、風向和星宿的象徵。」（Needham 1971: 60-1）房屋在地形上的布局和屋內的陳

achieve such an ideal of one with Nature. Thus Gao Lian quoted extensively from literati and hermits of old on what is considered as the ideal setting: to be one with Nature, and achieve calmness in oneself. (Gao: 7.7a) Wen's ideal dwelling place is similarly narrated. In the prologue to the section on dwelling, he suggested:

The best place to dwell is among the hills and water, or in the villages, or in the suburbs. If we have to live in urban houses and cannot follow the footsteps of well-known recluses to live among the mountains, at least, our gate and courtyard should be elegant and clean, our house and room pure and beautiful. ... So much so that those who dwell in it would forget that their age has advanced, those who come to live for a short time would forget to return home, and those who come to visit would not feel tired. ... However, if one is only interested in ornate construction and seeks after colourful appearance, [the house] would be just like a pair of handcuffs or a cage for birds or animals. (Wen: 18)

To Wen, the first and foremost requirement of a house is to be in the natural setting. If one has to dwell in the city, the house has to also create the same lingering and refreshing effect as one finds living in nature. (Fig. 11)

It was for this purpose of absorbing nature that gardens were created next to the house. (Fig. 12) Contrasting the house to the garden, Ji Cheng said that houses are orderly and have to be built in proper sequence, while the garden should be planned naturally so that it might be like a picture and that the desire for the hills and the water might be fulfilled. (Ji: 72) Likewise, Li Yu expressed that:

Fig. 11 A view into a courtyard of the Zhang house, Zhouzhuang. The plant in the courtyard serves as a reminder of nature.
圖11　周莊張廳小庭，庭中的盆景乃大自然的縮影。

設，是要達至天人合一的理念。因此，高濂從歷史中列舉了大量文人隱士對理想環境的意見─外適內和。（《遵生八牋》卷七：7a）文震亨理想中的居住環境亦近似，在室廬部份的引言中指出：

「居山水間者為上，村居次之，郊居又次之。吾儕縱不能棲岩止谷，追綺園之蹤，而混跡塵市，要須門庭雅潔，室廬清靚。… 令居之者忘老，寓之者忘歸，游之者忘倦。… 若徒侈土木，尚丹堊，真同桎梏、樊檻而已。」（《長物志》卷一：18）

文震亨認為房屋最好是建在大自然環境中，若要住在市鎮，房屋亦必須營造出在大自然環境中生活那種令人依戀、別有韻味的效果。（圖11）

為了融入大自然，人們便在房屋旁邊建設園林。（圖12）房屋跟園林相比，計成認為房屋方正，須依序而建，園林則應順自然而設計，做到與圖畫相似，滿足人們對山水林泉的渴好。（《園冶》卷一：72）李漁亦表示「幽齋磊石，原非得已。不能致身岩下，與木石居，故以一卷代山，一勺代水，所謂無聊之極思

It is only with regret that [we have to build] a secluded studio and [to pile] strange rocks. Since it is not possible to place the body under the cliff, or to dwell next to the wood or stone, thus a scroll [painting] is used to represent the mountain and a ladle [filled with water] the water. (Li: 180)

Thus clearly, this ideal of dwelling in nature is taken to be fulfilled in the garden of the house.

Another symbolic aspect of the living environment is its representation of the milieu of antiquity, the chief concern of the literati at the time of the Ming dynasty. This respect for the past is perceived by Clunas as a symbol of Chinese culture. (Clunas: 91-2) In the internal layout of the furnishings and placement of objects, simplicity and naturalness are the keys, as well as the representation of the past, as Gao Lian explained:

Outside the studio are ivy climbing up the wall, with miniature pines and cypress placed in the middle of the wall. Green and fragrant grass would grow through the cracks of the stair to create a sense of greenness permeating in the air. In the studio, a bowl with five or seven goldfish should be placed under the window, this is to observe the natural life. A long table is positioned in the centre of the studio, on which are arranged an ancient ink stone, an old bronze water dropper, a porcelain brush rest from an ancient kiln, a bamboo brush holder, a brush wash from an ancient kiln, a box for sticking paste, and a bronze paper weight. To the left of the table is positioned a small wooden bed, a rolling foot stool is placed by its side. At the head of the bed is placed a small table on which is a bronze vase or a vase of *ge* kiln. On the wall is hung an ancient *qin*, in the centre of the room is laid a long wooden bench, and a painting is hung on the wall. There are two genres of paintings that may be hung on a studio wall — landscape or

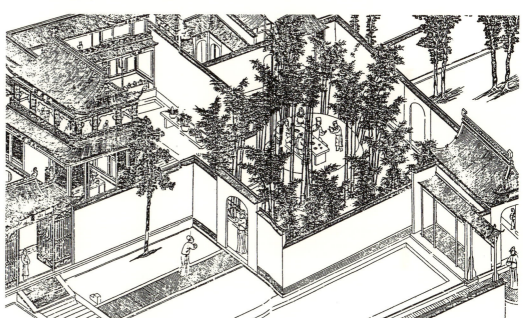

Fig. 12 A woodblock print of a house with a garden. *Huancuitang yuanjing tu* [Views of the garden of Huancui Hall], painted by Qian Gong, engraved by Huang Yingzu, Suzhou, Ming Wanli (1573-1620) edition. From *Jinling gu banhua*, Zhou Wu ed., Nanjing: Jiangsu Meishu Chubanshe, 1993, pp. 252-3.
圖12　錢貢繪《環翠堂園景圖》，黃應組鐫，明萬曆版。（轉載自周蕪編：《金陵古版畫》（南京：江蘇美術出版社，一九九三年），252頁。）

flower. One should not hang paintings of figures, or birds and animals. On the side of the wooden bench are placed four objects: a censer, a vase, a chopsticks holder, and a fragrance box. The selection of these objects would be determined by scholar of great learning. On the wall may also be hung a flower vase. As for the chair, the studio may have six stools and a meditation chair. On the right wall of the studio may be placed a bookcase. (Gao: 7.30b-31a)

亦表示「幽齋磊石，原非得已。不能致身岩下，與木石居，故以一卷代山，一勺代水，所謂無聊之極思也。」(《閑情偶寄》卷四：180) 由此顯明，居於大自然這理想，可從園林中實現。

懷古是生活環境的另一象徵意義，是明朝文士關心的事。Clunas把思古的悠情，理解為中國文化的象徵。(1991:91-2) 簡單自然是室內家具陳設和裝飾的關鍵，亦代表了懷古，如高濂解釋：

「窗外四壁，薜蘿滿牆。中列松檜盆景或建蘭一二，遠砌種以翠芸草，令遍茂，則青蔥鬱然。… 近窗處，蓄金鯽五七頭以觀天機活潑。齋中長卓一、古硯一、舊古銅水注一、舊窯筆格一、班竹筆筒一、舊窯筆洗一、糊斗一、水中丞一、銅石鎮紙一。左置榻床一、榻下滾腳凳一、床頭小几一，上置古銅花尊，或哥窯定瓶一。…壁間掛古琴一，中置几一，如吳中雲木几式佳。壁間畫一，書室中畫惟二品，山水為上，花木次之，禽鳥人物不也，…凡外爐一、花瓶一、匙筋一、香盒一。四者等差遠甚，惟博雅者擇之。…壁間當可處懸壁瓶一，四時插花坐列。吳興筍凳、六禪椅一。」(《遵生八牋》卷七：30b-31a)

Wen Zhenheng's specification for a mountain studio is similar to Gao Lian in its surrounding of plants, miniature plants and moss growing on the steps. Wen also went into great detail about the selection of furniture and objects to be placed in the house. The criteria are again elegance, loftiness and antiquity. Thus he advised that in a small room, one should not have too much furniture, a table of narrow width just as in the old style is sufficient. (Wen: 353) In a pavilion should be placed objects that are old and natural. (Wen: 355) Thus both the outside and the inside of the house work together to achieve a sense of naturalness, the cosmological symbol, and of antiquity, the cultural symbol.

THE DIALECTIC OF THE LIVING ENVIRONMENT

We have discussed the three values of a house as seen in its setting, construction, design and the furniture housed inside. By taking a holistic view, we are able to see the meaning of the living environment of the seventeenth century. This view may just be a fragment of the actual picture of the time, nevertheless, it provides us with the opportunity to discuss the key concepts that were applied by the literati on both the house and the furniture. These concepts are represented in words such as antiquity, elegance, simplicity, refinement, austerity and naturalness, and their complementary dialectics: modern, vulgar, complexity, coarseness, ornateness and overtly man-made.[16] In using these qualitative terms, the literati had advanced their concept of the ideal living environment, to be achieved in the design and placement of the house and its furniture.

文震亨對山齋指定的要求與高濂相似,四週要有植物、盆景,階間有苔蘚。他亦頗詳細講述屋中擺設的家具要古典高雅,小室不宜擺放太多家具,放一張古製狹邊書几便足夠。(《長物志》卷一〇:353)此外,亭內則應置古樸自然的物件。(《長物志》卷六:355)故此,房屋內外均共同發揮作用,以達至自然古雅的感覺,象徵著宇宙浩瀚和悠古文化。

生活環境的辯證關係

我們從房屋的環境、建築、設計及室內擺設的家具中討論三種價值,透過整體的角度,可見十七世紀生活環境的意義。這角度或許只可反映當時部份的實況,但卻可為我們提供一個機會,討論文人對宅屋和家具的重要概念,以古、雅、簡、精、樸、自然等為正,現代、俗、繁、粗、過份修飾、過份人工化為反。[16]在利用這些辯證詞語來描述生活環境時,文士已提出理想生活環境的概念,並要從宅第設計和營造,家具的陳設中達至這最高理念。

16 Some of these key terms are explained in the glossary in Lin Yutang: *The Importance of Living*. London: William Heinemann Ltd., 1938: 442–60.

16 林語堂在 *The Importance of Living*. London: William Heinemann Ltd., 1938:442-60中解釋部份詞彙。

REFERENCES CITED
徵引書目

Bourdieu, Pierre. *Distinction: A Social Critique of the Judgement of Taste*. Trans. by Richard Nice. London: Routledge & Kegan Paul, 1979.

Clunas, Craig. *Superfluous Things; Material Culture and Social Status in Early Modern China*. Urbana and Chicago: University of Illinois Press, 1991.

Gao Lian. *Zunsheng bajian* [Eight Notes on Respectful Living]. 19 *juan*. Published in 1591. 1884 edition.
【高濂：《遵生八牋》，十九卷，1591年初刊，1884年版。】

Li Yu. *Xianqing ouji* [Occasional Records of Leisurely Sentiment]. 6 *juan*. First published in 1671. Hangzhou: Zhejiang guji chubanshe, 1985.
【李漁：《閑情偶寄》，六卷，1670年初刊。杭州：浙江古籍出版社，1985年。】

Ji Cheng. *Yuan ye* [The Making of Gardens]. 3 *juan*. First published in 1631. Annotated edition by Chen Zhi. Beijing: Zhongguo jianzhu gongye chubanshe, 1981.
【計成：《園冶》，三卷，1631年初刊，陳植注譯。北京：中國建築工業出版社，1981年。】

Needham, Joseph. *Science and Civilisation in China, vol. 4, part III*. Cambridge: Cambridge University Press, 1971.

Wen Zhenheng: *Zhangwu zhi* [Treatise on Superfluous Things]. 12 *juan*. Compiled in 1615–20. Annotated edition by Chen Zhi. Nanjing: Jiangsu kexue jishu chubanshe, 1984.
【文震亨：《長物志》，十二卷，1615年至1620年初刊，陳植注譯。南京：南京科學技術出版社，1984年。】

Further Studies of Furniture In Alternative Woods – Reflections on Aspects of Chinese Culture

從中國民間家具反映中國文化

John Kwang-Ming Ang

洪光明

As a utilitarian object, furniture tells us much about its owners and their cultural backgrounds. The form, type and wood used not only reflect where and how its owner lived, but also indicate his economic and social status, while its style and quality of craftsmanship reveal the owner's artistic sensibilities.

However, with only a relatively small number of books written on hardwood furniture, particularly *huanghuali*, the understanding of Chinese culture through its furniture is very limited. So far what most of us can see is only a vague glimpse of the lives of an extremely small and exclusive strata of Chinese society – the very wealthy aristocrats, officials and scholars who lived during the period when *huanghuali* wood was readily available i.e. between the mid-Ming to mid-Qing dynasties (sixteenth to eighteenth centuries).

In order for Chinese furniture to be a window through which we view Chinese culture, we have to look at both *huanghuali* furniture and the immense range of furniture in other woods, a subject that has not yet been fully explored. Several examples of furniture in alternative wood from the Kai-Yin Lo collection provide the opportunity to examine different types of vernacular furniture and their decoration, woods used, styles and special features to give a deeper insight into Chinese culture.

TYPES OF FURNITURE AND THEIR DECORATION

The long narrow *kang* table is a type of furniture which immediately reveals its owner's origins and lifestyle. The *nanmu* (a variety of cedar) table in the Kai-Yin Lo Collection (plate 19) has small everted flanges, *ruyi* shaped spandrels and openwork carved panels of an upright *ruyi* (a mushroom-like decorative motif symbolising the fulfilment of wishes) on each of its side panels. On the side panels above each *ruyi* is an opening in the shape of two leaves with their tips meeting at the centre. In the centre of each leg on both front and back sides is an additional beaded line running vertically from top to bottom.

家具屬於實用的物品，它能夠充分反映物主的身份及當時的文化背景。家具的種類、造型以及木質不僅能夠顯示物主居住的地區及生活方式，同時也能顯示其財富及社會地位。至於它的造型及工藝水平，更可顯示物主的藝術品味。

但是，目前有關中國硬木家具的書籍，特別是以黃花梨為題的數量有限。因此。要藉家具去了解中國文化仍是有限制。明中葉至清中葉（十六世紀至十八世紀）期間，黃花梨木充裕，而目前我們可見的，僅是此時期貴族以及文人的生活方式，只是中國社會的極少部份。

故此，若要從中國家具去探視中國淵博的文化，我們除了要去認識黃花梨家具，更要認識其他不同木質的家具。羅啟妍女士收藏的多種木質家具，可讓我們了解民間家具的種類、裝飾、木質、造型及特點，藉此來進一步認識中國的文化。

家具的種類和裝飾

長條炕几可直接反映物主居住地區和他的生活方式。羅女士所收藏的一件楠木炕几〔圖版19〕，兩端略往上翹，帶如意牙頭，兩側檔板透雕有向上的如意圖案，如意上端則有一開光，造形似兩葉相交。此外，前後四支腿足的中央，有一上下垂直的一柱香線。

Not being easily portable, they were thus more often seen placed on the *kang*, the permanent hollow heated brick bed of northern Chinese homes, than on the *chuang*, the movable couch-bed of southern China. In both northern and southern China, small portable square or oblong low tables were placed in the centre of beds for the convenience of eating or drinking. Long low side tables generally belong to the north, where they are arranged against the back or side walls of the heated brick *kang* as altar tables or side tables for placing decorative, ritual or utilitarian objects.

Fig. 1   19th century elm wood altar table from Shanxi showing use of *ruyi* side panels. 180 cm (w) x 54 cm (d) x 92 cm (h).
圖1　十九世紀山西榆木翹頭案帶透雕如意檔板．180 x 54 x 92公分．

The Kai-Yin Lo table is striking in its beautiful and elegant long, narrow proportions and use of the simple carved openwork single *ruyi*. The *ruyi* panel is a traditional decorative form often seen on altar tables illustrated in late Ming woodblock prints, but time, use, ravages of war, or perhaps a loss of popularity contributed to its apparent decline. Instead, many of the altar tables found in various provinces of China and illustrated in books, more often use reticulated carved dragons, openwork lattice panels and other decorative designs.[1] It is only in the last decade that a large number of altar and *kang* tables of both *huanghuali* and alternative woods with *ruyi* side panels have been found, many of them from Shanxi. As the majority are from Shanxi, this author believes that the Kai-Yin Lo *kang* side table with everted flanges is also from this province. A Shanxi provenance is even more convincing when we notice that even the shape of the decorative opening above the *kang* table *ruyi* is strikingly similar to that of the Shanxi elm wood altar table illustrated above. (Fig.1)   The two beaded lines in the centre of the legs of

Fig. 2   18th/19th century elongated elm wood *kang* side table with *ruyi* spandrels from Shanxi. 145 cm (w) x 39 cm (d) x 35 cm (h).
圖2　十八～十九世紀山西榆木帶如意牙頭長條炕几．145 x 39 x 35公分．

this altar table also remind us of the beaded line on the legs of the *nanmu kang* table. An elm wood *kang* table with similar elongated proportions is another example of a *kang* table from Shanxi. (Fig.2)

The Kai-Yin Lo softwood table with everted flanges features, on its side panels, an unusual *lingzhi* carving symbolising double or triple longevity (Plate 29). Shanxi people seem to favour

由於長條炕几不便攜帶，在北方民居它們通常是固定放置在炕上使用；而南方的床榻由於比較靈活，所以很少使用炕几。雖然，在中國南方與北方，均有在床上放置方形或長方形的小几作飲食的習慣，但是特別長的炕几應在北方使用。在炕上內面或側面的牆邊，通常會放置裝飾品、供品或用品。

羅女士這張桌子，比例不僅優雅修長，透雕清簡，更刻有簡潔如意鏤雕。如意雕板是常見的裝飾圖案，在晚明木刻版畫中所繪的供桌上常出現。但是隨著時間的流逝和戰亂，它已漸漸不流行。從中國許多不同省份出現的供桌上，或是書籍上看到的大多是雕龍、透格以及其他裝飾圖案。[1] 直至最近十年，黃花梨和其他木質的供桌、炕几桌上，才出現不少如意檔板設計。這類桌子大都來自山西，所以羅女士的炕几，極有可能來自同一地方。此外，炕几如意紋上方的開光，跟一張山西的榆木供桌近似，（圖1）而這張供桌腿足中央的兩條一柱香線，亦類似楠木炕几桌腳上的陽線。另一個來自山西的例子，是一張榆木炕几，比例亦很修長。（圖2）

羅女士的軟木翹頭案側面檔板上的靈芝紋，象徵兩重或三重長壽。（圖版29）山西人喜愛靈芝紋圖

1. See altar tables in: Kates, George N. *Chinese Household Furniture*. N. Y. and London: Harper & Brothers, 1948.; Ecke, Gustav. *Chinese Domestic Furniture*. Rutland, Vermont and Tokyo: Charles E. Tuttle Co., 1962; Ellsworth, R. H. *Chinese Furniture*. New York : Random House, 1970.

1   見英文注釋1。

Fig. 3 Detail of an 18th century black lacquered elm wood altar table with group of *lingzhi* in side panels from Shanxi.
圖3. 十八世紀山西黑漆榆木供桌帶多個靈芝紋檔板局部.

the *lingzhi* variation of the *ruyi* motif to symbolise longevity. An interesting black lacquered elm wood Shanxi altar table with a cluster of large and small *lingzhi* carved on both of its side panels is another known example. (Fig.3) Although not identical, both tables highlight the individualistic forms of *lingzhi* seen on various examples of altar tables recently emerging from Shanxi.

Although there has been some study of popular Shanxi vernacular auspicious motifs found in paper cuts, embroidery and paintings on walls surrounding the *kang*, apparently no study has yet been made on the symbolic motifs frequently found on Shanxi furniture.[2] Perhaps further research on the innumerable *ruyi* and *lingzhi* decorations seen on many types of softwood Shanxi furniture may reveal why the people from this area had such a special affinity with these two motifs.[3]

Portable folding furniture gives insight into how social customs influence furniture design, and the well-crafted elm wood folding stool in the Kai-Yin Lo collection is a good example (Plate 7). According to Wang Shixiang, the few surviving *huanghuali* folding chairs were originally chairs of honour reserved for dignitaries.[4] However, the plethora of softwood examples that have recently been discovered in Shanxi remains perplexing. According to this writer's observations, no other province has yet yielded as many softwood folding chairs and stools of considerable age as Shanxi.[5]

Early evidence of the popularity of folding furniture in Shanxi is found in many Ming dynasty excavated lead glazed figures who carry folding stools over their shoulders. (Fig. 4) One way to understand why such an abundance of folding furniture was and continues to be used in Shanxi is first to investigate the need for folding furniture, and then to ascertain whether or not Shanxi people had such requirements.

Fig. 4 Ming dynasty excavated lead-glazed figure of a servant carrying a folding stool. Probably from Shanxi. From *Journal of the Classical Chinese Furniture Society*, Summer 1994: 13, fig. 15.
圖4. 明代出土的鉛釉帶交机待從像。此像大概來自山西。轉載自 *Journal of the Classical Chinese Furniture Society*，夏季1944：13，圖15。

案，取其長壽之意。與此相似的，是一張出於山西的黑漆榆木供桌，兩側檔板上雕刻著大大小小的靈芝紋。（圖3）雖然兩者不完全相同，但它們都有突出的靈芝紋，與近期在山西出現的供桌的共通。

雖然過去有不少剪紙、刺繡與炕上壁畫的研究，是與山西民間的吉祥裝飾圖案有關，但是山西家具上的裝飾圖案，卻未有加以研究。[2]若對山西軟木家具上的如意和靈芝紋多加研究，可以幫助我們了解何以山西人對於此一圖案情有獨鍾。[3]

透過折合家具，我們可以看到社會風俗如何影響家具設計。而羅啟妍女士收藏的一張榆木折凳，正是一個好例子。（圖版7）根據王世襄的說法，黃花梨交椅原屬於顯貴人士的坐椅。[4]但是最近在山西出現的許多軟木交椅，令人不解。據本文作者的觀察，目前其他省份並未如山西省一樣，出現那麼多具相當年代的交椅與交凳。[5]

明代出土了許多鉛釉陪葬俑肩扛著交凳，是山西折合家具早期普遍使用的例證。（圖4）要了解山西使用並且保存了那麼多折合家具，我們應該要先了解折合家具的特殊用途，然後再進一步分析山西需要此家具的原因。

2. Lee Shan. *An Overview of Shanxi Customs; The Vernacular Art of Shanxi People.* Beijing: China Publishing House, 1933: 345-57.
3. The *lingzhi* motif is found on furniture of many provinces but its use in both soft and hardwood Shanxi furniture seems much more prevalent. It is found on mirror stands, backsplats of chairs, ends of scroll tables, and display stands, to name a few. Perhaps one of the main reasons is the conservatism of Shanxi people. Many traditional symbols long forsaken in other provinces have continued to be used in Shanxi until the present.
4. Wang Shixiang: *Connoisseurship of Chinese Furniture.* Hong Kong: Joint Publishing Co. Ltd., 1990: 45.
5. In the last year, from 1996-7, many folding lamp hanger chairs have been found in Zhejiang province, however, most of them have no patina and seem to date to the early twentieth century.

2 李杉：《山西民族大觀・山西民間工藝美術》，中國旅游出版社，北京，1933：345-57。
3 靈芝紋在中國許多省份的家具中都有用到，但是在山西軟木及硬木家具中出現更多：包括鏡架，椅子靠背板上，下卷桌的兩端，陳列架等等。可能主要原因之一是山西人的保守個性，很多已被其他省份遺忘的圖案在山西卻一直使用到現在。
4 王世襄：《明式家具珍賞》，香港三聯書局，1990年：45。
5 在去年，也就是1996-1997年之間，在浙江省出現了很多燈掛交椅。但是,它們大多數沒有皮殼，年代應該是二十世紀初。

It is said that folding furniture was created to save space – when folded, it reduces in size, and stacks up for storage in bulk in smaller areas. Another reason for its existence is its portability. When folded, it of course become easier to transport. When storage and transportation are convenient, folding furniture becomes extremely practical, if not ideal, for outdoor activities. Evidence that Shanxi people used folding chairs and stools for outdoor activities can be found in the Yuan dynasty frescoes at Yongle Palace in Ruicheng county. In one detail, for example, we see a Daoist immortal healing a woman seated on a folding stool outside her home. (Fig. 5)

If outdoor activities necessitated the use of folding chairs and stools, then Shanxi's many outdoor activities created a definite need for them. As an important Buddhist and Daoist religious centre, Shanxi has been famous since the Tang dynasty for its religious temple gatherings known as *miaohui*. The ten most important *miaohui* of Shanxi are still held regularly every year, and although considered extravagant events today, are probably only a dim reflection of their original immensity of scale. During *miaohui* such as the Donkey Horse Festival at Wutai Mountain held on the 6th month of every lunar year, almost 20,000 donkeys and horses are brought together for sale and barter and an even greater number of people are gathered. This festival is considered a *miaohui* because during the celebrations all the Wutai Mountain temples, large and small, open their doors to worshippers. The weather during this festival is considered at its best, sunny but not unbearably hot, and thus appropriate for many outdoor ceremonies and performances, like the numerous Shanxi drum dances, story telling (*shuoshu*), temple mask dances, and stilt walking, to name a few.[6]

Fig. 5   Daoist immortal healing a woman seated on a folding stool. Yongle Palace, Ruicheng county, Shanxi. From *The Yongle Palace Murals*. Beijing: Foreign Languages Press, 1985: 84
圖5.   十七―十八世紀榆木交凳帶腳踏.

Although there is no direct evidence, it seems quite logical that the many examples of folding furniture discovered in Shanxi would have been used by participants of such outdoor

一般折合家具的特點是收合後可縮小體積、可重疊且便於存放。另外，它又便於攜帶、運送，最適宜在戶外活動時使用。芮城縣元代永樂宮的壁畫，是山西人在戶外活動時使用交椅與交凳的一個好例子。畫中我們可以看見一位道士坐在一張交凳上，在一房子外面為一位女士治療。（圖5）

如果因為戶外活動而需要交椅與交凳，那麼山西經常舉行一些戶外的活動，則絕對有需要使用折合家具。山西為佛教與道教的重鎮，自唐代起即有著名的宗教活動、廟會。今天，山西每年仍然舉行十個重要的廟會，規模上可能無法與昔日的盛況相比。在舉行這些廟會時，例如每年陰曆六月在五台山所舉行的驢馬節慶，幾乎有將近兩萬頭驢和馬在市集上出售及交易，因此聚集的人更多。這類活動也是一種廟會，因為節慶期間，五台山區的大小寺廟均會開放給信徒們。這段期間的氣候晴朗怡人，因此有許多的戶外活動舉行，例如山西的擊鼓舞、說書、面具舞和踩高蹺等。[6]

山西出現大量的折合家具原是供當時戶外活動使用的說法，雖沒

6.   Complete descriptions of all the *miaohui* and outdoor activities that accompany them can be found in *An Overview of Shanxi Customs*: 435–50. For other descriptions of outdoor activities in Shanxi see Wen Xin and Xue Faxi, *Shanxi Folk Customs*. Taiyuan: Shanxi People's Publishing House, 1991.

6   有關山西所有廟會以及戶外活動的詳細描述，可以閱讀*An Overview of Shanxi Customs*：435–450.
另外，其他有關山西戶外活動的介紹，可以參閱溫幸及薛發喜主編的山西民俗，山西人民出版社，太原，1991.

performances. Recent photographs of Shanxi outdoor activities show performing musicians seated on modern folding chairs.[7] This clearly demonstrates that folding chairs, old or new, are indeed integral to Shanxi outdoor life.

Opera is yet another outdoor activity which probably required the widespread use of folding chairs and stools. Shanxi people's love of opera is documented in the numerous temple wall paintings and relief sculptures of opera scenes[8] and by over a hundred open air opera stages dating from the Yuan to Qing dynasties.[9] Through centuries of patronage, four major opera styles have developed to entertain a wide range of people.[10] From many of the photographs taken of Shanxi opera today, we find that the performances are still held outdoors where people either stand or lean on their bicycles to watch.[11] It is difficult to ascertain whether or not the Kai-Yin Lo elm wood stool is from Shanxi. However, since many examples are still being found there, and this author has seen few, if any, very old folding chairs and stools from other provinces, it may be safe, for the time being, to assume that it is.

This elm wood folding stool carved in raised relief, with a pair of facing dragons on the uppermost front strip, shows considerable age in its worn surface and high patina, especially around the edges that were often touched. (Plate 7, detail) A pair of similar examples in *huanghuali* can be seen in the Great Mosque in Xian in Shanxi,[12] and a single example, also in *huanghuali*, is in the Mimi and Raymond Hung Collection.[13] The fact that the Kai-Yin Lo example is not *huanghuali* suggests that this type of furniture did not only belong to the wealthy scholar officials, but also to a wider range of ordinary people who might have used it for one of the several abovementioned outdoor activities. However, among folding stools, those of a height similar to the Kai-Yin Lo one, measuring 50–55 cm from the ground and with carved

有直接的證據支持，但此推斷亦合符邏輯。在一本介紹山西戶外活動的書中，從一張照片中可看見山西的樂師們坐在交椅上在戶外表演，[7]這也可證明許多的山西折合家具，是供戶外活動時使用。

戲劇是另一種可能需要使用交椅及交凳的戶外活動。從許多山西寺廟的壁畫與浮雕上出現的戲劇題材，可證明山西人很喜歡戲劇。[8]而且，自元朝至清朝，已有超過上百個戶外的戲碼。[9]由於數個世紀以來，戲劇都受到人們的喜愛，它已發展出四類主要的劇種，以滿足觀眾不同的偏好。[10]從今天我們看到拍攝山西戲劇表演的許多照片中，發現戶外表演仍然活躍，有些人們更站著或靠著腳踏車觀賞。[11]

羅女士收藏的這張榆木交凳，作工精細，但我們尚未能確定它是否來自山西。由於山西仍有不少此類凳出現，而本文作者又未曾見過其他省份出現年代古舊的交椅及交凳，故此暫且假設它是來自山西。

這張榆木交凳座面前端的木條上浮雕一對相向的龍，從其表面磨損的情形和很厚的皮殼，尤其是在接角經常被觸摸的地方，可看出它已有相當的年代。（圖版7，局部）在山西西安的大清真寺，出現了一對類似的黃花梨木交凳。[12]洪王家琪女士的收藏中，亦有一張黃花梨木製的。[13]羅女士收藏的一張不是黃花梨木，似乎說明此類家具並不只限於達官貴人使用，一般人在戶外活動時也

7. *Shanxi Folk Customs*: 455.
8. For a wall painting of opera activities see the Yuan dynasty fresco in the Hall to King Mingying in the Temple of the Water God in Guang Sheng Monastery in Hongtong. *A Panorama of Ancient Architecture in Shanxi*. Taiyuan: Shanxi People's Publishing House, 1986: 255. For brick sculpture of actors see the Jin dynasty tomb of Dong Ji Jian in Houma. *A Pictorial Guide to the History of Chinese Music*. Beijing: People's Music Publishing House, 1988: 116.
9. For photographs of several of these ancient opera stages see *Shanxi Folk Customs*: 500.
10. The four major Shanxi operas styles are Jin Ju, Pu Ju, Bei Lu Bang Zi and Shang Dang Bang Zi. Besides these operas there are also many other minor local opera styles. *An Overview of Shanxi Customs*: 268 - 82.
11. *Shanxi Folk Customs*: 497.
12. Illustrated in *Journal of the Classical Chinese Furniture Society* (JCCFS) Summer 1994: 21, fig. 28.
13. Ellsworth, Robert H. et. al. *Chinese Furniture; One Hundred Examples from the Mimi and Raymond Hung Collection*. New York, 1996: 43, pl. 1.

7 參閱《山西民俗》：455。
8 有關元代戲劇活動的壁畫，參閱洪洞水神廟明應王殿壁畫，見《山西古建築通覽》，山西人民出版社，太原，1986：255。有關演員的磚雕，參閱侯馬董圯堅金代的墓內，見《中國音樂史圖鑑》，人民音樂出版社，北京，1988。
9 有關山西古代戲劇的圖片，參閱《山西民俗》：500。
10 山西戲劇主要分為四大類：晉劇，蒲劇，北路梆子及上黨梆子，除此之外，還有一些小型的地方性風格，參閱 *An Overview of Shanxi Customs*：268－282。
11 參閱《山西民俗》：497。
12 圖片請參閱 *Journal of the Classical Chinese Furniture Society*，夏季刊，1994：21，圖28。
13 《洪氏所藏木器百圖》1996：43，圖版1。

decoration, are not as common as plain uncarved lower folding stools. The Kai-Yin Lo collection folding stool must thus have been made for someone of a certain level of importance.

VARIETIES OF WOODS USED

Through careful examination of the different woods used in Chinese furniture one can learn various aspects of the local areas where these woods were grown. The quality and types of woods used, together with the craftsmanship employed determined the price of the furniture, and thus throw light on the social status and economic background of their owners.

Nanmu (a variety of cedar) is grown mainly in Sichuan and Yunnan, and although a softwood, was considered precious and used in furniture manufacture all over China. Therefore like *huanghuali* furniture, which was also used throughout China, the provenance of *nanmu* furniture is usually difficult to pinpoint.

Nanmu has always been prized for its resistance to warping, its fine grain, and the sweet aroma which deters wood-loving insects. It was also an expensive wood since there was only a limited supply of large timber in Sichuan and Yunnan provinces. In fact, in the eighteenth century the wood almost became extinct when, in 1790, the Qianlong emperor spent 72,000 taels of silver to complete the immense *nanmu* Hall of Simplicity and Sincerity at the Summer Palace at Chengde in Rehe province.[14] Heshen, a favourite official of the Qianlong emperor, helped to cause the virtual depletion of *nanmu* forests. Sentenced to death in 1799, one of his many offences was the extravagant use of *nanmu* for his palatial mansions.[15]

Besides using the wood for architecture, some *nanmu* was also used for furniture. Most of the examples found today in China are extremely well-crafted in simple and classic styles, usually dating from the Ming to mid-Qing dynasty. The *kang* table discussed earlier (Plate 19) and a simple two-shelf bookshelf on a stand with three drawers from Suzhou (Plate 31) are good examples. The majority of *nanmu* furniture has been found in Jiangsu (especially Suzhou,

可使用。類似羅女士的凳子，帶有雕刻裝飾，離地約五十至五十五公分，較一般素交凳高，屬於少見的例子。因此羅女士這張凳子，應該原屬於一個身份地位比較重要的人物。

不同的木質

如果仔細檢查中國家具中不同的木質，可以了解這些木材生長地區的一些文化。 而從木質及作工的優劣，不僅可以決定它們的價格，也可以看出它主人的社會地位和經濟狀況。

楠木主要在四川及雲南生長，雖然木質較軟，但中國各地仍視之為製作家具的珍貴木質。因此，楠木家具的製造地，如黃花梨家具一樣，是很難確認的。

楠木受人喜愛是因為它不變形、質地細緻、味道香甜而且防蛀。四川及雲南出產大木幹的數量很少，所以楠木是很珍貴。事實上，在十八世紀時，楠木已幾乎絕種。單是乾隆皇帝，便在1790年花了七萬二千兩銀子，在熱河承德的避暑山莊內，以楠木建造了一個大規模的"澹泊敬誠"殿。[14]此外，他的寵臣和珅在1799年遭處死刑，罪行之一就是奢侈揮霍，使用楠木建造自己的豪華宅第。[15]

除了使用於建築外，楠木也用來製造家具。今天在中國各地出現的一些楠木家具，大多數作工細緻，而且樣式簡單典雅，年代介於明代至清代中期。前面討論過的一張炕几，（圖版19）以及一件平素帶三屜及底座的蘇州雙層書架（圖版31）均是很好的例子。大部份的楠木家具來自江蘇（特別是蘇州、

14. *China - A Land of Beauty - Chengde.* Shanghai: Shanghai People's Publishing House, 1980: 4.

15. Murck, Freda and Fong, Wen. *A Chinese Garden Court - The Astor Court at The Metropolitan Museum of Art.* New York: The Metropolitan Museum of Art, 1980: 60.

14 《江山多嬌‧承德》，上海人民出版社，1980: 4.

15 見英文注釋15。

Dongshan and Nantong), Anhui and occasionally Shanxi.[16] From the preciousness of the wood, refined workmanship and simplicity of styles, we can generally assume that *nanmu* furniture was the property of wealthy scholar officials of the seventeenth–eighteenth century.

Fig. 6   Pair of 18th century *jichimu* square stools from Suzhou, Jiangsu. 54 cm (w) x 54 cm (d) x 47 cm (h) .
圖6.   十八世紀江蘇省蘇州雞翅木方凳乙對.
54 x 54 x 47 公分.

Jichimu (chicken-wing wood) is another precious material. When Wang Shixiang published his books on Chinese furniture in the 1980s, there was very little *jichimu* furniture to examine. According to his research, the wood was mostly used in the Ming to the mid-Qing. However, after Wang's books were published, many pieces of *jichimu* furniture appeared on the market between 1989–1992, almost all of it discovered in Fujian province and dated to the eighteenth–nineteenth century. In Fujian, however, old logs of *jichimu* have been found but no *jichimu* trees have been located. This may indicate that the wood was imported, rather than grown locally. Although so far there are no known records regarding the importation of *jichimu* into Fujian, we can safely assume that such trade occurred since much *jichimu* has been found in Southeast Asia, especially Vietnam, a country that traded with Fujian.[17]

Fig. 7   Late 18th/early 19th century *luohan* bed with inset burl wood side panels and thin cabriole legs from Fujian.
圖7.   十八世紀晚期~十九世紀初期福建雞翅木帶嵌癭木圍板與扁平彎腿之羅漢床.

Although the majority of *jichimu* furniture we find today comes from Fujian, there is also *jichimu* furniture found in other provinces such as Jiangsu. Generally the Suzhou style of *jichimu* furniture is classic, following the traditional standard forms of Chinese furniture. The pair of square stools with bridle-joined spandrels and stretchers on four sides are good examples of typical Suzhou-style *jichimu* furniture. (Fig. 6) Fujian *jichimu* furniture, on the other hand, is often more provincial looking, incorporating local designs not previously encountered. An example is a *luohan* bed with oddly shaped thin flattened cabriole legs. (Fig.7)

東山與南通）和安徽、間中亦有來自山西。[16] 從木材的珍貴價值、作工的精巧和文雅的形式，我們可推論楠木家具是十七至十八世紀時較富有的文官所使用。

雞翅木是另一種珍貴的木質。當王世襄在80年代出版他的著作時，並未出現太多的雞翅木家具可供檢視。根據王氏的研究，此一木材大多數使用於明代至清代中期。但是，當他的著作發行後，在1989年至1992年間，市場上突然出現了大批雞翅木家具。這些雞翅木家具幾乎全部出自福建，而且年代屬於十八至十九世紀。但是，在福建僅可見到老的雞翅木幹材，卻無法看到新的雞翅木樹。這或許表示此材料是進口木質，而非本地出產。雖然至今尚未發現關於福建進口雞翅木的記錄，但是我們應可假設當時曾經存在此一貿易，因為在東南亞，特別是越南，產有大量的雞翅木，而越南和福建曾經有貿易往來。[17]

雖然，今日我們所見的雞翅木家具們大多來自福建，但是其它地區如江蘇蘇州，亦出現一些雞翅木家具。大體上説，蘇州的雞翅木家具多屬於傳統的古典造型，與其它木質如黃花梨的式樣接近，例如一對四面有夾頭榫及根子的方凳，即是典型的蘇州雞翅木家具。（圖6）福建的雞翅木家具，近民間造型，加入了一些地方特色，是以前未曾見過的設計，其中一個例子是一張扁平彎腿羅漢床。（圖7）

16. During the writing of this article this writer was aware that there are differing opinions as to where the Kai-Yin Lo collection's *nanmu kang* table (Plate 19 and described on page 63) originated. However, as there is no direct evidence so far, differing opinions should be kept in order to stimulate more curiosity for further research into the actual source of such tables.

16 本文作者在寫這篇文章時，發現很多人對羅女士所收藏的楠木炕几的來源意見不同（圖版19及頁63），由於目前尚未有確切的証據，應該將這些意見整理保留下來以便激發今後証實此類桌子真正來源的進一步研究.

Fig. 8   18th century pine wood recessed-leg side table with foldable legs and humpbacked stretchers from Fujian.
圖8.   十八世紀福建杉木帶可折合腿與羅鍋根條案.

The design of the *jichimu* recessed-leg table in the Kai-Yin Lo Collection is most unusual (Plate 22). The upper third section of the table can be lifted up and separated from the legs that form the lower two-thirds. The upper section can then be used as a low table for the *kang* or couch-bed. This type of design, however, which has precedents in *huanghuali*[18] and lacquered elm wood[19] cannot be clearly ascribed to either Suzhou or Fujian by stylistic means alone, since it is neither the standard classical style which we often see in Suzhou nor the localised style we see in Fujian.

The origins of this unusual design become clearer when we examine the provenance of some of the recently discovered softwood furniture. It seems that of the several provinces where softwood furniture is being found, similar types of recessed-leg tables with removable legs are restricted to Shanxi and Fujian. An example in pine wood was recently discovered in Shadi, northern Fujian. (Fig. 8) In this example, the slight differences are the legs which fold under the table and the ends of the humpback stretchers that meet the legs are carved in the shape of dragon heads. The short legs of the upper third section, however, closely resemble the short legs of the Kai-Yin Lo table, and since hardly any *jichimu* is found in Shanxi, it is more likely to be from Fujian.

Two pieces of furniture in the Kai-Yin Lo Collection are constructed from unusual wood. These are a small round-corner sloping stile cabinet (Plate 33)[20] and a table with its edges ribbed to simulate bamboo (Plate 25).[21] Their wood has a reddish brown colour with stripes ranging from dark brown to translucent gold. Because the stripes of this wood resemble that of tiger's skin, it had been referred to by many dealers and collectors as "tiger maple" or "curly birch". However, the wood has now been clearly identified as that of the *longyan* fruit tree from Fujian province. So far no furniture made of this type of striped *longyan* wood has been found outside Fujian.

羅女士收藏的一張雞翅木條案式樣很特別（圖版22）。桌子的上半部三分之一與桌子的下半部的三分之二可以分離。上半部可變成一張矮几或炕桌。雖然黃花梨 18 與櫸木漆 19 家具都有這種式樣，但是我們無法單獨從其式樣來斷定它是屬於蘇州還是福建雞翅木家具，因為它既不屬於蘇州的古典造型，也不屬於福建的民間造型。

只要留意最近出現的一些軟木家具，即可了解這些設計獨特的家具的出處。在許多出現軟木家具的省份中，只有山西省與福建省有類似桌面跟桌腳可分離的條案。最近在閩北沙湜所找到的兩張杉木條案便是好例子。（圖8）這些條案的腿足可以折合至桌下，與桌腳相交的羅鍋根尾端雕刻有龍頭。上面可收合的四支較短的腿足，近似羅女士桌子的短腿足。由於山西很少出現雞翅木條案應該是來自福建。

羅女士的收藏中，有兩件家具的木質很特別，一件是小圓角櫃（圖版33），20 另一件是仿竹裹腿的方桌（圖版25）。21 它們的顏色偏棕紅，帶有暗咖啡色至金色的細紋。由於它的紋路很像老虎皮的斑紋，因此很多古董商及收藏家稱之為虎皮楓或鍛木。不過，這木質現已被正式確認為龍眼木，是產自福建省的龍眼樹。目

17 Vermeer, Eduard B., et. al. *Development and Decline of Fukien Province in the 17th and 18th century.* Leiden, The Netherlands: E. J. Brill, 1990: 178.

18 Ellsworth, Robert H. et. al. *Chinese Furniture; One Hundred Examples from the Mimi and Raymond Hung Collection:* 121, pl. 40 and Christie's (New York). *Important Chinese Furniture, formerly the Museum of Classical Chinese Furniture Collection,* September 19, 1996, Lot 43.

19 This lacquered elm wood example looks extremely old, perhaps dating to as early as the seventeenth century. The pudding stone top suggests a Shanxi origin. Sotheby's (New York). *Fine Chinese Ceramics and Works of Art.* November 29 - 30, 1993, Lot 468.

20 For a similar example see Sotheby's (New York). *Fine Chinese Ceramics and Works of Art.*   December 1 - 2, 1992, Lot 656.

21 For a similar example see Sotheby's (New York). *Fine Chinese Ceramics, Furniture and Works of Art.*   March 22, 1995, Lot 385.

17 見英文注釋17。

18 《洪氏所藏木器百圖》：121，圖40。第43件, 及Christie's (New York). *Important Chinese Furniture, formerly the Museum of Classical Chinese Furniture Collection,* September 19, 1996, Lot 43.

19 這件漆櫸木家具看起來很老。年代可能早到十七世紀，桌面為角礫石應該來自山西。Sotheby's (New York), *Fine Chinese Ceramics and Works of Art,* Nov. 29-30, 1993, Lot 468.

20 相似的例子，參閱Sotheby's (New York), *Fine Chinese Ceramics, and Works of Art.* Dec. 1 & 2, 1992, Lot 656.

21 相似的例子，參閱Sotheby's (New York), *Fine Chinese Ceramics, Furniture and Works of Art.* Mar. 22, 1995, Lot 385.

As the wood is quite beautiful, hard and durable, there seems to be no reason why it would not have been readily accepted outside Fujian. Perhaps it was either unknown beyond Fujian or the wood was so popular locally that there was not enough for outside consumption.

From the frequency of *longyan* wood furniture appearing at auctions between 1990–95,[22] we assume that it was quite popular in Fujian and a large quantity must have been made. Looking at several examples of *longyan* wood furniture the following questions arise. Firstly, why are many of the styles are not classical, but new and unique to Fujian? An example is an ancestral tablet cabinet. (Fig. 9) Secondly, from the styles, patina and wear, why can hardly any be considered earlier than the Qianlong period? Thirdly, why is there the existence of extremely large timber of this wood? Some panels surrounding the sides of *luohan* or canopy beds can measure as much as 40–50 cm in width.[23]

Fig. 9   19th century *longyan* wood ancestral tablet cabinet from Fujian. 55cm (w) x 26 cm (d) x 71.5 cm (h)
圖9.   十九世紀福建龍眼木供祖先牌位神龕. 55 x 26 x 71.5公分.

The answer to these questions lies in the province's economic history. Fujian has limited arable land. Three quarters of the province is mountainous and only a small area along its coast is suitable for sedentary life. As a result, the Fujianese have been forced to live off the sea as merchants or fisherman. With no primary products of their own, the Fujian merchants since the Song dynasty have mostly acted as middlemen. They imported, exported and redistributed goods from other provinces and foreign countries. By the mid-Ming dynasty, however, the Fujianese were insistent on developing their own source of primary products and thus spent great efforts to make their land arable. The hilly slopes were terraced and irrigated for the cultivation of cotton, tea, lychee (*lizhi*) and *longyan*. Because these crops flourished in Fujian's climate, they soon became the main trade commodities of many local merchants.[24] In fact, dried Fujian *longyan* fruit, know as *fuzhou guiyuan*, is famous all over China and Southeast Asia even today.

By the early to mid-Qing period, the lychee and *longan* trees in Fujian would have ranged

前除了福建省外，其它地方並沒有出現過龍眼木家具。這木材既美又堅硬，不知道為何其它地區沒有採用。或許是由於不知道此種木質的存在，或者是龍眼木在福建很受歡迎，產量不夠供應外銷。

1990至1995年間，拍賣會上頻頻出現龍眼木家具，[22] 可以推測龍眼木在福建曾經很流行，並且製成了不少家具。當我們去看這些龍眼木家具時，會有以下的疑問：首先，為何它們大多數並非古典造型，而是新的、福建特有的造型？其中一個例子是一件祖先牌位神龕〔圖9〕。其次，從它們的樣式及皮殼判斷，為何幾乎全都屬於乾隆以後時期？第三，為何有這麼多大塊的木料？有些羅漢床或架子床的檔板，寬度達四十至五十公分寬。[23]

以上的問題，在福建的經濟史中可找到答案。福建耕地有限，四分之三的土地為山陵地，僅沿海一帶適合耕作。因此，很多人都是集中居住在沿海一帶，從事商業或捕魚活動。由於福建本身沒有主要產品，當地的商人自宋朝以來多扮演仲介的角色，他們自其它省份或國家進出口買賣。但是到了明代中期，福建人開始自己種植一些主要作物，努力開墾農作地，把山坡開發成梯田，加以灌溉，種植棉花、茶葉、荔枝、龍眼等作物。由於福建的氣候適宜，這些作物生長得很好，而且很快變成了福建商人經營的主要商品。[24] 實際上，福建的龍眼乾燥果實肉，一般稱為桂圓，到了今天在中國各地甚至東南亞一帶都很著名。

到了清初至清中葉期間，福建的荔枝樹及龍眼樹已有二百五十至

22. At least six to seven pieces appeared yearly from 1992 - 95 in the New York auctions. Many examples were also seen in Taiwan, Hong Kong and Singapore galleries.

23. For *luohan* and canopy beds with large *longyan* wood used for their side panels see Sotheby's (New York). *Fine Chinese Ceramics and Works of Art*. June 1–2, 1993, Lot 566 and Sotheby's (New York). *Fine Chinese Ceramics, Furniture and Works of Art*. May 31–June 1, 1994, Lot 54.

24. *Development and Decline of Fukien Province in the 17th and 18th Centuries*: 163–9.

22 從1992年至1995年間，每年在紐約的拍賣會上，至少出現六至七件；在台灣、香港、新加坡的古董店亦很常見.

23 以大塊龍眼木作檔板的羅漢床及架子床，參見Sotheby's (New York). *Fine Furniture and Works of Art*. June 1–2. 1993, Lot 566; 及Sotheby's (New York)/*Fine Chinese Ceramics, Furniture and Works of Art*. May 31–June 1. 1994, Lot 54.

24 見英文注釋24.

between 250–350 years old and were of enormous size. As fruit trees bear less fruit when they become older, they are eventually felled for their wood. *Longyan* wood was no exception, and must have been the favoured wood for furniture since it has beautiful tiger-striped pattern not found in lychee wood.

With mature trees only available in the early to mid-Qing period, we can now understand why earlier examples of *longyan* wood furniture do not exist. The appearance of more local styles seen in furniture of this wood is also the result of Fujian's economy. The wealthy Fujianese merchants of the Ming dynasty seemed to emulate the tastes of the well-to-do scholar officials of Suzhou. Thus early Fujianese furniture such as a large *huanghuali* flush-sided corner leg side table, formerly in the Museum of Classical Chinese Furniture,[25] tend to keep to simple and restrained classical forms. However, in the late seventeenth–early eighteenth centuries when the Fujian economy reached its height of prosperity, new forms of furniture were created, perhaps revealing Fujianese merchants' new confidence in their own tastes.

Local Fujian characteristics can be noticed in the Kai-Yin Lo collection's two examples of *longyan* wood furniture – the pointed *ruyi*-shaped opening in the corners where the apron meets the spandrels under the small cabinet and in the simulation of bamboo on the table edges. The use of *longyan* wood may also indicate the increased general economic wealth of a region demanding greater quantities of furniture, thus encouraging the use of local woods when imported woods became insufficient.

Zhajing is another local wood that may perhaps also demonstrate the increased wealth of a region – in this case, northern Jiangsu. A pair of southern official's hat chairs which will be discussed later (Plate 12) and a low seat with a reclining back (Plate 15) are two such examples. The frame of this seat is of *zhajing* wood and the central section forming its reclining back, is constructed of many bamboo strips. *Zhajing* wood for some inexplicable reason is found in great abundance only in and around the vicinity of Nantong in northern Jiangsu. Like *longyan* wood, it has been appreciated for its hardness and beautiful wood grain. Furniture of this wood can be found not only in Nantong, but also in Shanghai and Suzhou, indicating that the market for it was more extensive than just local. Impetus for its use may have arisen from the

三百五十年的樹齡，因此果樹長得相當巨大。由於果樹年紀愈老，果實愈少，因此被砍伐作木材。龍眼木具有漂亮的老虎斑紋，而荔枝木則缺乏此一特點，在此情況下，它便被製成受歡迎的家具。

由於龍眼木是在清初至清中期以後才出現，因此我們可以理解為何龍眼木家具並未在此時期之前出現。它們的造型，多屬於本地的樣式，這跟當地的經濟有關。在明代，福建的富賈商人仍多仿傚蘇州地區文人的品味，如中國古典家具博物館曾經收藏的一件早期福建家具，是一張大的黃花梨四面平桌，[25] 造型簡單古典，但是到了十七至十八世紀，當福建的經濟繁榮之時，新的樣式出現了，也反映了福建商人對自己的品味增加了信心。

羅女士收藏的龍眼木小櫃子和桌子，櫃下面牙條及牙頭相交處的尖頭如意形開光，以及桌抹邊仿竹的作法，可看到一些福建地方特色。使用龍眼木或許也說明了當時社會經濟富裕，需要大量的家具，而逐漸使用本地的材料，以補足進口材料的不足。

柞榵木是另一種與當地經濟成長有關的木質。在羅女士的收藏中有兩個例子，一對南官帽椅（圖版12），我們稍後再加以討論；以及一件矮躺椅（圖版15）。躺椅座框部份是柞榵木，而靠背中央則由許多竹條組合而成。我們尚無法得知為何柞榵木僅大量出現於蘇北的南通一帶。如龍眼木一樣，柞榵木木質堅硬，木紋優美，受到人們喜愛。柞榵木製成的家具，除了南通以外，在上海及蘇州一帶亦有出現，這說明此一木質並不限於供應當地。柞榵木的流行或許與南通成為主要的織品製造城市有

25. Christie's (New York). *Important Chinese Furniture*. Sept. 19, 1996, Lot 22.

25 見英文注釋25。

increased prosperity of Nantong as a textile manufacturing town. Since the Ming dynasty Nantong has been famous for its locally grown hand-spun and hand-woven cotton indigo dyed fabrics. In the Qing dynasty the cotton trade of Nantong further developed until the city become one of the more important industrial textile centres of China.[26]

VARIETIES OF STYLES

Huanghuali wood has wide appeal because of its hardness and durability. Had they not been constructed of *huanghuali*, popular styles and forms of the Ming dynasty, in particular flush-sided corner-leg tables and recessed-leg tables with double-mitred inserted-shoulder joints, could not have withstood the ravages of time because of their rather weak joinery system.

Softwood examples of the above two styles were hardly known until the 1990s when several examples began appearing at auctions. When the origins of these were traced, virtually all examples known to this author can be said to come from Shanxi and Shandong provinces. The age of these softwood flush-sided corner-leg tables and double-mitred leg tables from Shanxi ranged from the Ming to the late Qing dynasty. However, the few extremely rare softwood examples not from Shanxi, such as recessed-leg side table discovered in Nantong, and another from Shandong province appear to be quite old and may date to as early as the Ming dynasty. (Figs. 10 & 11) The lack of later period softwood examples from these provinces indicates a discontinuity of their production. Perhaps the weakness of their joints rendered them impractical and therefore they lost their popularity by the Qing dynasty.

Fig. 10 Leg of 17th century elm wood recessed-leg side table with double-mitred inserted shoulder joints from Nantong. 圖10. 十七世紀南通櫸木插肩榫條案之腿足. 攝於 1993年.

Fig. 11 Detail of 17th/18th century elm wood recessed-leg altar table with double-mitred inserted shoulder joints from Shandong. 圖11. 十七~十八世紀山東榆木插肩榫供案. 攝於1994年.

The recessed-leg side table with double-mitred inserted shoulder joints from the Kai-Yin Lo Collection (Plate 20a) is a standard example from Shanxi province. Its burgundy coloured lacquer and patina place it around the eighteenth century. Earlier examples from Shanxi usually have a thicker black or burgundy lacquer with a complex crackled surface, while later examples are less finely made and

關，自明代以來，南通即以生產手紡及手織的靛青棉布料馳名；至清代，它的棉紡貿易更加發達，成為中國織品工業的重要城鎮之一。[26]

造型的不同

黃花梨家具堅硬耐用，所以不少能留存至今天。在明代曾經流行的造型，特別是四面平及插肩榫兩種樣式，因為它們的結構較弱，如果不是像黃花梨木質較硬實，是無法經歷長時間的使用。

在1990年的拍賣會之前，我們從未見過上述兩種樣式的軟木家具。根據本文作者的考查，發現它們幾乎全部來自山西與山東省。這些來自山西的四面平桌或插肩榫桌，年代介乎明至晚清之間，但是那幾件並非來自山西的家具，例如一件江蘇南通的插肩榫桌，以及另一件年代久遠，來自山東省的應該同屬於明代（圖10及11）。由於這些地區並未出現較晚期此樣式的軟木家具，或許表示到了晚期它們經已不存在。此外，或許它的結構較弱又不耐用，故到了清代已不再流行。

羅女士收藏的一件插肩榫邊桌，是一件典型來自山西的家具。它酒紅的漆及皮殼，可定為十八世紀之製作（圖版20a）。早期的山西家具通常上較厚的黑漆，因此表面會產生錯落的裂紋。而晚期的則不講

26. "Nantong - An Ancient City of Textiles" China Tourism No. 70, Hong Kong: China Tourism Press: 74-9.

26 "南通—織品的古代城市"，《中國旅遊》第70期，香港：中國旅遊協會：74-9.

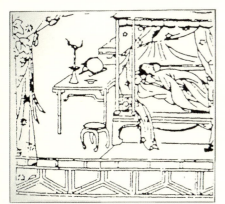

Fig. 12 17th century woodblock print shows use of table with 3 spandrels to each leg and humpback stretcher on all sides, from Shanxi. From John Kwang-Ming Ang, *The Beauty of Huanghuali*, Taipei: Artasia, 1995: 43.

圖12. 十七世紀山西木刻版畫中帶羅鍋棖之一腿三牙方桌. 參閱洪光明著"黃花梨之美", 亞細亞佳, 台北, 1995年: 43.

have a thinner coating of lacquer, usually in black. The different periods of these Shanxi tables show a continuation of a style that is no longer popular in other provinces. This continued patronage of long forgotten styles reflects the conservatism of its owners.[27]

Shanxi people's conservatism can be confirmed by the province's abundance of many other older styles of furniture. From the Kai-Yin Lo collection an eighteenth–nineteenth century cypress square table with spandrels from Shanxi (Plate 24a) is a style continued from the late Ming dynasty as seen in woodblock prints of that period (Fig. 12) and Ming period excavated miniature pottery furniture from Shanxi. (Fig. 13) Although many types of tables in this style still exist in abundance in Shanxi today (Fig. 14), the Kai-Yin Lo table with plain spandrels, particularly the one with three affixed *ruyi* motifs, are examples of fine proportion and well-executed details.

Fig. 13 Ming dynasty pottery tomb miniature table showing the early use of one leg with 3 spandrels. From *Journal of Classical Chinese Furniture Society*. Summer 1992: 17, fig. 10.

圖13. 明代迷形基葬陶器家具中可看見早期已有使用一腿三牙之造形, 參閱"中國古典家具學會季刊", 1992年夏季: 17, 圖10.

Another table demonstrating Shanxi people's conservatism is the eighteenth century *tieli* wood side table with a beaded curvilinear apron and short cabriole legs that extend to the floor as round-membered legs. (Plate 23) There are humpbacked stretchers on all sides that join at the points where the cabriole legs end and round legs begin. This type of table may have continued to develop from earlier Ming dynasty *huanghuali* tables that have the same short cabriole feet extending downward as round legs. The differences are the more ornate relief carving on the aprons and waist, the giant's arm braces with *lingzhi* decoration, and dragon-shaped spandrels that stretch diagonally from each leg to the carved-relief aprons.[28]

The Shanxi provenance of *tieli* wood table in the Kai-Yin Lo Collection can be confirmed by several softwood Shanxi examples in almost similar forms. Although the Kai-Yin Lo table cannot be dismantled, the legs of some softwood examples can be taken off or loosened and folded underneath the table. (Fig. 15 a, b)

究, 上漆較薄。從這些不同時期的山西桌子看, 一些已不在其它省份流行的樣式仍在山西使用, 這種對傳統樣式的保留, 或多或少反映了山西人保守的性格。[27]

山西人保留了許多古老樣式的家具, 印證了他們保守的個性。羅女士收藏的一件十八至十九世紀山西柏木一腿三牙方桌 (圖版24a), 其樣式自晚明延續而來, 這可從當時的版畫 (圖12) 以及自山西出土的一些明代陪葬陶製家具 (圖13) 看到。今天, 在山西雖然仍可看到此一樣式 (圖14), 但是羅女士這件收藏很特別, 因為它的牙頭為如意造形, 非一般所見的平素牙頭。

另一張十八世紀的鐵力木桌, 可看出山西人保守的個性。此桌帶有流線形並起陽線的牙條, 短的彎腿向下延伸接續圓形直腿 (圖版23), 四邊均有羅鍋棖, 位置在彎腿及圓腿相接的地方。這類桌子可能延續了明代早期黃花梨桌短彎腿連接圓直腿的樣式。兩者的差異, 在牙條及束腰上較複雜的浮雕, 霸王棖上有靈芝紋飾, 以及每支腿足上有龍頭形牙頭, 牙板對角連接浮雕牙條。[28]

Fig. 14 Detail of a section of a Shanxi home today showing use of a table with 3 spandrels to each leg and humpback stretchers. From Qi Ju, et. al. *A Collection of China's Folk Art*. Taipei: Hua-I Bookstore, 1994: 40, fig. 44.

圖14. 山西今日家居中亦可看見使用一腿三牙方桌. 參閱中國民間美術全集(4), 起居篇, 華一書局, 台北, 1994年。

27. For a detail discussion of double-mitred inserted-shoulder jointed recessed-leg tables see John Kwang-Ming Ang, "Enduring Traditions of Shanxi Furniture" *Orientations* May 1996: 57-9.

28. See Berliner, Nancy. *Beyond the Screen; Chinese Furniture of the Sixteenth and Seventeenth Centuries*. Boston: Museum of Fine Arts, Boston, 1996: 135, pl. 22.

27 有關插肩榫案的詳細討論, 參閱John Kwong-Ming Ang, "Enduring Traditions of Shanxi Furniture", *Orientations*, May 1996: 57-9.

28 見英文注釋28.

Fig. 16 1609 woodblock print from the *San Cai Tu Hui* illustrating a southern official's hat chair with protruding armrests. From *Journal of Classical Chinese Furniture Society.* Autumn 1994: 61, fig. 6c.
圖16 1609年之木刻版畫" 三才圖會" 中所繪帶出頭扶手之椅子.參閱" 中國古典家具學會季刊",秋季,1994年:61,圖6c.

The *zhajing* wood southern official's hat chairs with armrests that extend beyond the front posts (Plate 12) in the Kai-Yin Lo Collection come from Nantong in northern Jiangsu, the wood's only known source. Although it is difficult to pinpoint an exact period to this style of chairs, an approximate late eighteenth-early nineteenth century dating can be ascribed to it since virtually all other *zhajing* wood furniture known to this writer have only shown stylistic features of the mid to late Qing period. The patina and wear of this example also correspond to its mid-Qing dating. The only known record of this style of southern official's hat chair is found in the sixteenth century Ming dynasty encyclopaedia *San Cai Tu Hui.*[29] (Fig.16) So far no Ming dynasty examples are known to have surfaced, but as several pairs of this style of chairs in softwood dating to as early as the Qianlong period (1736-96) have recently appeared in Shanxi (Fig. 17), the style might have been revived on a national level.

Revivalism is a form of archaism when old styles, once popular, become neglected for a certain period, and are then revived. This should not be confused with conservatism where styles were never neglected but were continually being used. In China conservatism tends to exist in pockets of regional isolation. On the other hand, archaism seems to occur on a more national level.

Fig. 15 18th/19th century elm wood side table from Shanxi with short cabriole legs that extend downward as round-membered legs. The upper section can be separated from the legs. 104 cm (w) x 62 cm (d) x 107 cm (h)
圖15 十八~十九世紀山西榆木帶彎腿延伸圓腿之條案,下部之四個腿足可折合於桌面下。

Archaism was also a national movement in many of the arts of the Qianlong period. Song dynasty imperial *guan, ge,* and *longquan* wares, along with Yuan to Ming dynasty blue and white porcelain, were all revived by the ingenious Tang Yin, the official in charge of the imperial kilns of Jingdezhen during the Qianlong reign. In jade carving, Tang to Ming styles were imitated, while bronze vessels repeated many Shang to Han forms. Although archaism was never an official national movement, its prominence in the arts, especially the imperial arts, shows the emperor's obvious encouragement of it. Reasons for Qianlong's desire to revive old styles may be very complex, but some scholars believe it was to show his love and knowledge of China's past, a pattern of behaviour foreign rulers followed to gain respect of the Chinese people.

Fig. 17 Detail showing inscription under chair reading "made in the 53rd year of the Qianlong reign (1789) in the Southern Court"
圖17. 椅子下部年款之局部" 乾隆五十三年 (1789年) 南廷製"

我們可以確定羅女士這張鐵力木桌是來自山西,因為在當地已經出現了幾張樣式相同的軟木桌。雖然羅女士的桌子不能拆合,但是有些這個樣式的軟木桌子,桌面與四個腿足可以分離,或者腿足可折下收藏於桌子底下。(圖15a, b)

羅女士收藏的一對柞榴木南官帽椅非常有趣,它的扶手超出前端的支柱 (圖版12)。這對椅子應是來自蘇北南通,因為柞榴木出自此一地區。雖然這類椅子的年代尚未能確定,但是可大致定為十八至十九世紀之間。據本文作者所見過的柞榴木家具,幾乎全部屬於清中期至晚期的式樣,而這對椅子的皮殼及使用狀況,應該也屬於清中期的年代。有關這類南官帽椅的史料,唯一見於十六世紀明代的《三才圖會》(圖16)。[29] 雖然我們未見過明代的例子,但是最近看到幾對在山西出現,跟乾隆年代 (1736-1796) 相同樣式的軟木椅子 (圖17),因此這個款式可能全國普遍使用,而非某地方特有。

復古主義是指一種曾經流行的式樣,在忽略了一段時間後,再度復興;保守主則只是把一些樣式一直保留使用。在中國一些較偏遠的地區,保守主義依然存在,而復古的情況,則各地可見。

乾隆時期,復古之風更加盛行全國。宋代的官、哥、龍泉窯,元、明代的影青陶瓷器,皆由唐英監督下,在景德鎮的官窯生產製作。玉雕方面,許多唐代至明代的名件亦被模

29. See Wang, Qi, ed. *San Cai Tu Hu* [1585]. Shanghai: Shanghai Guji Publishing House, 1988, ch. 20: 1329.

29 參閱王圻,《三才圖會》〔1585〕,上海:上海古籍出版社,1988:第20章:1329.

While the Manchu Qianlong emperor tried to obtain Chinese approval of his reign by reviving certain aspects of the country's past, at the same time he also simultaneously tried to demonstrate his power by changing many aspects of traditional Chinese culture by experimenting with new designs in all the major arts. Together with the introduction of new western concepts entering China at that time, a major overhaul of many traditional styles in Chinese art occurred.

Paintings from the Qianlong era show an even further advance in techniques of western perspective and chiaroscuro. Porcelain imitating other materials such as cinnabar lacquer, pudding stone, bronze and wood, a technique that started in the Yongzheng period, was brought to its height of perfection in the Qianlong era. In the realm of furniture the few small changes that began in the Kangxi and Yongzheng periods increased manifold by the Qianlong times, leading to a major transformation of classical styles. The forms of so-called "Ming-style" furniture – represented by the simple four-protruding end official's hat chairs, recessed-leg tables, waisted-corner leg tables with horsehoof feet, to name a few – had actually been in continuous existence since the northern Song dynasty as demonstrated in frescoes and paintings of that period.[30] By the Qianlong period, these classic forms, popular from the tenth to eighteenth centuries, were suddenly exchanged for the more elaborate "Qing-style" furniture.

The period when "Ming-style" changed to "Qing-style" can be estimated to fall between the late seventeenth–eighteenth century. During this transitional or experimental period it can be surmised that many works produced were either successful and thus continued to be produced or were unsuccessful, having been tried and discarded.

A few examples of furniture with unprecedented forms from the Kai-Yin Lo collection fit well into this experimental period from 1680–1780. Many examples from this period look classic except for a few small new details which cannot be classified as either "Ming" or "Qing" style. The pair of black lacquered elm wood official's hat chairs with four protruding ends with latticed railings

仿雕刻；而從商代至漢代的一些主要銅器造型，亦被翻製模仿。雖然復古運動並非明文規定之政令，但是乾隆皇帝對此的熱衷，可在藝術方面，特別是宮廷藝術方面看到。至於他提倡復古的原因，可能很複雜，很多學者認為他一方面是為了顯示個人對中國文化的學識，另一方面則以此作為一種手段，博取中原漢族對外族統治者的支持。

事實上，南通與山西相距甚遠，但是在同一時期內，卻同時製作出樣式古遠而非共時的椅子，說明這些家具的工匠們，亦可能受到皇帝所倡行的復古藝術風潮的影響。因此，在我們對復古運動的影響還未完全了解時，羅女士的椅子可以算是印證這歷史運動的一種具體文物。

當乾隆皇帝一方面在提倡復古運動，以換取更多人民支持的同時，另一方面為了表示他個人的權力，亦改變了一些傳統中國文化。這可以從他在不同藝術加入了新的設計看出。此外，再加上他引進了許多西方觀念到中國，令中國藝術傳統發生了明顯的變化。乾隆時期的繪畫，引入了西方透視的技術；陶瓷上力圖模仿不同木質，如朱漆、角礫石、銅器及木器等。此一做法雖然在雍正時期已經開始，但是在乾隆時期達到高峰。家具方面，在康熙、雍正時期，僅有小幅的改變，但是在乾隆時期，整個中國家具的古典式樣卻發生了重大的改變。古典式樣即我們所一般習稱「明式」，例如有簡單的四出頭、南官帽、縮腿的案以及束腰馬蹄足的桌....等等的樣式，它們自北宋已經存在，可從當時的一些壁畫或繪畫上得到證明。[30] 到了乾隆時期，這些在中國從十世紀至十八世紀一直流行的古典造形，卻突然變成了較為繁複的「清式」家具。

---

30. The Song dynasty frescoes show recessed-leg tables and lamp hanger chairs not unlike those of the Ming dynasty. See wall paintings from tombs at Pai-sha Tomb no. 1 dated 1099 in Su Bai. *Pai-sha Sung Mu*, Beijing: Wen Wu Press, 1957.

30. 在宋代的壁畫中所看到的案及燈掛椅，與明代的不同。有關白沙宋墓1號墓，1099年的壁畫，參閱宿白：《白沙宋墓》，北京文物出版社，1957年。

under each armrest (Plate 11) and the pair of large black lacquered elm wood southern official's hat chairs with backsplats that slant back to an exaggerated angle (Plate 12), both from Shanxi, look classic in form from a direct frontal view. However, when we look at their side profiles, we see the unusual latticed railings under each armrest of the first pair and the exaggerated slanted backsplat in the second pair. These unusual features are not peculiar only to these particular types of chairs. Lattice rails can also be found on other types of chairs such as a pair of black lacquered elm wood southern official's hat chairs from Shanxi (Fig. 18) and the exaggerated slanted backsplat can be found on a low black lacquered elm wood southern official's hat chair with a backsplat that extends over the rail of the chair (Fig. 19 a, b). These examples show not only the individual evolution of each style of furniture, but also an overall transformation of traditional styles. New ideas would be experimented on several types of furniture instead of only one particular type.

Fig. 18   Pair of black lacquered elm wood official's hat chairs from Shanxi with four protruding ends and latticed railing under armrests. 57.5 cm (w) x 47.5 cm (d) x 117 cm (h) Seat Height 52 cm.
圖18.　山西黑漆榆木扶手帶欄杆之南官帽椅乙對.

The Shanxi elm wood stool with double-curved legs and carved decoration of tendrils in relief in the Kai-Yin Lo Collection (Plate 3) is an unprecedented form which is difficult to place in the development of Chinese furniture styles. However, if we have identified certain stylistic trends that furniture may have followed, such as conservative, archaistic or experimental, it would fit best into the experimental phase. Possibly this is an example whose style did not receive widespread acceptance and thus did not continue to be produced.

Fig. 19   Two views of 18th century black lacquered elm wood low-seat reclining southern official's hat chair with protruding armrests and extended backsplat. 59 cm (w) x 51 cm (d) x 95 cm (h) Seat Height 50 cm.
圖19   十八世紀黑漆榆木帶出頭扶手與後彎靠背之矮南官帽椅.59 x 51 x 95 公分，座高40公分.

The nineteenth century twin southern elm wood cabinets from Suzhou (Plate 30) which may be related to a twin low northern elm wood cabinets from Shanxi (Fig. 20) of the same period can also be said to be experimental forms since earlier examples of this twin form are not known. They may also reveal that the experimental period continued into the nineteenth century. If the relationship between these two twin cabinets can be clearly traced it would add more evidence that there may have been a conscious national movement in experimenting with new styles in Chinese furniture.

十七世紀晚期至十八世紀，家具由「明式」轉變成「清式」。在這段期間，很多藝術造型得以繼續使用，有些則被放棄或遺忘。

羅女士收藏中幾件造型較特別，以前從未見過的家具，可以歸納為1680至1780年間此一實驗期。它們基本上是古典樣式，但是多了許多細節，看上去非明非清。其中一對黑漆榆木官帽椅，扶手下方出現幾何紋欄杆（圖版11），以及一對大黑漆榆木南官帽椅，背板向後彎曲，角度相當誇張（圖版12），均來自山西。從正面看，它們樣式古典，但從側面看時，則發現第一對椅子多了少見的小欄杆，而第二對椅子靠背板過度彎曲。這些新增的特點，不只出現在同一類型家具上，比如說扶手下的小欄杆，亦在另一對山西黑官帽椅上出現（圖18）；在另一張黑漆矮背榆木南官帽椅上，亦可看到背板超出搭腦（圖19a，b）。這些例子說明傳統風格在整體上作出了變化，而非個別家具形式上的轉變。要實驗新的意念，並不單限於某一類家具，而是以多種家具作出嘗試。

Fig. 20   19th century low twin catalpa cabinets from Shanxi. 140 cm (w) x 48 cm (d) x 83 cm (h)
圖20.　十九世紀山西楸木雙聯矮櫃. 140 x 48 x 83公分

羅女士收藏的一張雙C形彎腿浮雕卷草紋山西榆木凳子，樣式從未出現過，我們很難將它歸類入中國家具的類型當中（圖版3）。但是如果依照家具造型分保守、復古或實驗期風格，那麼這張凳子則應該歸入實驗期。這些家具的樣式，或許得不到普遍接受而逐漸消失。

這對十九世紀蘇州櫸木雙聯櫃（圖版30），與山西的一對榆木雙聯櫃（圖20）以前並未出現過，所以可同時歸入實驗時期，而這亦表示實驗期一直

With more examples of both hard and softwood furniture available, there is now more material to reconstruct the context in which they evolved. For example, when we see softwood folding stools, we are now able to associate them with Shanxi opera or *miaohui*. When we see *longyan* wood furniture, we will be able to relate it to the Fujian merchants in trading their own primary products cultivated with great effort in a province of limited arable land.

Conservatism, archaism and experimentalism were important artistic trends in China that kept the culture viable. At present, from the pieces of softwood furniture made available for study through collections such as Kai-Yin Lo's, we can only surmise that the development of Chinese furniture types and designs were influenced by these artistic movements. If such influence can be proven through further research, then furniture can be legitimately viewed as one of China's artistic expressions instead of being treated as mere utilitarian objects. Thus no matter whether imperial or vernacular, hard or softwood, all examples will be more carefully preserved and a clearer picture of the historical development of Chinese furniture can be reconstructed.

There are already indications of an increasing awareness of the importance of vernacular furniture. Recent exhibitions of small collections with alternative wood furniture were shown at the San Francisco Craft & Folk Art Museum in 1992 [31] and at the Peabody Museum in Essex Massachusetts in 1995. [32] The Kai-Yin Lo Collection of both hard and softwood furniture, made available for research through this catalogue, adds to this body of knowledge and represents a new trend in Chinese furniture collecting.

延續至十九世紀。如果我們多了解這對櫃子的關係，或許可以證明在全國各地，均不斷對家具的造型進行實驗。硬木和軟木家具出現的數量增多，可以幫助我們了解它們演變的背景。例如山西出現很多的軟木交凳，我們可以將它與山西的戲劇與廟會活動聯繫起來；而龍眼木家具則有助了解福建商人如何在本省耕地貧乏的情況下，努力開墾，成功種植重要的農作物。

保守、復古以及實驗主義在中國是很重要的藝術風潮，它們推進了中國文化的發展。羅女士收藏的硬木及軟木家具，為我們提供了很好的研究題材。我們逐漸能證明中國家具的種類及造型的變化，是受到了藝術運動的影響。如果我們能再繼續此研究，相信可以證明中國家具不僅屬於實用性工藝，而應該視為中國藝術的一支。本文中每件家具，都值得我們細心欣賞。因此，不僅是宮廷家具或民間家具；硬木家具或軟木家具，都應盡力保存和研究，相信這樣才可將中國家具的歷史更清晰地建構起來，幫助我們探視中國文化的不同層面。

人們對民間家具和它的重要性愈來愈感興趣。例如在1992年和1995年，美國舊金山工藝與民藝博物館 [31] 和波士頓皮奧博迪博物館 [32] 就分別展出了多類木質家具。羅女士這次出版的家具圖錄，有助日後的研究，標誌了中國家具收藏的新趨勢。

31 Mason, Lark. et. al. *Classical Chinese Wood Furniture*. San Francisco: San Francisco Craft & Folk Art Museum, 1992.
32 Berliner, Nancy and Handler, Sarah. *Friends of the House; Furniture from China's Towns and Villages*. Salem, Mass: Peabody Essex Museum, 1996.

31 見英文注釋31。
32 見英文注釋32。

Vernacular Dwellings and Furniture in Northern China

中國北方民居與家具

Chen Zengbi
陳增弼

The scorching summers and harsh winters of China's vast northern regions – here taken to include all the area above latitude 35° N, including the Yellow River valley north of the Qinling Mountains, the Tarim Basin of China's north-west and the valleys of the Liao, Songhua and Heilong rivers in China's north-east – create dramatic climactic conditions. The average winter temperature in most of northern China is below 0°C, and in a few areas falls below minus 20°–30° C. As a result, protection against the cold and the conservation of warmth are problems that housing in the north must address and solve. As time passed, northern houses came to develop thick outer walls, higher and lower floor levels, and a plain exterior, as well as special features such as heated floors, internal walls and *kang*. These features of northern housing naturally also influenced interior architecture and furniture.

Northern vernacular furniture displays boldness, lack of restraint and a rugged strength, and makes liberal use of available materials. The interior architecture and furniture of northern homes are quite different in style and arrangement from those in the Yangtze and Pearl river valleys, and their distinctive features make them an important type of traditional Chinese furniture. Vernacular furniture represents the enrichment and enhancement of the cultural significance of homes. The tendency to study vernacular furniture removed from its domestic context is misguided; moreover, to focus on the

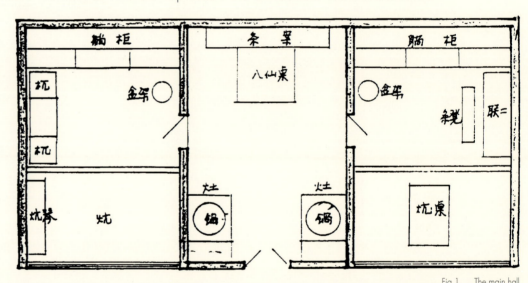

Fig.1 The main hall (*tingtang*) is flanked by two shaded side rooms which serve as bedrooms.
圖1 北方民居一明兩暗，炕、灶及家具佈置示意圖。

architecture of vernacular dwellings while overlooking its furniture is short-sighted. This essay stresses the principle of investigating and researching vernacular furniture within the context of its domestic environment and architectural framework.

本文「中國北方」一辭，是指北緯卅五度以北的西北、華北和東北的「三北」地區，也就是秦嶺以北黃河流域、塔里木河流域以及遼河、松花江、黑龍江流域。在這遼闊的北國，最大的自然條件就是冬有嚴寒、夏無酷暑。冬季平均氣溫大都在攝氏零度以下。少部份地區在二十度至卅度以下，因此防寒保暖就成為北方民居首要考慮和解決的問題。在長期歷史流變中，北方民居形成了外牆厚、層高低、外輪廓簡潔以及火坑、火地、火牆的使用特點。北方民居這些特點也必然對民居的室內、家具產生影響。北方民間家具粗獷有力、用料大、裝飾紋樣豪放，與長江流域、珠江流域地區的室內和家具在風格上、布格上都有很大的不同，在中國傳統家具中佔有重要的地位。民間家具是民居建築功能上的補充，也是民居文化內涵的豐富與加強。因此，在離開民居建築的空間環境下研究民間家具，會是一種偏頗。而研究民居建築，忽視民間家具的客觀存在，也是不可取的。民間家具與民居存著「裡」與「表」的關係。我們主張把民間家具放置在具體的民居建築環境中來探討與研究。

THE ARRANGEMENT OF FURNITURE IN NORTHERN HOMES

In order to maximise direct sunlight and reflected light, the main room generally faces south. Normally the main hall (*tingtang*) has most sunlight and is flanked by two shaded side rooms which generally serve as bedrooms. (Fig. 1) These rooms – the main hall and bedrooms – also happen to be those in which most items of furniture are placed. The variety of furniture and its arrangement in the main hall and bedrooms of northern Chinese homes have their own distinctive features and differ greatly from those in southern areas. (Fig. 2)

剖视图

Fig.2   Arrangement of furniture in a northern Chinese home.
圖2.東北民居家具布置

THE IMPORTANCE OF THE EIGHT IMMORTALS' TABLE AT THE CENTRE OF THE MAIN HALL

In wealthier households, the bright central room usually serves as a reception hall for guests and as a centre for family activities, being used, as occasion demands, for weddings or funerals, as a place for welcoming back the spirits of the departed and venerating ancestors, and for celebrating seasonal festivals and ceremonies. Among the various rooms of the Chinese home, the main hall is generally reserved for activities involving the whole family, and most seats set out in it are high, enabling people to sit erect with their feet up off the ground. In a frequently seen arrangement of furniture in the northern house, the Eight Immortals' table (*baxianzhuo*) is placed at the centre of the room; along the northern wall of the room a flat topped table (*pingtou'an*), a table with upturned ends (*qiaotou'an*) or a low display table (*jiaji'an*) is placed, and on them are positioned a screen set with stone (*yanping*), a large vase (*danping*) or an ornamental mantle clock. The Eight Immortals' table is positioned in front of the long table, and a chair is placed on either side of it – in a more formal setting, these would be chairs with armrests. A high stand for a brazier is placed in front of the table. A frame for a wash basin,

北方民居室內的家具布置

北方民居為了爭取更多的陽光、日照，院落的主房一般是坐北朝南，一明兩暗式布局。明間多為廳堂，兩側次間則用作臥室。（圖1）而擺放家具最多的房間，也正是民居中的廳堂和臥室。北方民居的臥室與廳堂中家具的布置和品種都有自己的特點，與南方地區有很大的不同。（圖2）

以八仙桌為中心的廳堂家具布置

在富裕的家庭，明間作為會客和起居之用，有時還用於婚喪嫁娶、祭祖迎神、四時節氣舉行儀禮的地方。在民居各類房間中，它具有更多的家庭活動性質。從家具類型來看，廳堂布置的家具多屬可供垂足坐的高型家具。常見的格局是以八仙桌為中心，布陳家具：靠北牆放平頭案、翹頭案或架幾案，上擺硯屏、膽瓶、自鳴鐘。案前放在一張八仙桌，桌兩側放兩把椅子，講究一些的會放扶手椅。桌前還擺放有高型的火

half-moon tables, stools or round stools (*zuodun*) are placed at either side of the bright central room. The room and its furniture could thus serve the needs of the family, whether partaking of meals or entertaining guests.

Fig.3   Tang dynasty murals, Cave no.85, Dunhuang depicting use of square tables.
圖3   敦煌第82窟（唐）屠狗圖上之方桌

In average homes, guests are fewer, and the sunny room is reserved as a kitchen and storeroom. On each side of this room is a "stove platform", connected by a flue to the *kang* in the adjoining room. In the kitchen meals are cooked, water boiled and even the food for the pigs prepared. Against the northern wall, an Eight Immortals' table, a long table (*tiaozhuo*) or a sloping storage cupboard (*tanggui*) is placed, as well as a cupboard for kitchenware and even small agricultural implements. In the sunny room, there can be more or less furniture according to economic circumstances, but an Eight Immortals' table is considered a must. Since the Eight Immortals' table is essential in the northern home, and is the centrally positioned piece of furniture in the main hall, it warrants closer scrutiny.

The Eight Immortals' table is a fairly large square table, its upper sides ranging from 96–116 cm in length and its height ranging from 84–86 cm. These dimensions ensure that two persons can be seated at each side, for a total of eight persons dining or banqueting at it, hence its name. The Eight Immortals' table of China serves a number of functions in the main

盆架，明間兩側多為擺放面盆架、半桌、凳、坐墩等，為全家用膳、會客時使用。

一般民居客人較少，明間只作廚房和倉儲之用，兩側各有一灶台，與次間的火炕相連，做飯、燒水，甚至煮豬食都是在這裡進行。靠北牆擺放八仙桌、條桌或是儲糧的躺櫃、豌櫃，甚至小型農具等。明間的其他家具，可以根據狀況有所增減，但一張八仙桌卻是多數民居廳堂必備之物。八仙桌既然是北方民居必備家具，而且是北方廳堂家具布置的中心，因此有必要對它進行深層的考察。

八仙桌是一種較大的方桌，桌面約為96厘米至116厘米見方，高度約84厘米至86厘米，每邊可停坐二人。一桌可供八人就餐、宴飲，故名曰八仙桌。中國的八仙桌在廳堂中具有多種功能：就餐宴飲、議事會客、

hall; at such a table meals are eaten, banquets spread, discussions held, guests entertained, marriages celebrated, funerals observed, ancestors worshipped and spirits of the departed received. In the majority of homes, everyday events, religious activities and ritual observances all make use of the Eight Immortals' table. In the context of world furniture history, the Eight Immortals' table of China is unique, and it even exerted influence on Southeast Asian countries.

The square table (*fangzhuo*), the prototype of the Eight Immortals' table, most probably made its appearance in the mid or late Tang period. The earliest depiction of a square table appears in Tang dynasty murals decorating Cave no. 85 at Dunhuang in Gansu. (Fig.3) We see such tables later depicted in the Five Dynasties period paintings *Night Revels of Han Xizai*

(*Han Xizai yeyan tu*) and *Collating Books* (*Kanshu tu*). Although the square table was fashionable only among the upper echelon of society in the Tang and Five Dynasties periods, by the time of the Song, Liao and Jin dynasties, it was prevalent among all classes of society. Evidence of this general use can be seen in the depiction of a rural inn and an urban wine shop in the Song dynasty paintings *Ascending the River on Qingming Festival* (*Qingming shanghe tu*) (Fig.4) and *The Jigger* (*Panche tu*). By the Ming and Qing dynasties, the square table attained its full maturity. This is apparent in its technical finesse, perfection of form and full variety of styles. It was also in Ming times that the square table most probably came to be termed the Eight Immortals' table. In the Ming scholar Wen Zhenheng's *Zhangwu zhi* [Treatise on Superfluous Things] we read: "The square table ... has in recent times come to be made in the Eight Immortal and other styles reserved for banqueting".[1] In Chapter 55 of the Ming dynasty novel *Jin Ping Mei* [Golden Lotus] we read how the protagonist Ximen Qing "ordered Dai'an to lay out vegetable dishes, crusty rice, steamed dimsum and light wine at an Eight Immortals' table where everyone could eat and drink".[2] In the Ming and Qing times, Eight Immortals' tables were of various types – they could have flat sides,

Fig.4　Song dynasty painting showing widespread use of square tables
圖4　　宋・張擇端《清明上河圖》飯館・酒肆中之方桌

婚喪嫁娶、祭祖迎神。大凡民家日常生活、宗教活動、儀禮活動都使用八仙桌。八仙桌在廣闊的北方地區，使用十分廣泛。從世界家具史看，八仙桌是中國所獨有，並對周邊國家生產影響。

從中國家具史看，八仙桌的原型—方桌，大約出現於中世紀的中、晚唐時期。中國方桌形象最早見於甘肅敦煌第八十五窟（圖3），唐代屠師圖的壁畫上，共繪有兩張方桌。其後在五代的《韓熙載夜宴圖》、《勘書圖》上都有反映。如果説方桌在唐、五代只在上層社會流傳使用，那麼到了宋、遼金時代，方桌已經普及到社會各個階層了，這可從宋代的《清明上河圖》（圖4）、《盤車圖》上的鄉間驛站、市井酒肆的普遍使用得到證實。明、清時期，從方桌的結構科學、完美造型、多樣品種可看到它的發展已十分成熟。而把方桌稱為「八仙桌」大約也是在明代。明文震亨《長物志》：「方桌……近制八仙等式，僅可供宴。」[1] 明《金瓶梅》第五十五回：「西門慶就叫玳安里邊端出菜蔬、嘎飯、點心、小酒，擺著八仙桌兒，就與諸人燕飲。」[2] 明、清八仙桌有四而

1　Wen Zhenheng. *Zhangwu zhi*. Nanjing: Jiangsu Publishing House, 1984: *juan* 6: 233
2　Xiaoxiao-sheng. *Jin Ping Mei cihua* Beijing: People's Literature Publishing House, 1985: *hui* 55: 730

1　明・文震亨：《長物志》，方桌條・江蘇科學技術出版社，1984年：卷六：233。
2　明・蘭陵笑笑生：《金瓶梅詞話》，人民文學出版社，1985：第55回：730。

straight legs, (Fig 5a) horse-hoof feet (Fig. 5b), one leg with three spandrels, inturned feet, (Fig. 5c; see also Plate 24 a & b) and three cabriole legs. The Eight Immortals' table was the most distinctive category of classical Chinese furniture, as well as the item with the broadest range of domestic uses.

THE ARRANGEMENT OF FURNITURE IN THE BEDROOM WITH THE HEATED *KANG* AT ITS CENTRE

Because of the cold weather in the north, the bedrooms had to be heated.   A universal mode of heating employed is the *kang*, a distinctive and essential form of construction. In colder areas, the floors and walls are also internally heated. In addition, a low brazier is used to augment the sources of warmth and maintain the heat. The *kang* is a fixed bed, usually made of tamped earth, brick or stone, with a cavity underneath. The area above is plastered, and this cavity is connected with the kitchen stove by a flue. The heated air from cooking and boiling water passes through this cavity before finally escaping out through the chimney, and so this superfluous hot air becomes a source of warmth for heating the house. (Fig. 6) The *kang* is usually installed beside the windows on the south side of the room, which is a fairly bright part of the room that catches the direct rays of the sun in winter. Mats (*xi*) are laid out on the *kang* and sometimes a layer of woollen rugs is placed on top. The adjoining wall can be papered, painted or decorated with colourful *kang* paintings. Most activities on the *kang* basically entail sitting cross-legged, kneeling or semi-reclining; at the same time, low furniture placed on it. Such items include the *kang* table, *kang* bench (*kangji*), *kang* "lute" (*kangqin*), bedding holder (*beige*) and low brazier holder (*ai huopenjia*). The northern lifestyle of *kang* activities can be seen as a survival of the ancient lifestyle of living on mats.

a.

b.

c.

Fig.5   Ming dynasty Eight Immortals' tables
a. flat sides, straight legs type
b. horse-hoof type
c. one leg, three spandrels type
圖5   明代八仙桌類型
a. 無束腰式
b. 有束腰內翻馬蹄式
c. 一腿三牙式

平齊式、直腿式（圖5a）、內翻馬蹄式（圖5b）、一腿三牙式（圖5c，另見圖版24a及b）、裏腳式、和三彎腿式。八仙桌是中國古典家具中極具特色的一種品類，也是廣大民居中使用廣泛的一種家具。

以火炕為中心的臥室家具布置

北方天寒，臥室內必須取暖。取暖普遍使用火炕，再冷的地方還有火地、火牆。此外，尚有矮形火盆，用以輔助取暖和保存火種。

炕即是固定的床，一般用土坯或磚、石砌成，其下盤成孔洞，上抹灰泥，與灶相連。作飯、燒水的熱氣盤桓櫃中，最後從煙囪排出，利用這些餘熱取暖。（圖6）一般沿南向靠窗搭設。此處室內光線比較明亮，冬季也是爭取陽光直接照射的地方。炕上鋪席，席上有的還鋪一層毛氈。沿牆或糊紙、或油漆、彩繪炕牆畫。人在炕上活動，基本上是盤腿坐或跪坐式，或自由坐式，同時炕上擺放的家具，從家具類型來看，都是屬於低型家具，如矮的炕桌、炕幾、炕琴、被格、矮火盆架等，因此北方民間火炕上的生活方式，也可以看作是古代席地而坐的生活方式的一種遺存。

The *kang* is actually a distinctive construction for sitting, lounging and sleeping, with very early origins in China, although there are few extant materials to document this. In a section of *Old History of the Tang* (*Jiu Tang shu*) titled "The Account of Koryo" (*Gaoli zhuan*), we read: "In the winter months, a long *kang* is constructed under which a fire is made to provide warmth".[3] The Song dynasty writer Zhu Bing in a piece titled "Sleeping on a *Kang*" (*Kangqin*)

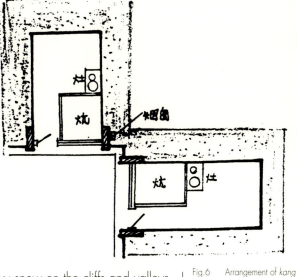

Fig.6 Arrangement of *kang* and stove in a cave dwelling in Shanxi
圖6 陝西單體窰洞民居炕、分布示意圖

wrote: "Customs are different in the north and south, and the customary practices are also not the same. ... I linger as the year ends; and there is a heavy snow on the cliffs and valleys. I try keeping out winter with furs, but only feel comfortable curled up on the *kang*".[4] The Ming dynasty scholar Gu Yanwu in his famous work *Rizhi lu* wrote: "The northerners fashion a bed from earth and hollow out the section below it in which they light a fire and this is called a *kang*".[5] The Qing dynasty scholar Gao Youji wrote in *Jiqiu zachao* [Miscellaneous Writings on the Beijing District]: "In the Yan [i.e. Beijing] area the weather is bitterly cold and the people there do not use beds for sleeping, but a *kang*".[6] An anonymous Qing dynasty work *Yantai kouhao yibaizhong* [One Hundred Jottings of Beijing] contains the following: "When Ji Kang stoked the furnace, he was a master; and everyone knows how hot a *kang* is when first lit. But when sleeping, one must guard against burning one's back. Otherwise you'll start cooking away".[7] Today the *kang* can be seen in rural villages throughout Shanxi, Hebei, Shandong, the north-west and the north-east of China. (Fig 7) Within the context of Chinese furniture, the *kang* is a unique type of fixed bed.

Fig.7 Placement of *kang* in a vernacular dwelling, central Shanxi
圖7 山西晉中民居火炕分布示意

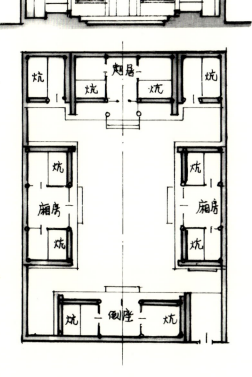

炕又是很具中國文化特色的一種臥具。不了解炕在北方民居中的地位和重要性，就無法詮釋北方民居臥室內空間環境的特殊性和文化內涵。

炕在我國起源很早，但目前我們看到的史料不多。《舊唐書·高麗傳》：「冬月皆作長炕，下燃火以取暖」。[3] 宋朱幷育《炕寢》云：「風土南北殊，習尚非一躅。……淹留歲再殘，朔雪滿崖谷。御冬貂裘弊，一炕且全伏。」[4] 明顧炎武《日知錄》云：「北人以土為床，而空其下，以發火，謂之炕。」[5] 此外，清高佑記《薊邱雜鈔》云：「燕地苦寒，寢者不以床，以炕。」[6] 另同時期佚名之《燕臺口號一百種》謂：「嵇康鍛灶事堪師，土炕燒來暖可知。睡覺也須防炙背，積薪報火始燃時。」[7]

炕在山西、河北、山東、西北、東北諸省的農村十分普遍，隨處可見，是中國家具中一種獨具特色的固定式床。（圖7）

3 *Jiu Tang shu* (Zhonghua Shuju edition) 1985, *juan* 199: 5319
4 *Gujin tushu jicheng: Kaogong dian*, (Qing edition) *juan* 215 (*Chuangta section*) *ji* 797:46
5 Gu Yanwu. *Rizhi lu* (from *Gujin tushu jicheng: Kaogong dian* (Qing edition) *juan* 215 (*Chuangta* section)
6 Gao Youji. *Jiqiu zachao*, ibid.
7 Anonymous. *Yantai kouhao yibai zhong*. Beijing: Guji chubanshe, 1982: 31

3 後晉·劉昫：《舊唐書》，高麗傳，中華書局，1985年：199卷：5319。
4 清《古今圖書集成·考工典》，第215卷，（床榻部），第797冊：46。
5 明·顧炎武：《日知錄》，轉引自清《古今圖書集成·考工典》第215卷，床榻部。
6 清·高佑祀：《薊邱雜鈔》，同上。
7 清·佚名：《燕臺口號一百種》，北京古籍出版社，1982：31。

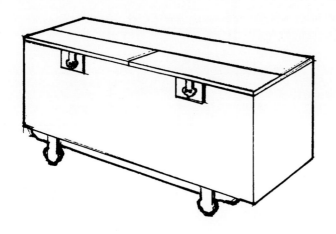

Fig.8   Commonly used *tanggui* in rural villages in northern China
圖8   北方農村使用普通的躺柜

Apart from the large amount of space occupied by the *kang* in the bedroom, there are two main types of furniture placed on the ground below the *kang*. In wealthier households, one can find upright cupboards with chests on top (*dingxiangligui*), chests for clothing (*yixiang*), dressers (*ligui*), long tables (*tiaozhuo*), tables with drawers (*choutizhuo*), stools (*deng*) and footstools (*wudeng*). Most average home feature a sideboard (*tanggui*) along the northern wall, and in front of that, plank stools (*bandeng*) and stools (*dengzi*).

Here we need to discuss a unique northern item of furniture – the *tanggui*. The *tanggui* was usually constructed *in situ* by local carpenters using local timber. The unique feature of this imposingly large chest-style cupboard is its extensive capacity. There are double and triple *tanggui*. They range from 150–300cm in length, and are around 120 cm in width and 100 cm in height. They are used for storing clothing, bedding and grain, and some also double as tables. One can place household articles, such as mirrors, pitchers of drinking water and study materials on them. The basic sideboard consists of a division into two compartments. They form a solid cupboard when placed against a wall and are not meant to be moved. Objects can be placed on the top surface whose front can be detached, raised or removed, with a lock fitted to the front so that it can be fastened.

Another type of *tanggui* common in central Shanxi (Jin), northern Shanxi (Yan) and other areas features a fixed upper surface, with each side opening out like a door to allow the storage or removal of clothes. (Fig.8) In southern Shanxi, Shandong or Hebei, we encounter another type of useful furniture called *xianggui* – the upper section is a chest, but the lower section is a low cupboard allowing the two sections to be separated.

臥室內除大面積的火坑外，地下擺放的家具大致也可分為兩種：富裕之家，會在地上擺放頂箱立櫃、衣櫃、立櫃、條桌、抽屜桌、凳、机凳等；一般農家則大多沿北牆一字排開擺放躺櫃，櫃前擺放板凳、凳子等。

在此要談一談北方特有的家具─躺櫃。一般躺櫃是農村木匠就地取材打做成的，它的特點是容量大，基本上是放大加長的大箱子。躺櫃有二聯和三聯之分，長約150厘米至300厘米，寬約120厘米左右，高則約100厘米，用來儲存衣物、被褥、糧食等，又可當桌案使用。櫃上可擺放生活用具，如鏡、飲水具、學習用具等。它的構造基本上是把櫃面分成兩部份，靠牆處為固定式櫃面，不掀起不移動，上面擺放器物；靠前面為活動的櫃面，可以掀起、拿下，並在前面中間邊緣處安有扣吊，可以上鎖。

在晉中、雁北等地有另一種躺櫃，上部櫃面全為固定式，而在前面做成左右可開啟的門，使用時把門打開，可裝入或取出儲存的衣物。（圖8）晉南或山東、河北等地還有一種箱櫃，上部是箱子，下部是一個短櫃，可分開搬動，使用很方便。

THE TYPES OF FURNITURE IN NORTHERN HOMES AND THEIR CONSTRUCTION MATERIALS

Because of economic restraints, vernacular furniture is usually plain and simple with emphasis on utility. There are seven major types of furniture, each with numerous subtypes:

Fig.9   *kang* table
圖9   炕桌

(a) furniture for seating: long stools (*bandeng*), stools with single planks (*tiaodeng*), square stools (*fangdeng*), chairs with backs (*kaobeiyi*), "hanging lantern" chairs (*dengguayi*), round-back chairs (*quanyi*), straight-back folding chairs (*zhibeijiaoyi*), and round-back folding chairs (*yuanbeijiaoyi*);

(b) tables: *kang* tables (*kangzhuo*) (Fig.9), small *kang* tables (*kangji*), full-length *kang* tables (*kang'an*) (Fig. 10), Eight Immortals' tables (*baxianzhuo*), half-moon tables (*yueyazhuo*), long tables (*tiaozhuo*), tables with recessed legs (*pingtou'an*), tables with upturned ends (*qiaotou'an*), and tables with shelves (*jiaji'an*);

(c) storage chests: small chests (*xiaoxiang*), medicine chests (*yaoxiang*), clothing chests (*yixiang*), small cosmetics' cabinets (*guanpixiang*), small cupboards (*xiaogui*), bookshelves (*shugui*), bookcases (*shuge*), upright cupboards (*ligui*), upright cupboards with chests on top (*dingxiangligui*), double compartment cupboards (*lian'ergui*), triple compartment cupboards (*liansangui*), and *kang* cupboards (*kanggui*) (Fig.11);

Fig.10   Full-length *kang* table
圖10   炕案

(d) beds: single couch-beds (*ta*), luohan beds (*luohanchuang*), canopy beds (*jiazichuang*), and heated kang (*huokang*);

(e) shelving and stands: wash basin stands (*mianpenjia*), accessories' stands (*jinjia*), clothing stands (*yijia*), lamp stands (*dengjia*), and mirror stands (*jingjia*);

北方民居家具類型及用材

民間家具受經濟條件限制，一般因陋就簡，注重功能，大略可分為七類，常見的包括了：

(a) 坐具：板凳、條凳、方凳、靠背椅、燈掛椅、圈椅、直背交椅和圓背交椅；

(b) 承具：炕桌（圖9）、炕几、炕案（圖10）、八仙桌、月牙桌、條桌、平頭案、翹頭案和架几案等；

(c) 庋具：小箱、藥箱、衣箱、官皮箱、小櫃、書櫃、書格、立櫃、頂箱立櫃、聯二櫃、聯三櫃升和炕櫃（圖11）；

(d) 臥具：榻、羅漢床、架子床和火炕；

(e) 架具：面盆架、巾架、衣架、燈架和鏡架；

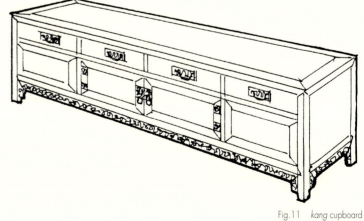

Fig.11   *kang* cupboard
圖11   炕櫃

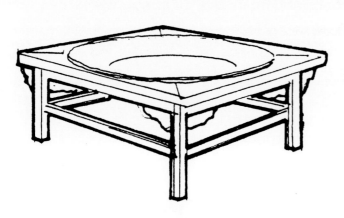

(f) screens: standing screens (*zuoping*), and folding screens (*zhediepingfeng*);

(g) others: foot rests (*jiaota*), tea trays (*chapen*), brush pots (*bitong*), and *kang* braziers (*kanghuopenjia*) (Fig.12)

The use of local materials is the principle governing furniture in dwellings. There are many different types of trees and timber in the north – elm (*yumu*), cypress (*baimu*), locust (*huaimu*), mulberry (*sangmu*), oak (*zuomu*), a type of catalpa (*qiumu*), linden (*duanmu*), purple elm (*ziyumu*), willow (*liumu*), as well as pine (*songmu*) and spruce (*shanmu*). After working with timber over a long period of time, carpenters become thoroughly familiar with local types of trees and timber – their grain, strength, flexibility and colour. The ability to extract maximum function from the materials at hand is essential and an unwritten set of rules govern which types of furniture make use of which materials, as well as the combination of materials in one piece. For example, chairs and stools are mostly made from elm, locust, oak and mulberry; tables and beds from elm, and catalpa; cabinets from elm, catalpa, spruce and willow; and screens from catalpa and *nanmu*.

THE PRODUCTION OF NORTHERN CHINESE DOMESTIC FURNITURE

The three main levels in the manufacture and production of northern homestead furniture are: fairly crude items of furniture made by farmers themselves or by village craftsmen; furniture manufactured in workshops and furniture shops in urban centres and smaller towns; and custom-made furniture.

(f) 屏具：座屏和折疊屏風；

(g) 其他家具：腳踏、茶盤、筆筒和炕火盆架。（圖12）

「就地取材」是民居家具的用材原則。北方樹種多為榆、柏、槐、桑、柞、梓、椴、櫟、紫榆、松、和杉。在長期實踐的基礎上，民間木工對當地的樹種、材性、紋理、強度、韌性和色澤等都十分了解。因此，本著材盡其用的精神，什麼家具用什麼材種，在民間已形成了一種習慣的做法，而且在同一件家具上，不同材質的搭配，也有不成文的一套規度。如椅凳多用榆、槐、柞、桑；桌案和床榻多用榆、楸、槐、梓；櫥櫃多用榆、楸、杉、楊；屏風多用楸、楠等。

農民和農村土木匠打做的家具

由於長時期封建經濟的束縛，導致生產力下降，農村普遍貧苦，北方的農村大多使用簡陋的家具。農民日用的家具，不少由自己打造，或是由土木匠打造。這類家具的特點是因地制宜，就地取材，制作比較粗糙，大多白茬使用，或是塗飾桐油而已。然而，這類家具卻更多保存了古老家具的訊息。其技藝，其造型世代相傳，延延不息。通過這些比較原始的民間家具，可以看到古代家具的文脈。例如在山西北部或東北、內蒙一些地區，現在還可以看到遼代短桌造型的遺存。在晉中地區的農村，一些家具尚與金代墓壁畫上的家具相似。此外，河南北部某些村落中的家具，仍保留了宋式家具的遺風。

SIMPLE FURNITURE MADE BY FARMERS AND VILLAGE CRAFTSMEN

Because of long-term economic hardships, villages were generally poor, with only low levels of production, and so throughout most of rural northern China simple and plain furniture was in use. For everyday use, many farming families either made their own furniture or had it made by the village carpenter. The main characteristic of such furniture was that it was made on the spot, made use of local materials and featured fairly crude workmanship. Most were left unpainted (*baicha*) or were simply coated with *tung* oil. Most furniture of this type, however, preserved the styles of ancient furniture. The techniques and designs had been passed on from generation to generation without interruption. In these fairly rudimentary items of furniture we can discern the pulse of ancient furniture craftsmanship. For example, in northern and north-east Shanxi and in parts of Mongolia ,we can still see survivals of the prototypical low table of the Liao dynasty, and in central Shanxi villages, some items of furniture preserve the types we know from Jin dynasty tomb murals. The furniture in some villages in northern Henan province also preserves a residual style dating back to furniture of the Song dynasty.

FURNITURE MANUFACTURED IN URBAN WORKSHOPS

Urban workshops and shops producing furniture in smaller towns drew on carpenters who had left the villages; most establishments of this type consisted of shop fronts with residences behind. Carpentry skills were passed on from father to son and from master to apprentice. The carpenters' skills provided them with reasonably stable living conditions, and market economic incentives demanded an increasingly improving level of workmanship, resulting in furniture of higher standards of aesthetic appeal and technical finesse.

The furniture shops produced various everyday items of furniture, and sometimes agricultural implements as well, which became the major source of vernacular furniture in the north. A passage from chapter 9 of *Jin Ping Mei* demonstrates how common furniture stores had become in urban settings: "When Ximen Qing's concubine (Pan Jinlian) arrived, she fixed up three rooms in the garden to serve as her home. ... Later he spent 16 silver taels to buy a black lacquer canopy bed with gilding, ... tables, chairs, embroidery and stools, so that it was all well appointed". Fan Lian's Ming dynasty work, *Yunjian jumu chao* states: "After Mo Tinghan arranged for his daughters to marry the sires of the Gu and Song families, he purchased fine timber and also purchased materials from Wumen [today's Zhejiang and adjacent areas]. From the Longqing (1567–1572) and Wanli (1573–1619) periods... Anhui cabinet makers

市、鎮的家具作坊、家具舖製作的家具

這類家具作坊、店舖，則是從農村土木匠分離出來的木匠，大多是前店後宅的手工業作坊。在木工技藝上，父子相承或師徒相繼。由於他們具有一技之長，生活相對比較穩定；由於市場經濟規律的促使，技術精益求精，使家具有較高的藝術質數，在造型上也日求完美。

這些家具舖製作的各類生活日用家具（有時也包括農具、鞍馬具），成為北方民間家具的主要來源。《金瓶梅》第九回謂：「西門慶娶婦人（潘金蓮）到家，收拾花園內樓下三間與他做房。……旋用十六兩銀子買了一張黑漆歡門描金床，……桌椅錦杌，擺設整齊。」此亦反映了遍及市鎮的家具舖的存在。明范濂《雲間據目鈔》云：「自莫廷韓與顧，宋兩家公子，用細木數件，亦從吳門購之。隆萬以來……，徽之小木

("small-scale carpenters") competed fiercely in the large urban centres for business, and so all the wedding furniture business was in their hands".[8]   The term "small-scale carpenter" that appears in this passage is a term for cabinet makers, in contrast with the "large-scale carpenters" who built houses.   The passage also describes the fierce competition that existed among shops making furniture in the Suzhou-Yangzhou district in the Ming dynasty, but a similar situation probably also prevailed in the middle-sized and small towns of northern China.   Further evidence of this is provided by the rows of furniture joineries and workshops that were crowded into the carpenters' district of southern Beijing in the late Qing and Republican periods.

The large number of pieces of old furniture we now encounter on the market are mostly products of the various furniture workshops that were spread throughout the countryside and towns in northern China.

CUSTOM-MADE FURNITURE

Very well-to-do families, retired officials who had returned to their hometowns or merchants who had been successful in business, as well as those who were not so affluent, but who were culturally sophisticated, had particular needs when it came to furniture.   They provided their own specifications for dimensions, appearance, materials and decoration, and would request that the expert craftsmen comply with these requirements, and even add some creative touches to the commissioned piece.   Obviously this was furniture made for the upper classes in past times.   In Chapter 17 of the novel *Honglou meng* [*The Dream of the Red Chamber*] written in the Qianlong period of the Qing dynasty the following revealing passage appears: "Jia Zheng asked, 'In the residences that make up this mansion, do all tables, chairs and other internal furnishings, and not to mention the hangings and screens, the objets d'art, and antiques, not match each with the other?' Jia Zheng replied, 'So many orders for internal furnishings were filled in the past. ... yet still they are incomplete.   When the project got underway at that time a lot of designs were drawn up and a lot of measurements made, and people were sent out to have the orders made up'."   This passage clearly describes the special commissioning of objects not available ready-made on the market.   The novel, in its description of the Xiaoxiang-guan

匠，爭列肆於郡治中，即嫁妝器，俱屬之矣。」[8]文中之「小木匠」是與建造房屋的大木匠相對，是指製作家具的細木匠。文中述說的雖然是明代蘇、揚地帶細木匠「爭列肆中」的情況，但北方的中、小城市，細木匠「爭列肆中」的情況，也會大體相類，這可以從晚清、民國時期北京南城魯班館一帶家具舖、作坊毗鄰接壤的盛況得到進一步的證實。

我們現在在市場上看到大量的古舊家具，大多數出自遍及北方城鄉的各類家具作坊。

特別製作的家具

退居故里的官員，或是經商致富的商賈，不是財力特別殷實，就是有較高的文化素養，因此有條件對家具作特別的要求。他們可以在尺寸上、造型上、用材上和紋飾上命題，聘請家具作坊中技術精湛的匠師製作，甚至親自參予家具的創意，是古代在較高層面上製作的家具。《紅樓夢》寫於清乾隆時期，其第十七回云：「賈政道：『這些院落屋宇並幾案、桌椅都算有了，還有那些帳幔、簾子並陳設玩器、古董，可也都一處一處合式配就的麼？』賈珍回道：『那陳設的東西，早已添了許多……還不全。那原是一起工程之時就畫了各處的圖樣，量準尺寸，就打發人辦去的。』」家具造型和尺寸要「畫了圖樣」和「量準尺寸」，以便「合式配就」，不同於市面上一般之物。在對瀟湘館的描寫中，所指的

8   Fan Lian. *Yunjian jumu chao: juan 2*

8   明・范濂：《雲間據目鈔》：卷二。

states more explicitly: "Observe how when one enters the serpentine corridor, the stones at the foot of the stairs resemble a narrow road, above which the three little rooms, one sunny and the other two dark, match the beds, tables, chair and desks at every step."[9] The fact that the furniture in these rooms matched the viewer "at every step" clearly shows that the measurements and appearance of all the items of furniture in these three unusually small rooms were made to suit the customer.

The combination of a cultured patron with substantial funds and an experienced artisan with skill sufficient to interpret and realise his patron's exacting demands created furniture of outstanding quality. Such socio-economic circumstances have played a critical role in the creation of superb pieces of furniture known to us today.

更為具體：「只見進門便是曲折游廊，階下石子漫成甬路。上面小小三間房舍，兩明一暗，裡面都是合著地步打就的床、幾、椅、案。」[9]這裡「合著地步打就」更是根據建築的室內空間的要求，訂造合適尺寸和造型的家具。

由於業主財力充實、文化藝術素養高，對家具的造型、紋樣、材質以及工匠技藝水平的要求，都會較一般市民高。此外，坊間能工巧匠的參予，就有可能製造出一些高水平的家具。這些社會歷史背景，也許説明了我們今天仍可從大量傳世的古舊家具中看到一些精美的製作。

9   Cao Xueqin. *Honglou meng.* Beijing: Renmin wenxue chubanshe , 1957: *hui* 17: 190-1

9   清·曹雪芹：《紅樓夢》，人民文學出版社，1957：第17回：190-1。

The Main Hall – Nucleus of The Chinese Home

廳堂意蘊之構成

Wang Qijun
王其鈞

The main hall (*tingtang*) was the nucleus of a well-structured traditional Chinese home. Here, in a core room symbolic of the unity and continuity of the family, male members carried out rituals to the gods, honoured their ancestors, received guests, and entertained relatives and friends. While serving formal and ritual functions, main halls sometimes were used for more mundane purposes as multi-functional centres for family life. It was here that seasonal festivals such as at the New Year and periodic weddings and funerals were all celebrated. Here, too, important household decisions were announced and young family members sometimes were tutored. Serving as the formal focus for almost all the major activities of a household, the main hall expressed not only the social status and economic power of the family but also the level of their cultural refinement and artistic tastes. In traditional China, one only had to enter the main hall and glimpse its furnishings to know a great deal about the status of both living and dead members of the family.

Why did people pay so much attention to the arrangement of furniture in the main hall? Central to answering this question is the realisation that Chinese traditionally had an implicit faith in the coexistence of three realms – an illusory paradise in a world beyond, a nether world that transcended the present, and the immediate sphere itself in which humans lived – realms belonging to gods, ghosts, and mortals. These three realms existed not only in the human mind and in the daily behaviour of a family, but also were reflected in the layout of furniture in the main hall.

Here within the traditional dwelling, the human realm occupied intermediate ground and was subject to regular inspection by household gods and infrequent visitations from unquiet ghosts who sometimes disturbed the peace of those living within. Inhabiting the ground where gods and ghosts intermingled, each family was obliged to carry out rituals directed towards both groups. Sacrifices and supplications to gods were made in order to obtain their protection and enlist their power in order to drive away harmful ghosts. Household members also sought to ingratiate themselves with ghosts in the hope that they would not cause trouble among the living and would happily remain as mere ghosts. Each year, on the 15th of the first lunar month, the Chinese equivalent of All Souls' Day, people were required to placate all the ghosts waiting in

廳堂是中國傳統民居的核心空間。在這裡，人們祭祀神天、供奉祖宗、接待賓客、宴請親朋。同時，廳堂又是一個多功能的家庭活動中心。歡度節日，紅白喜事，以及家長宣佈重大的決定，教育子女等也在廳堂舉行。正因為廳堂幾乎集中了所有家庭重大的活動，所以它的家具和布置代表了家庭的社會地位、經濟實力，以及房主人的文化修養、藝術愛好等。在過去，祇要一進入某一家的廳堂，就可大致了解其家庭情況。所以我們常常可以在一些文人的宅邸中，感受到房主人某些心性品格，甚至其學養襟抱。

為什麼人們如此重視廳堂的家具布置呢？因為在過去，人們認為有三個世界同時存在：虛幻的天國、超現時的冥府、人間現時環境。換句話說，也就是神、鬼、人居住的境地，簡稱為三界。人們的頭腦中存在這三個境地，而廳堂的家具布置，也間接反映了這三個境地。

由於人間是一個中性的境地，所以神僊常來巡狩，而不安份的妖魔歷鬼，也出沒無常、騷擾凡人。居住在神鬼交征之地，人不得不舉行迎送、祭拜酬謝神明的儀式來祈求神明保佑，並渴望假神力逐鬼驅魔。另一方面，人也要討好鬼，希望它們不要來人間惹事生非而安心作鬼。因此每年都要中元普渡、安撫陰間眾鬼。在這種觀念下，傳統民居的廳堂，就是一個表露人界環境，既能祭拜、酬謝神明，又能安撫、紀念自己已經死去成鬼的長輩和親人，祈拜他們轉為神靈的特殊場所。

Hell. In line with these beliefs, it was essential that the family's main hall provide a locus for ritual and commemoration, including sacrificial worship to gods and filial remembrance of departed ancestors.

For these reasons the main hall of the traditional Chinese home was a space in which gods, ghosts, and humans coexisted. In the main hall people would welcome the gods in their quest for protection and peace. After one's ancestors died they became ghosts who, requiring food for sustenance, frequently returned to the main hall in order to be nourished by the offerings of food left for them. The arrangement of the furniture in the main hall was guided by each of these elements in order to suit the needs of mortals, gods, and ghosts. Both the furniture and ornamentation throughout the main hall were dominated by auspicious themes that summoned good fortune and welcomed benign spirits who were capable of bringing peace to both the living family and their ancestors. The principal function of the most important items of furniture in the main hall – the altar table (shenlong anzhuo) and long side table (da tiaoji) – was to facilitate the offering of sacrifices and prayers to the gods using incense and offerings of food and to situate a shrine and memorial tablets for the ancestors (shenwei). In addition, households typically incorporated decorative features outside their main halls and even on the exterior walls and doors of their dwellings in order to ward off malevolent spirits, especially the ghosts of those who had died without descendants.

Even though there were differences in the structured space of Chinese dwellings from region to region, there were certain conventions that governed the placement of furniture within main halls wherever they were found. Ancestral tablets, for example, were generally placed along the northern or back wall of the main hall either in a case attached to the wall or on an altar table. In either case, a long and high altar table (shenlong anzhuo), was positioned along the wall to hold ceremonial paraphernalia such as incense as well as offerings. Each of the upper ends of this imposing table curved upwards and was carved with decorative motifs that were austere in content. The top of the high table was not well adapted to the height of mortals so that the edge of the tabletop met the eye of a person of even modest height. Just in front of the altar table was a bench-like table called a changji that was of moderate length and served mostly for displaying objects. The surface of this long table could be either flat, curved upwards or downwards at either end. Below it was normally a square table called an Eight Immortals' table (baxianzhuo), a necessary piece of furniture that was always used when entertaining

正因為如此，傳統民居的廳堂是一個神、鬼、人三者共存的空間。人們在廳堂中歡迎神明來保佑平安。自己的祖宗死後成鬼，但鬼也是需要食物的，所以要經常回到廳堂來攝取家人祭祀的食物。廳堂的家具布置，受到以上的因素制約，要神、鬼、人皆宜。人們還在民居的大門及外部，設置了一些鎮鬼驅鬼的裝飾物，以防鄰家沒有後代祭祀的孤魂野鬼溜進自己家中。民居廳堂內的家具裝飾物，都是取吉祥的主題，用意在於迎接神明安居家中、並歡迎自己的祖宗返回取食。廳堂中的主要家具，如神龍案桌、大條几等的主要功能就是祭祀神明及祖宗，安放神位及祖宗牌位，供奉香火、擺放食物。

儘管各地民居的建築空間形式有很大的不同，但廳堂的家具布置卻有一定的規律。一般來說，祖宗牌位是設置在廳堂北側正中的位置。祖宗牌位的下方是既高又大的神龍案桌。神龍案桌是一種尺度較大的長條形桌子，放置在空間較大的祖堂，靠牆擺放祖宗牌位或放置香火、供品。桌面兩端起翹，雕刻圖案內容嚴肅。其桌面高度已經不太符合人的尺度，幾乎與一個中等高度的人的視平線等平。神龍案桌的前方是長几，長几是一種中等尺度的長條形的桌子，多用作置放供品和陳設品。几面有平直的、兩端起翹的和兩端向下捲起的類型。長几的前方是八仙桌。桌是僅次於椅的一種必不可少的廳堂家具，主要用來接待客人。八仙桌的兩側各放一把靠背椅，椅是廳堂中數量最多的一種家具，根據擺放的位置和主人的喜好，椅子有

guests; this table was normally flanked by a pair of backed chairs (*kaobeiyi*). Chairs of various types were the most numerous furniture type in Chinese main halls and were generally placed according to the preferences of the head of the household. Besides chairs, small round or rectangular stools or benches (*dengzi*) were placed around the main hall and were used to supplement chairs when needed. Functional tables (*zhuo*) of various types were quite numerous, usually square pieces of furniture that were second only to chairs in number. Tall, small tables (*huaji*) for holding either living plants or cut flowers in pots were often as high as the altar table. Low tables called teapoys (*chaji*) were placed between a pair of chairs, and were designed to place a tea cup within a hand's reach of each person in the adjacent chairs.

Although these commonalities can be seen widely, there are of course differences that reflect each household's economic circumstances and variations in customs. Generally speaking, the choice of furniture was tempered by a family's budget and taste. While some furniture clearly was grander and more elaborate than others, in most cases the actual layout of the furniture was similar — formal and sober with a clear sense of hierarchy. Symmetry and the presence of a central axis that conveyed a sense of seriousness and awe were dominant organising principles in the placement of the furniture. In this way, the furniture layout of a main hall was quite unlike that of Chinese bedrooms and kitchens, each of which was decidedly informal and often quite random in terms of how furniture was situated.

While the items of furniture vary little from place to place, there were changes from dynasty to dynasty as well as some variations in how individual pieces were positioned from one region to another. The Ming dynasty, for example, represents a pinnacle in the development of Chinese furniture with forms that are austere yet refined. Made of fine grained timbers, each piece is structurally sound and held together with intricate joinery. Very few fine examples of Ming furniture survive except in museums and in private collections. Qing dynasty furniture, on the other hand, is rather common and is still seen in Chinese homes that can be visited today. The overall style of traditional Chinese furniture is relatively simple with only limited regional variations. At this juncture, let us examine some of the regional differences in the arrangement of furniture in the main halls of large houses in Shanxi, Jiangsu and Zhejiang, southern Anhui,

多種不同的形式。除了椅子以外，凳子也是廳堂常用的一種坐具，凳子移動方便，使用靈活，可以根據情況隨時增減數量。另外，花几、茶几等在廳堂中也經常使用。花几一般較高，有的和神龍案桌一樣高。花几是用來擺放花瓶或花盆以作廳堂裝飾。茶几的尺度較矮，高度與椅子的扶手等平，一般都擺放在兩把椅子之間，供人們擺放茶杯。

這是廳堂家具擺放的常見形式。當然，因各地、各家的經濟情況與習俗不同有所變化，廳堂家具的陳設所體現的思想境界，反映出房主人的日常生活情趣和真實情感。一般來說，祖堂中使用的家具比較規整、厚重、典雅，並按等級制度布置，在不超越自己身份的情況下，盡可能的顯示出隆重的氣派。對稱是其最重要的原則，這樣可以顯示出中軸線，流露出莊重的氣氛。廳堂家具不像臥室家具或廚房家具那樣，不同地區的家具風格有較大差異。廳堂家具本身的模式在各地變化不大，其主要變化在於家具的布置。

明代家具是中國家具發展史上的高峰，特點是造型簡樸洗煉，構架嚴謹，榫卯精密合理，木紋細膩，但遺存至今的並不多。讓人見到後不禁引起時序更迭、流年暗換的慨嘆與迷惘。一些富有人家廳堂中保存的古家具僅是清代家具。

中國傳統家具的風格比較單一，特別是廳堂家具，各地都相差不大。南、北方廳堂家具布置的區別主要是因為民居空間的形式不同。這裡我們介紹一下在中國具有代表性的山西、江浙、皖南以及福建民居中的廳堂家具及布置。（圖1）

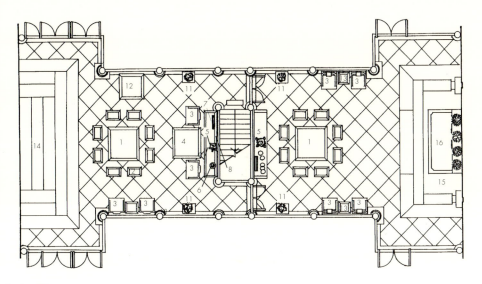

and Fujian provinces. (Fig. 1)

Even though the courtyard-type dwellings of Shanxi province can be seen as representative of a northern Chinese type, the large manor houses of Qixian district in the central portion of the province are qualitatively superior. This is attributable to the fact that many people from this district were engaged in lucrative trading activities that took them to all parts of the country. On returning home, they constructed magnificent rambling manorial homes with many courtyards and surrounding three and five-bay wide structures. When entering the main hall of manor homes in Qixian one notices first that the room is strikingly shallow. This is because in the northern latitudes of China, sunlight is needed within the dwelling in winter. If the room were too deep, sunlight would not penetrate the room during the cold months. Since the main room is rather shallow, the overall space in the room also was not large, and as a result there was room only for limited furniture. While a long side table (*changyi*) to hold the memorial plaques of ancestors was common in each Shanxi main hall, a full-length altar table (*shenlong anzhou*) was not generally used. In addition to the side table, there typically was an Eight Immortals' table and on each side chairs with backs and along the northern wall display stands for decorative objects and other items would be placed. (Fig. 2) Because the main hall was generally in the middle of a three-bay structure, it was common for alcove-type beds to be placed in each of the adjacent bays. Alcove-type beds are large, relatively enclosed chambers, veritable rooms within rooms, that served not only as places for sleeping but during the day provided space for leisure, study, and even some appropriate domestic tasks as sewing and embroidery.

Fig. 2   Furniture in one of the halls of the Qiao family compound in Qiaojiabaocun, Qixian, Shanxi province. A typical furniture arrangement favoured by affluent households in northern China during the Qing dynasty, conveying prominent social status and a life of luxury.
圖2.　山西：山西省祁縣喬家堡村喬家大院某廳堂家具陳設。這是清代典型的北方大戶人家的家具布置形式。從中可以看出房主人的顯達地位和奢靡生活。

山西民居在北方民居中最具代表性，其中以晉中祁縣一帶的民居質數最好。當地人能建起這麼好的住宅，主要是在歷史上曾經有一段時間，他們外出到許多省市做生意，而且非常成功。致富以後，便回鄉營造了漂亮的宅邸。祁縣民居的廳堂進深不大，主要原因是北方需要陽光。假如房屋的進深過大，必定會影響採光。廳堂的進深淺，室內的空間也不是太大。在這種情況下，祁縣民居的廳堂家具相對布置較少，一般只設長几，而不設神龍案桌。祖宗牌位就放在長几上。另外祁縣民居的廳堂通常是一個三開間或五開間的開敞空間，所以除了廳堂正中擺放長几、八仙桌、以及八仙桌兩側各擺放一把靠背椅以外，只在廳堂北側靠牆的部位再設置一些花架、八寶格之類富有裝飾性的家具。八仙桌正前方的兩側不再擺放靠背椅、茶几之類的家具。（圖2）由於廳堂是三間開敞的空間，所以在山西民居廳堂兩側的次間中，往往可以見到床。床很大，就像是一個小房間，除了睡覺外，還有許多功能。山西民居的家具在厚重之中表現沈情，婉轉含蓄，風格蘊藉，神韻卓絕，尤堪玩賞。

The houses of southern Anhui provide a striking contrast with those of Shanxi. A large number of the residents of southern Anhui were prosperous merchants, like those in Shanxi, but here they travelled throughout the productive provinces of central and southern China. On returning home after acquiring wealth, they also built well-appointed houses and filled them with fine furniture. Homes in southern Anhui are unique in that they are usually compact and at least two storeys high. Each was constructed around a central open space called a skywell that was like a small courtyard, providing a focal area for light and air to enter the structure. The main hall was positioned on the northern side of this open space and was open to it, without a wall separating interior from exterior space. The back of the main hall, that is its northern side, was taken up by a timber wall termed "the teacher's wall" (*taishibi*), to either side of which was an

open doorway without door panels that afforded access between the front and rear courts. In front of the "teacher's wall" was a long side table and an Eight Immortals' table. Several high backed chairs were placed symmetrically on the eastern and western sides of the main hall; these chairs generally were in pairs with a teapoy between them. Decorative items would be placed on the long side table. In the homes of less cultured persons or merchants, these objects sometimes functioned as auspicious rebuses using homophonous associations. For example, a vase (*ping*) placed on the east and a mirror (*jing*) placed on the west together connoted tranquillity (*pingjing*). Even though the main halls in homes in southern Anhui were invariably small, two or four chairs would always be placed against each side wall with a plaque hung above them. Generally such plaques contained marble insets in which the grain of the marble resembled mountain landscapes. With an inscription carved into the corner of the marble, a "landscape painting" was created.(Fig. 3)

Fig. 3 A view of the front hall of Chengzhitang in Hongcun, Yixian, Anhui province. During the late Qing period, this was a popular setting among the merchant class in southern Anhui.

圖3 皖南：安徽省黟縣宏村民居承志堂內第一個廳堂的家具布置，是皖南一帶清末商人的家具布置方式。

In south-western Fujian, co-habitation by members of an extended clan was the customary norm. The main halls of dwellings here were structurally high and quite formal with elaborate and stylish ornamentation. A tall altar table, about 3.3 metres in length, .66 metres deep, and at least a half metre taller than the side table, held ancestral tablets and dominated the main

與山西民居相對應的是皖南民居。在歷史上，皖南地區相當比例的居民都做過商人，與晉中商人相似的，是他們也曾有過一段成功的時期，其經商的範圍也包括南方不少省份。這些商人賺錢後，回鄉建起相當數量的宅邸，並在宅邸中設置了許多豪華家具，有綺席凝塵，香閨掩霧的閒靜感。皖南民居的特殊形式決定了其廳堂不一般的設置。皖南民居都是兩層以上的樓房，中間圍合一個很小的天井，廳堂就設置在天井的北側。廳堂與天井之間不設任何牆壁或門窗，廳堂是開敞的空間。廳堂的背後（也就是廳堂的北牆）是木質的太師壁，太師壁的兩側是門（不裝門扇），使民居的前後院相連。太師壁的前面設置長几、八仙桌等家具。廳堂的東西兩側，對稱的擺放幾把靠背椅。一般兩把靠背椅為一組，兩把靠背椅之間放一個茶几。人們還喜愛在長几的上面擺放一些器具作為裝飾，有神無跡，如輕霜溶水，泯融無痕。在一些文化修養不高的人家或商人家中，往往利用擺放的物件取得諧音，以獲得心理上的滿足。如左（東）側擺一只花瓶，右（西）側擺一面鏡子，取"平"（瓶）"靜"（鏡）之意。儘管皖南民居的廳堂很小，但在廳堂的東西兩側卻靠牆擺放著各兩把或各四把椅子，椅子上方的牆壁上，一般都掛有掛屏，掛屏的屏芯是大理石，大理石的花紋像似高山流水，在石頭的一角刻有題跋，如同一幅潑墨山水畫，婉轉含蓄，情致纏綿。（圖3）

福建民居集中體現了中國人聚族而居的傳統習俗。福建民居的廳堂建築結構高大，形體規整，而且裝修浩繁，與其他地區民居的溫潤風格頗有不同，有激言烈響的氣勢。正面當首的是高大的神龍案桌，上面設置祖宗牌位。神龍案桌比長几高出半尺到一尺，桌面沿牆橫向展開長達一丈，前後寬度近兩尺，兩端飛足起

hall. Although the upper portion of the altar table curved upwards, the overall appearance of the table was that of an expansive flat space that was at once lofty and imposing. In front of the altar table there usually was a lower side table on which incense and offerings were arranged. In front of this stepped table would be placed a square Eight Immortals' table used for entertaining guests or for periodic family meals. Flower stands were positioned at both ends of the altar table, and sometimes also at both ends of the side table. A single chair was placed to both the right and left of the Eight Immortals' table. (Fig. 4) Overall, the furniture increased in height and width from the Eight Immortals' table to the side table and on to the altar table, imparting a sense of clearly defined hierarchy. At either side of the main living room, a large number of chairs, teapoys, square tables, and half-tables were symmetrically placed. This formal and articulated layout appeared stately yet dynamic, fully expressing the feudal protocol that governed large families.

Fig. 4   A hall of Fuyuantang in Ma'anxiang, Minqingxian, Fujian province, with furniture in a style commonly found in peasant households of this area.

圖4　福建：福建省閩清縣馬安鄉民居福圓堂的廳堂家具。這是典型的南方農村清代家具形式。

The homes of Jiangsu and Zhejiang are the quintessential Chinese dwellings. Here in the catchment area of Lake Taihu, well-appointed dwellings reflected the prosperity of the region. In the modern period, especially, a large number of wealthy people from Shanghai and other cities built villas in the Lake Taihu area, further increasing the splendour of dwellings here. There are several types of main halls in the homes of Jiangsu and Zhejiang and, unlike the houses of Shanxi, southern Anhui, and Fujian, these generally were not reserved to function principally as ancestral halls. Indeed, there often were multiple main halls in Jiangsu and Zhejiang dwellings, each serving specific or multiple functions, including not only spaces or rooms to commemorate ancestors (zutang) but also to serve a family's need for a parlour (huating), and a drawing room to receive and entertain guests (keting).

Although the ancestral hall was usually located in a central position in the dwelling, other main halls could be placed in the rear or adjacent to a private garden. There was a broad range of furniture in the main halls of large dwellings in Jiangsu and Zhejiang. Apart from the items of furniture mentioned earlier, there also were couches and screens as well as other assorted pieces. An exquisitely carved couch (ta), used for sitting but also resting, was often placed in

翹，整體結構舒展平直，氣勢高昂，體態龐大。神龍案桌的前面是長几，上面擺放香火和供品。長几的前面是八僊桌，用來接待客人或當餐桌。神龍案桌的兩端各設置一個花几，有的在長几的兩端也設置花几。八僊桌的左右兩側各設椅子一把。（圖4）從八僊桌、長几到神龍案桌，家具一個比一個高，一個比一個寬。感覺上寬窄有序、層次分明。在廳堂的兩側，對稱布置大量的椅子、茶几、方桌、半桌等，格局清晰，布置整齊。整個大廳顯得莊嚴熱烈，嚴肅寧靜，充分體現了大家庭的封建禮儀。福建家具是對房主人品格的寓托，淡而有味，富於畫意，著筆無多，沖和閒雅，自成一格。

江浙民居是中國民居中的精品。太湖流域在歷史上一直是一個經濟發達、富庶的地區。尤其是近代，許多在上海等城市居住的富戶，在太湖一帶建了不少別墅，更為江浙民居增添光彩。江浙民居的廳堂顯得蕭疏明麗而有脫塵絕俗的風致。江浙民居的廳堂有許多種類，不像山西、皖南、福建民居的廳堂，主要功能局限於祖堂。江浙民居的廳堂可以分為祖堂、花廳、客廳、四面廳等多種形式。除祖堂設在民居的正中外，其他廳堂也可以設置在民居的後花園（即私家園林）之中。江浙民居廳堂的家具種類很多，除前面提到的，還用榻、屏等家具。江浙民居的客廳正面中央往往設置精巧華貴的榻，這種榻，以坐為主，兼可睡

the middle of Jiangsu and Zhejiang drawing rooms. To the right and left front of the couch, large or small tables, stools, flower stands, and display cases (*babaoge*) were placed. In the centre of a parlour, one usually found a set of furniture comprised of a round table with round stools surrounding it. Chairs and teapoys were placed symmetrically to either side of the room. The form of the furniture in such parlours was flexible, including a variety of styles that were descriptively named: "flowering crabapple" type, "plum blossom" type or "high waisted" type. Most chairs had carved or decorated backs that expressed a simplicity of line and purity of form. (Fig. 5) Calligraphy, painting, and suspended screens usually were hung on all four walls and decorative lamps were suspended from the ceiling, together conveying a sense of a lively and dynamic domestic space.

In conclusion, while each item of furniture in the main hall of a traditional Chinese home had a clearly defined special function, each served to complement the other pieces in the hall. The furniture in the main hall represented the material form in which a family expressed its status, as though it were the outward face of the family itself. In traditional China, one only needed to see the furniture in a family's main hall to appreciate the household's social position, economic power, and cultural level. In terms of elemental design principles, Chinese homes typically faced inward and were framed by balanced structures. Internal space was hierarchically organised and ritually centred in ways that heightened the significance of the main hall, the nuclear space of the family within.

With contributions to the English version from Professor Ronald G. Knapp

臥。榻的前方左右兩側，或放置桌子、几案，或擺放花架、八寶格。江浙民居的花廳中心，常擺放一堂圓桌圓凳，兩側是對稱擺放的椅子和茶几。花廳的家具造型非常靈活，圓桌圓凳常用海棠式、梅花式、束腰式等，而椅子大都為線條簡潔、形體清秀的屏背椅、花背椅等。（圖5）江浙民居的廳堂布置極富變化，四周牆面上一般都掛有書畫、掛屏等裝飾，上方懸掛有花燈，環境氣氛生動活潑、充滿活力。

總之，中國傳統民居的廳堂家具，在突出使用功能的同時，明確體現了烘托廳堂氣氛的特點。人們將廳堂家具作為自己家庭形象的物質體現，就像是自己的臉面。故此，在往日祇要看了廳堂家具，便可以了解一個家庭的社會地位、經濟實力和文化修質。

Fig. 5   Reception hall of Bishuizhai in Suzhou, Jiangsu province, furnished in a manner characteristic of affluent households in the Jiangsu and Zhejiang region. Its elegant setting and tranquil atmosphere reveal the cultural accomplishments and developed aesthetic taste of the occupants, probably scholars enjoying great leisure.

圖5   江浙：江蘇省蘇州市民居碧水齋的花廳家具。這是清代江浙一帶富人住宅的客廳家具布置方式，清幽平靜，表現了房主人的文化休養和審美愛好，與及讀書人的閒情逸致。

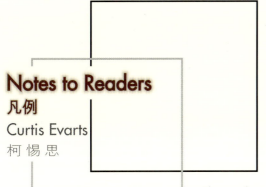

Notes to Readers
凡例
Curtis Evarts
柯惕思

Although advances have been made over the last decade, dating Chinese furniture remains an inexact science, and specialists do not always agree.

The growing interest in traditional furniture produced from the many miscellaneous deciduous and coniferous woods native to China has also resulted in varying opinions and levels of knowledge regarding wood classifications and their terminology. This author looks forward to the aid of botanical scholarship combined with local and regional knowledge to yield further advances in this area of study over the next decade.

When possible, regional provenance of the catalogue objects has been noted. Those for which the regional provenance is unknown, or are without an identifiable regional style, have been left unattributed.

The captions are divided into two parts, the first including general commentary surrounding individual categories, materials, historical background, artistic qualities etc. The second half is of a more descriptive nature, and emphasis is placed on the more noteworthy aspects of the objects' design and construction, while omitting the more redundant description of typical construction techniques. Readers unfamiliar with furniture construction may wish to refer to Wang Shixiang's *Connoisseurship of Classical Chinese Furniture* for further details regarding its construction and joinery.

在最近十年，鑑定中國家具年代的技術有很大的進步，但尚未發展成一門嚴謹的科學，即使專家之間也往往存有不同意見。

中國本土的落葉和長青樹木資源豐富，人們對這些不同木材製成的傳統家具興趣日濃，對木材的分類和有關術語亦意見紛紜，理解各異。本文作者盼未來十年的研究工作能從植物學入手，結合地方和區域特性的探索，令有關研究更上一層樓。

本圖錄盡可能列出各家具的出處。若是出處不明，或是沒有明顯的地方風格，則將不予列出。

本圖錄的文字説明會分成兩部分：第一部分簡介家具的種類、材料、歷史背景及藝術價值；第二部分著重介紹每一件家具的設計和製作的特點，至於一般的製作技術則不贅。

此外，對家具製作和結構有興趣的讀者，亦可參考王世襄著《明式家具研究》。

Platform in Three Sections
Nanmu (A variety of cedar)   18th century   Jiangnan Region
156 cm (w) x 62.5 cm (d) x 43 cm (h)

Low platforms were the earliest type of raised seating furniture to appear in China and were often used as honorific seats by high officials and religious dignitaries during ceremonies and sacrificial rites. Records from the Han dynasty (206 BC–220 AD) indicate that sitting platforms were called *ta*; the relatively longer *chuang* was used both for sitting and reclining. (Cui: 52) By the Tang dynasty (618–907), the platform had increased in height, and usually featured decoratively-shaped openings on each side. In addition to being used for seating and reclining, this popularised form also served, in a slightly higher version, as a large, low table. Evidence in paintings and woodblock prints indicates the box-style platform daybed continued to be used throughout the Qing dynasty (1644–1912), during the late Ming dynasty, men of cultivated taste praised its elegant antique form in preference to the newly fashionable daybeds with free-standing legs. (Wen: 6, 1ab)

This rare platform is constructed in three modular sections which can be easily set side-by-side to function as a single daybed-type platform, or used separately as smaller seating platforms, stands, or low tables. The frame members are typically joined using mitred, mortise-and-tenon techniques in the flat-sided (*simianping*) box-style construction. The seat surfaces are fit with flush panels; the two larger sections (62.5 x 62.5 cm) with two-piece panels; the smaller (31.2 x 62.5 cm) with a single panel; each is supported with a single transverse brace. Each side houses an open panel whose oscillating lines appear to pulse against the rectilinear framework.

一.

三件式組合榻
楠木　十八世紀　江南地區
156公分 寬 x 62.5公分 深 x 43公分 高

矮榻是中國最早的垂足式坐椅，專供高官和地位崇高的僧侶在慶典或祭祀儀式時使用，以示他們尊崇的地位。根據漢朝〔公元前206年—公元220年〕文獻記載，坐的器具稱為榻；可坐亦可臥，體形較長的為床〔崔：52〕。到了唐代〔618年—907年〕，榻的高度增加，兩側通常有裝飾性的圈口。除了用來坐和躺臥外，它亦可當作大的矮桌使用。箱型的榻一直沿用到清朝〔1644年—1912年〕，這從當時的繪畫和版畫可證明。晚明期間，流行無管腳根榻，但文人雅士卻偏好優雅的古典造型。〔文：6, 1ab〕

這組少見的榻為三件式構造，既便於將三件放在一起當榻使用，也可個別分開當成坐椅、腳踏或矮桌使用。榻的邊框以格角榫攢邊作成四面平的箱型構造，面板以平鑲式安裝，大的〔62.5 x 62.5公分〕兩件面板是由兩塊板拼合，小的〔31.2 x 62.5公分〕是獨板組合；三件皆有穿帶支撐。四邊以弧形板條造成的圈口，為方形的結構添上動感。

2. Daybed

Huanghuali   late 16th/early 17th century

221.3 cm (w) x 98.5 cm (d) x 53.6 cm (h)

The use of the daybed was manifold: during the day, it served as a sitting platform; at night, a bed for sleeping – when furnished with a small portable armrest, it was convenient for reading old texts; of relatively light weight, it was also easily carried into the garden where, enclosed within an awning, it provided a cool place to sleep.   This daybed exemplifies the quality of grandeur prized in furniture from the late Ming period, while retaining the antique elegance of the raised dais or platform that a respected nobleman or high priest might occupy.   The bold, uniform decoration of carved cloud designs creates an ethereal quality which masterfully balances a robust form. Tian Jiaqing ranks this as one of the three best examples of *ta* daybeds he has examined.   (see this book's foreword: page 14)

It is of typical waisted corner-leg form.   The mitred, mortise-and-tenon seat frame is woven with a soft cane seat.   The surrounding curvilinear aprons are decorated in relief with *lingzhi*-like cloud motifs and outlined with a boldly drawn line of raised beading which continues down the inside of the legs.   The short cabriole legs are curved with a *ruyi*-cloud lappet design on each shoulder, and terminate with a scrolled foot from which a leaf sprouts in relief.

Previously Published:

Handler, Sarah.   "Square Tables Where Immortals Dine." *Journal of the Classical Chinese Furniture Society* Autumn, 1994: 17

Wang Shixiang and Curtis Evarts.   *Masterpieces from the Museum of Classical Chinese Furniture*.   San Francisco: Tenth Union, 1995: 8

二. 榻

黃花梨　十六世紀晚期／十七世紀初期

221.3公分 寬 x 98.5公分 深 x 53.6公分 高

榻有多樣的用途：白天作為坐具，晚間用作睡覺。若在榻上放置一件小憑几，便於閱讀古籍；由於它並不沉重，可以輕易地搬到花園，擺放在布棚下，變成一個涼快的寢處。此榻充份體現晚明家具有勁有神的特色，同時也保留了貴族和高僧擁有的榻那份古雅。榻上優雅的祥雲裝飾，平衡了它堅實的造型。田家青更把此榻列為他所見過最好的三張之一。（見本書前言：頁14）

這榻屬典型有束腰桌形結構，邊框格角榫攢邊，帶籐編軟屜。四面牙子雕有靈芝紋，沿邊起燈草線與三彎腿足相接，三彎腿足成如意狀，並在足底部形成嫩芽的卷雲。

曾經刊載於：

見英文説明

Large Square Stool

3

Yumu (Northern Elm)   18th/19th century   Shanxi
63.5 cm (w) x 63.5 cm (d) x 53.5 cm (h)

The stool – a basic seating unit – was produced in hundreds of configurations; its uses multiplied it by another hundred. In the hierarchy of seating furniture, stools were relegated to a low position, and in any seated gathering, relative social status was reflected by those sitting in armchairs and on stools. Nevertheless, they were also made in various sizes, and large, well-proportioned stools were used in wealthy households by both men and women.

The rather charming decoration of this stool generally follows traditional motifs, yet has distinct provincial characteristics. Although of somewhat eclectic form, this large stool is of standard corner-leg construction. The original soft woven seat has been replaced with a hard panel. The seat frame and aprons are reticulated along each side to form shallow recesses between the projecting corners. Three long, beaded openings penetrate each waist section. Below, the apron is carved in relief with three bats, of which the central one holds a plum blossom in its mouth, leafy, scrolling grass reaches out along each end of the apron from the griffin-like *taotie* mask lightly curved on the shoulder of each leg. Each leg is uniquely shaped as a short C-curved leg terminating in a scroll and rests upon a lotus leaf pad, and which then stands upon a leg-extending C-curved bracket carved with a pendant leaf in full relief – all continuously shaped from a single piece of wood. The four legs are joined with a base stretcher, the original of which has been replaced.

大方凳

三.

榆木　十八世紀／十九世紀間　山西
63.5公分 寬 x 63.5公分 深 x 53.5公分 高

凳是基本坐具，可做成許多不同的式樣，用途十分多樣化。在坐具的品級中，凳屬較低層次，在任何聚會裡，只需看坐者是坐在有扶手的椅子還是凳上，即可知道其社會地位。此外，凳也可做成不同尺寸，體積大且比例勻稱的凳，亦為富家男女使用。

此大方凳基本上仿效傳統的裝飾，但卻帶有明顯的地方色彩。它的造型不拘一格，屬標準的桌形結構，原來的軟屜已改為硬屜，兩格角之間的邊、抹和其對應的束腰皆有一段凹陷的造型。束腰為弦紋三開光，牙板的中間部分有三隻蝙蝠浮雕，居中的蝙蝠口含盛放的梅花；其他部分則由浮雕卷草紋，連接腿足上方的饕餮獸面淺浮雕。鼓腿彭牙是一木連做，足底向內兜轉成圓形球狀，下有一瓣蓮葉，腿足至此再延展出另一截帶有懸垂葉雕刻的鼓腿。四足下原來的托泥，原件為新造取代。

4.

Meditation Stool

Tielimu late 16th/early 17th century

105 cm (w) x 70 cm (d) x 49.6 cm (h)

Variously termed "meditation platforms" or "single daybeds", the origins of such sitting platforms can be traced well into antiquity as seats of rulers, sages, monks and hermits. Gao Lian and Wen Zhenheng both note that low platforms were also called *Mile ta* (literally, a platform for the Buddha of the Future [Maitreya]), and that they were also well-suited to placement in a temple or a study for contemplative meditation (Gao: *juan* 8, 12b; Wen: *juan* 6, 1a). These entries, along with other furniture types, suggest that such sitting platforms were once more commonplace. Extant examples are rare to non-existent (cf. Wang and Evarts: 4; Christie's: 27, 57; Bruce 1991: 134).

This large platform is of waisted corner-leg construction. The soft-seat frame is typically constructed to minimise warpage of the frame members due to the tension created by the woven seat: a bowed stretcher across the centre is flanked by two straight stretchers near each; the latter are additionally fit with short lateral braces fit perpendicular to their midpoints. The apron/waist sections are single pieces. Spirited clouds carved in relief on the shoulders of each leg also appear as a *taotie* animal mask when viewed diagonally. Below, humpback stretchers are tenoned through the legs utilising the offset tenon technique so as to minimise a weak point in the leg. Beading along the aprons continues down the legs to a well-formed hoof-shaped foot.

四.

禪凳

鐵力木 十六世紀晚期／十七世紀初期

105公分 寬 x 70公分 深 x 49.6公分 高

「禪榻」或是「單人榻」的歷史可遠溯至古代，是統治者、賢士、僧人和隱者的坐椅。高廉和文震亨皆曾提出矮榻也稱為彌勒榻〔即彌勒佛之榻〕，這種榻極之適合置放於廟宇或供靜思的書房。〔高：卷8，12b；文 卷6，1a〕從這些家具可以看到榻在以前是比較普遍的，而傳世的例子卻非常罕見。〔比較 Wang 和 Evarts：4；Christie's：27，57；Bruce 1991：134〕

此件較大的有束腰馬蹄足桌形結體的禪凳，軟屜中央處安有典型的彎帶，在接近兩邊抹頭各安直帶一根，並在中間處以短木條與抹頭相接。束腰和牙板是一木連做。每支腿足的上端皆有祥雲浮雕，從側面看則呈饕餮獸面紋。羅鍋棖皆以透榫型式與腿足相接，一上一下的榫減輕腿足的承托力。線紋沿牙條邊起，一直伸延到內翻馬蹄足。

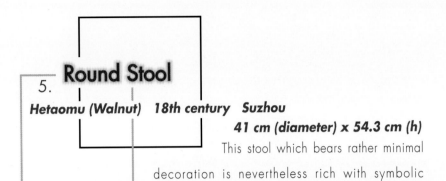

5. Round Stool

Hetaomu (Walnut)   *18th century*   *Suzhou*

41 cm (diameter) x 54.3 cm (h)

This stool which bears rather minimal decoration is nevertheless rich with symbolic interpretation: the rebus "five bats [blessings] bringing longevity" (*wufu pengshou*) is suggested by five bat-shaped cut-outs encompassing the round *shou* character-like seat. There is also an alternate reading, "five bats [blessings] have descended upon the house" (*wufu linmen*) as the five bats hover above each of the five *kunmen*-openings formed by the legs and aprons. Additionally, the decorative pattern described in the Ming dynasty carpenter's manual *Lu Ban jing — zhuanbi zhuangcao* — can also be seen when the cut-outs are viewed as the eyes of an elephant animal mask whose long trunk curves around to the foot where its curled end is carved with leafy foliage.

Pictorial evidence in Ming book illustrations and paintings would suggest that stools of round form were once quite common. However, that surviving ones are relatively rare points to a circular structural form which is both difficult to execute with linear wood members as well as relatively quick to degrade over time. This stool follows the basic waisted corner-leg construction pattern. The seat is formed with a segmented five-piece frame and single board panel. Below the concave waist are five apron sections each pierced with a simple cut-out resembling a bat. The legs meet the apron which utilises inserted shoulder joints and tenon to the seat frame above as well as to the base stretcher below.

五. 圓凳

核桃木　十八世紀　蘇州

41公分 直徑 x 54.3公分 高

此圓凳紋飾簡約，然寓意豐富。座面飾圓形"壽"字紋，周邊透雕五蝠，以示"五蝠(福)捧壽"。五腿間之券口牙字鏤成壼門輪廓，五蝠位於其上，取"五福臨門"之意。此外，券口牙子好比捲鼻低垂之象首，透雕蝠形恰如其目，捲鼻末端刻草葉紋，正是明代《魯班經》所描述的"轉鼻裝草"紋樣。

從明代文獻中的插圖與繪畫，可知圓凳曾流行一時。但由於凳身以彎材結合，不特難度較高，堅實度亦較遜，故此傳世實物不多。此圓凳採用基本的束腰和鼓腿式樣，座面邊框以五段弧形彎材攢接而成，中間嵌夾圓形板心。束腰底下為五道券口牙子，上方各有線條簡潔的蝙蝠形透孔。腿足上連牙子，下帶托泥，上下端皆採用插肩榫造法。

6.

Bench

Baimu (Cypress)   19th century   Beijing
176 cm (w) x 27.5 cm (d) x 36 cm (h)

Benches were commonly set in front of shops, next to or inside of the door. Pairs were often set opposite one another inside gateways, and thus acquired the term "gate benches". In restaurants they were placed around square tables as seats for two. As a stable workbench, they were, and are still utilised in countless ways by craftsmen. In temples, monks still kneel before benches arranged as tables while reciting sutras. All in all, perhaps the bench was the most ubiquitous piece of furniture found throughout China.

This bench, of recessed-leg construction, has a framed panel seat supported with two transverse braces and plain aprons below. The outside edges of the splayed legs are shaped with an indented moulding. Parallel humpback stretchers are tenoned into each pair of legs, the lower stretcher of which is additionally pinned to each leg with a bamboo peg. The underside retains some of its original lacquer and ramie undercoating.

六．

條凳

柏木　十九世紀　北京
176公分 寬 x 27.5公分 深 x 36公分 高

條凳通常是放在店舖門前、店側或店內使用。成雙的條凳一般放在大門通道兩側，故有「門凳」之稱。在酒樓食肆，可坐兩人的條凳會置於方桌的四邊。自古至今，工匠利用凳作不同用途。在廟宇裡，僧侶往往以凳為桌，蹲跪在前面誦經。總的來說，條凳是中國最常見的家具。

這張條凳為側腳造型，凳面以雙穿帶攢邊打槽裝板造法做成，牙子光素。側腳扁圓形腿足在看面兩邊壓邊線。凳的兩側各施兩根羅鍋棖，在下的棖子與兩腿相接處各安一根竹釘。內側仍保留了原來的漆和披麻。

7.

Folding Stool

Yumu (Northern Elm)   18th century   Shanxi

57.5 cm (w) x 37 cm (d) x 53 cm (h)   The folding stool has been used for centuries throughout China since its legendary popularisation by the Han Emperor Lingdi, who was recorded to have had a fascination with things foreign, including the "barbarian" seat (*huchuang*). It was common amongst nomadic tribes in the more remote northern and western regions where it was also used for mounting and dismounting horses. Its use spread throughout China during the following Sui, Jin and Tang dynasties. Being easily carried over the shoulder, it quickly became a popular seat for rulers and religious dignitaries when travelling or on hunting excursions, and its lightweight portability made it especially suitable for officers on military campaigns. The folding stool eventually became a popular form of portable seating furniture throughout all social strata. Even today in China, men and women can be seen relaxing on small folding stools by the side of the street, or while fishing along a canal.

The construction and style of this relatively large folding stool differs little from known hardwood examples (cf. Berliner: 92; Ellsworth: 43; Wang and Evarts: 30; Wang 1986: 71). Merit also lies in the well-carved confronting dragons stretched out in relief across the front seat stretcher and the scrolling grass motif lyrically creeps across the back. The original wrought iron hinge fittings are decorated with *ruyi* cloud heads and chrysanthemum design. The footrest has been replaced.

Previously Published:

China Art. *Antiques in the Raw.* Hong Kong: China Art, 1997.

七.

交杌

北方榆〔榆木〕 十八世紀 山西

57.5公分 寬 x 37公分 深 x 53公分 高

交杌在中國已使用了好幾個世紀。據歷史記載，漢靈帝喜愛胡床等舶來品，隨著他的提倡，交杌的使用亦普及起來。北方的遊牧民族和西邊的少數民族普遍使用交杌，同時也把它當作上馬和下馬的用具。隋、唐時代，交杌的使用遍佈中國。由於交杌便於攜帶，因此高官和高僧出巡或打獵時喜以此作為坐椅。此外，它的體型輕巧，特別適合武官在軍事上使用。交杌成為普及社會各階層的可攜型座具。到了今天，在中國仍能看到人們坐在交杌上在路旁休息，或是在河邊垂釣。

這張交杌體積較大，造型和式樣和那些為人熟知的硬木交杌有些不同。〔比較 Berliner：92；Ellsworth：43；Wang 和 Evarts：30；王1986：71〕正杌面龍浮雕，後橫材立面卷草紋浮雕，手工極為精細，是交杌優秀之處。原來的軸釘穿鉚有如意雲頭和菊花飾樣，腳踏則屬新做。

曾經刊載於：

《歲月中的家具》，香港：華藝，1997

8.
Side Chair (Set of four)

Huanghuali   late 16th/early 17th century

51.2 cm (w) x 44 cm (d) x 92.5 cm (h), Seat Height 43.2 cm

The quiet, simple form of these side chairs resembles those excavated from Song and Jin period tombs (Handler Spr 93: 11) as well as those depicted in early wall paintings. Their low seat height corresponds to their overall small proportions, a feature which may point to a relatively early date. Because of their less structurally integrated from, side chairs have survived in fewer numbers than other types. Extant sets of four side chairs are quite rare, although sets of four, eight or more were likely once commonly produced. Each of the soft cane seats is also framed with rarely found finishing strips wrapped with cane, the similar technique which appears on a carved lacquer throne chair dated to the Jiajing period (1522–66) (Wang 1990: A98) as well as the miniature wood chairs and beds excavated from the Wanli period (1572–1619) tomb of Pan Yunzheng. (Berliner: 83)

Each of these small side chairs is simply styled with a straight crestrail, a lightly curved backrest, and a simply moulded seat frame. Each chair retains an early style soft-woven seat which is trimmed along the edges with thin finishing strips wrapped with cane. The combination of exposed seat frame tenons of the back corner joints with blind tenons at the front corners is a rarely seen variation in seat frame construction. The small spandrel-head aprons below the seat frame are joined with the mitre and dovetail wedge technique. The undersides of all the chairs retain traces of a lacquer and cloth undercoating. Each footrest stretcher is protected with a *paktong* cover which is uniquely secured through three rosettes of *paktong* shaped and incised like scrolling hibiscus.

八.
靠背椅〔 一組四件 〕

黃花梨　十六世紀晚期／十七世紀初期

51.2公分 寬 x 44公分 深 x 92.5公分 高，座高43.2公分

這些優美、簡潔的靠背椅跟宋、金墓出土的文物〔Handler Spr 93：11〕、早期壁畫中的靠背椅類似。低椅盤的高度和椅本身較細小的體型合乎比例，顯示此組椅子屬較早時期的作品。因為靠背椅較少整合的結構，所以傳世的靠背椅數量較其他類型的椅子少。以往的靠背椅通常是一組四件、八件或更多件數，而現在留存一組四件的已很少見。每件座面壓條是以少見的裹籐條技法做成，與嘉靖時期〔1522年—1566年〕〔王1990：A98〕的一件雕漆寶座以及從萬曆年間〔1572年—1619年〕潘允徵墓出土的袖珍木椅和床的壓條相同〔Berliner：83〕。

四件小靠背椅皆造型光素、直形搭腦，獨板靠背中段稍向後彎，椅面的大邊與抹頭皆為素混面。每件椅面皆保持原先的軟屜蓆面，並以細木條裹上籐條做成壓條。後面邊抹以明榫相接，前面則以悶榫相接，座面極少以此法製造。椅面下的牙板以格肩穿銷的營造法相接，並有漆、披麻的痕跡。踏腳棖鑲有薔薇狀的白銅以作保護，白銅上雕有渦旋狀的芙蓉飾紋。

112

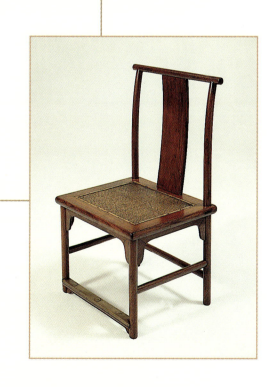

9. Yokeback Armchair (Pair)

Huanghuali   late 16th/early 17th century
59 cm (w) x 47.8 cm (d) x 115 cm (h), Seat Height 52 cm

In the hierarchy of seating arrangements, the yokeback armchair was positioned as a seat of high status. Its balanced sculptural form and artistic line also makes it one of the most favourite pieces of Chinese furniture. This pair is of the classical style – devoid of carved ornamentation, yet fluid in sculptural line – and of a form which can be compared to the miniature wood model excavated from the late Ming tomb of the official Wang Xijue in Suzhou (Suzhou: 51), as well as the typical yokeback chair form frequently depicted in many late Ming woodcut illustrations.

An overall quality of roundness and simplicity is contributed by the softly modelled crestrail and its smooth juncture to the plain, S-shaped splat. The armrests protrude beyond goose-neck supports which are without reinforcing spandrels. The tenons of the mitred, mortise-and-tenon seat frame are exposed, and its edges are simply rounded over. Underneath two curved transverse braces reinforce the seat; the original soft woven seat has been replaced with a hard panel. The front apron forms a well-rounded, arched and cusped opening, and is trimmed with neat beading; the half aprons at the side and back are plain. Traditional oval-shaped stretchers with a flat edge along on bottom reinforce the legs. The shape of the original aprons below the footrest are suitably proportioned to the width of the aprons above.

九.

四出頭官帽椅〔一對〕

黃花梨　十六世紀晚期／十七世紀初期
59公分 寬 x 47.8公分 深 x 115公分 高，座高52公分

這款四出頭官帽椅在坐椅品級中，是身居高位者的坐椅。它勻稱的雕刻和藝術的線條，成為最受人們歡迎的中國家具之一。這對四出頭官帽椅具有典型的樣式——全無雕刻飾品，卻有雕刻的流暢線條，可與蘇州出土的晚明王錫爵墓中的袖珍家具，以及常見於晚明木刻版畫中的典型四出頭官帽椅相比較。

此椅柔和的圓材形搭腦和雙曲線素靠背板流暢地相接，使整體產生圓潤及簡潔感。扶手在鵝脖處出頭，沒有強固牙板。椅盤以明榫格角榫攢邊法製造，在透眼處與抹頭齊；下有兩根彎帶加強椅面作用。原來的軟蓆屜已換成硬板，椅盤下安置弧度優美的起線壼門券口牙子；兩側及後面則為素牙子。傳統的橢圓下扁平形材板使腿足更加堅固。踏腳根下的牙子尺寸合宜，與上面的牙子相互配合。

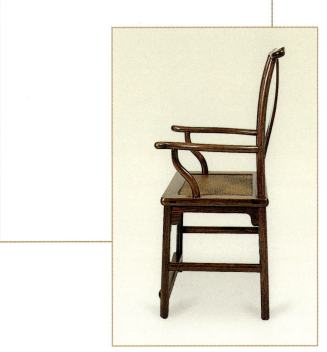

10.
Yokeback Armchair with Square Members (Pair)
Huanghuali 17th century

61 cm (w) x 46 cm (d) x 114 cm (h), Seat Height 52 cm

The yokeback chair is also called an "official's hat chair" (*guanmaoyi*) in reference to the protruding ends of the crestrail which appear like the wings of an official's cap. Although any use of this terminology has yet to be evidenced from known Ming or early Qing texts, the noble imagery conveyed by uplifted wings extending out behind the sitter could have certainly enhanced his status. The subtle variations found within the yokeback form are numerous; nonetheless, those of square-members are relatively rare. A similar style and form at the Victoria & Albert Museum (Clunas: 18) exhibit subtle differences, yet measuring 104 cm in height, are thought to have been reduced in height.

These yokeback armchairs are framed with square-cut members of which the surfaces are shaped with deep concave mouldings. Half-lap double mitres with mortise-and-tenon joints are used throughout to create seamless transitions between the subtly moulded members. The two S-shaped splats are matched, having been cut sequentially from the same timber. The curvilinear armrests are each supported by a tapered S-shaped side post of square section and protrude slightly beyond the atypical backward curving front post. Below the seat frame, deeply arched humpback stretchers with short pillared struts rigidify the framework.

十.
方形構件四出頭官帽椅〔一對〕
黃花梨　十七世紀

61公分 寬 x 46公分 深 x 114公分高，座高52公分

顧名思義，稱此類型椅子為官帽椅是因為它突出的搭腦，像古代官帽的展腳。雖然此說仍有待明、清文字記錄證明，椅背後向上伸展之翼顯示坐者擁有較高的地位。官帽椅的構件有不少組合，但方形構件是很少有的。倫敦維多利亞博物館〔Clunas：18〕藏有一件近似作品，風格和形式大致相同，但高度只有104公分，應是被截斷所致。

這對官帽椅是由方形的構件所組成，表面皆起大窪面。通體以合掌式榫卯接合，所以構件間精緻的窪面並無接縫。雙曲線靠背板花紋一樣，是裁自同塊木料。曲線形把手由方材的聯幫棍支撐，並在微向後傾的鵝脖處出頭。椅盤下，彎度極大的羅鍋棖和矮老強固了整體結構。

11.

Yokeback Armchair (Pair)

Yumu (Northern Elm) and Lacquer   *18th/19th century*   *Shanxi*
57.5 cm (w) x 47.5 cm (d) x 117 cm (h), Seat Height 51.8 cm

While softwood furniture is often of heavier proportion than similar hardwood forms, the slender shaping of frame members and overall proportions of these chairs can be compared with those constructed from more precious hardwoods. Nevertheless, the basket-like lattice under the armrest is a seldom seen variation, although, and can perhaps be compared to the double S-shaped side posts under the armrests of the chairs figured in Plate 12.

The construction of these chairs is generally typical, with sinuous hindposts tenoned through the yoke-shaped crestrail. The S-shaped splat is deeply carved to reveal a *ruyi*-shaped medallion in relief. Goose-neck supports hold up the end of the curvilinear armrests and frame the unusual basket-like latticework which appears to bulge outward to create a spacious seat space. The seat frame contains its original hard seat panel configuration; the tenons of the front legs are exposed. The front aprons are beaded to highlight the arched and cusped openings; the side and back aprons are beaded and fit with spandrel heads.

十一.

四出頭官帽椅〔一對〕

榆木和髹漆　十八世紀／十九世紀　山西
57.5公分 寬 x 47.5公分 深 x 117公分 高，座高51.8公分

以同樣的造型計算，柴木家具比黃花梨家具厚重。這對椅子細長的結構和整體比例可與其他較珍貴的硬木家具比較。雖然如此，扶手下類似花籃的欄杆卻是少見的造型，與圖版十二的扶手下的雙聯幫棍做法有異曲同工之妙。

這對椅子的構造非常典型，後腿上半部向外傾斜，和官帽展腳般的搭腦相接。雙曲線靠背板上有圓形如意深浮雕。鵝脖支撐帶曲線的扶手，後腿與鵝脖之間的扶手下有一向外彎的籃狀攢接結構，使座面空間變寬。椅面為原來的硬板造型，上有前腿的透眼。椅盤下安壺門券口牙子並起陽線加強其弧線；兩側及後面安有起線的牙子和牙頭。

Southern Official's Chair (Pair)

12.

Yumu (Northern Elm) and Lacquer   18th century   Shanxi

59.5 cm (w) x 48.5 cm (d) x 94 cm (h), Seat Height 48.5 cm

Chinese ideology emphasises the dual nature of all things, and it may well be that the terminology "southern official's hat" armchair (also a modern term) has been derived as an antithetical term for the "official's hat" chair. While one is typically constructed with protruding crestrail and armrests (also termed "chair with four protruding ends" (*sichutou*), the "southern official's hat" armchair typically has armrests and crestrail which flow continuously into its front and back posts. The large size of these chairs enables the occupant to sit with legs crossed or hanging pendant. The deeply curved backrest, which approximates that of a round-back chair, is extremely rare, yet comfortable to relax into. The lacquer on these chairs is generally well preserved, with significant wear only on the armrests, front edge of seat frame, and footrests. With the aid of a magnifying lens, the finish can be seen to be a mixed and layered coating of red and black lacquer – perhaps with the intended effect of imitating more expensive dense hardwoods.

Regarding the construction of these chairs, the single-piece crestrail which follows on exaggerated deep curve is notable, and at each end makes an unusual downward turn to meet the hind posts with an elongated pipe joint. The S-shaped splat is carved in relief with an abstracted variation of the longevity (*shou*) character within a round medallion. The unusual arrangement of double side posts under each armrest creates a baluster railing-like enclosure. The seat frame is relatively wide and houses the original hard panel seat. The round vertical posts pass through the seat frame to become legs of somewhat larger section, each retains a squared-timber shape on the inside, while the outside is rounded over with beaded edges. The full aprons – whose beaded openings are each delineated with a fluidly drawn arched-and-cusped line – fill the openings below on front, sides and back, and each is attached with wrought iron nails.

十二.

南官帽椅〔一對〕

榆木和髹漆 十八世紀 山西

59.5公分 寬 x 48.5公分 深 x 94公分 高，座高48.5公分

在中國哲學「陰陽」的觀念影響下，「南官帽椅」一詞〔也是現行用詞〕也許是為了對照「官帽椅」而產生。其中，典型官帽椅的搭腦和扶手皆出頭〔亦稱「四出頭」〕，而典型南官帽椅則是扶手以及搭腦和前、後腿上截流暢地銜接在一起。這種大尺寸的椅子可以用來盤腿坐或是掛垂懸物。彎度靠背極大，有點近似圈椅，是非常罕有的結構。椅子的漆大致還完整，只是扶手、椅盤前端和腳踏部分有顯著的磨損。若以放大鏡來檢視的話，可以看出一層一層混合紅色和黑色漆，造成了仿珍貴硬木的效果。

這些椅是一木連做，彎度極大的搭腦在盡端造成轉項向下，跟後腿以挖煙袋鍋法相接。雙曲線靠背板上有圓形抽象變化的壽字浮雕。扶手下少見的雙聯幫棍營造出圍欄般的外觀。椅盤寬且保有原來的硬屜。前後腿穿過椅盤的下截比例變粗，裡側為方材形式，圓看面起線腳。前、後以及左右皆有起陽線的券口牙子，上有鍛鐵釘。

13.

Low Back Southern Official's Style Armchair (Pair)

Zhajingmu/zhazhenmu   18th century   Jiangsu Region
55 cm (w) x 42.5 cm (d) x 86.5 cm (h), Seat Height 46.7 cm

Zhajingmu/zhazhenmu is indigenous to regions in Zhejiang and Jiangsu provinces. The wood is dark reddish-brown and layered with coffee-coloured tissue; it has a fine grain pattern with medullary rays visible in the radial cut. That the extant body of furniture made from *zhajingmu/zhazhenmu* is generally has a refined quality may suggest both rarity of the material, as well as a special reverence for its fine dark grain.

In variance from the standard form noted above (text, Plate 12), this unique pair of small low-back southern official's armchairs have protruding – rather than continuous – armrests. Nevertheless, their classical proportions are pleasing to the eye. The deeply curved crestrail is typically secured to the back posts with pipe joins. The sinuously shaped armrests terminate with a well defined scroll and are supported below with S-shaped side posts and goose-neck front post firmly tenoned through the seat frame. The frame retains its original soft woven seat configuration. Below, humpback stretchers with vertical struts lend visual support. The base stretchers are tenoned into the legs and additionally secured with wood pins.

十三 .

低靠背南官帽椅〔 一對 〕

柞榔木／柞針木　十八世紀　江蘇地區
55公分 寬 x 42.5公分 深 x 86.5公分 高,座高46.7公分

柞榛木/柞針木是江浙一帶特有的木料,呈深紅褐色,帶有一層層的咖啡色紋理,木紋細少,橫切面有放射木髓紋。目前傳世的柞榛木/柞針木家具一般比較精巧,由此可以看出當時它是罕有的木料,以及人們珍惜其深色木紋。

這對特別的小低靠背南官帽椅有出頭的扶手,而非扶手鵝脖相聯,與圖版十二的標準樣式不同。整體的古典造型十分悅目,彎度極大的搭腦在盡端造成轉項向下,跟後腿以挖煙袋鍋法相接。曲線形的扶手在盡端轉成一優美的渦漩頭,其下有聯幫棍和鵝脖緊密地和椅盤相接。椅座為原來的軟屜結構。羅鍋棖和矮老增添了視覺的樂趣,踏腳棖與腿足相接處另有木釘加固。

14

Rose Chair (Pair)

Huanghuali   17th/18th century

59 cm (w) x 45 cm (d) x 86 cm (h), Seat Height 51 cm

Rose chairs are characterised by their small size and low angular back and armrests, the latter being a feature which also makes them somewhat uncomfortable for sitting. Their basic form actually mimics that of small bamboo chairs, whose angular framework of bent bamboo is also typically filled with decorative panels. The association of the form to the ladies' quarters is based primarily on the effeminate, yet modern, term "rose chair" and as well, their diminutive size. It has also been suggested that their low height was well suited for placing under a window opening. That they were sometimes made in sets of four is suggested by another pair identical to these at the Victoria & Albert Museum. (Clunas: 30) Their feet, having also decomposed to lose considerable height, have since been restored with small ball-like pads. In all likelihood, all four chairs were once together and exposed to similar moist conditions – perhaps under leaking windows – for some period of time.

These exceptionally refined rose chairs are constructed of choice *huanghuali*. The members of the rectilinear framework are moulded with a variation of the melon profile, and are joined with mitred, mortise-and-tenon pipe joints. Aprons, curved in relief with angular scrolling on both sides, decorate and reinforce the backrest and armrests; below, a small balustrade-like railing – also "melon-shaped" in reduced scale – is fit to the top of the seat frame. The apron under the seat frame is juxtaposed with those above in its curvilinear profile with relief carving of scrolling grass. The *paktong* wrappings around the feet conceal restoration of height to feet which had deteriorated throughout centuries of standing and being moved about upon damp-to-wet surfaces.

十四．

玫瑰椅〔一對〕

黃花梨　十七世紀至十八世紀

59公分 寬 x 45公分 深 x 86公分 高，座高51公分

玫瑰椅的特徵是尺寸小、方形低靠背和低扶手，其中後兩點減低了椅子的舒適程度。它的基本樣式仿效小竹椅，方形的邊框通常都會加上裝飾的花板。由於玫瑰椅的尺寸較小，名稱雖現代卻又充滿女性味，常令人聯想起與閨房有關。由於它的後背矮，所以適合背靠窗臺置放。維多利亞博物館〔Clunas：30〕藏有一對相同的椅子，當初製作時應該是一組四件的，現在椅子已被削去相當高度，缺少部份補有球狀護墊。綜觀各種跡象，這四把椅子在某段時期間曾共處於潮濕的環境，也許是在漏水的窗臺前。

這對特別精緻的玫瑰椅是以精選的黃花梨製成，腿足開多種樣式的甜瓜稜，壺門式券口牙子，攢浮雕拐子紋，令搭腦和扶手更穩固；靠背、扶手和椅盤之間安一欄杆式造型的橫棖加矮老，橫棖和矮老皆起較小的甜瓜稜。椅盤下浮雕卷草紋牙板和牙頭之方形曲線，與上面的券口牙子同。腿足處白銅裹腿，是為了補回因暴露在潮溼環境時腐蝕了的部分。

15.
Low Seat with Adjustable Backrest
Bamboo and Zhajingmu/zhazhenmu   18th/19th century
Jiangsu Region   51 cm (w) x 34.5 cm (d) x 44 cm (h)

For centuries, low backrests and armrests were conveniences for sitting on the ground and on platforms; the backrest was also an accessory used for the enjoyment of erotic pleasure. Extant examples are relatively rare, with known examples numbering less than five. A black lacquer backrest in the Palace collection in Beijing is of somewhat similar construction to the piece illustrated here; furthermore, its acquisition from a workshop – also in the Jiangnan region – was noted in the Imperial Workshop archives after it was brought to the Palace in Beijing during the Yongzheng period. (Zhu 1: 110; Zhu and Wang: 117)

This unusual seat is comprised of three independent, yet interconnected, frames. Grooves cut along the inside edge of the seat and backrest side frame members house thin strips of bamboo to afford a cool, cushioned support. The seat frame extends behind the backrest to provide a base from where the support frame pivots into three adjustable positions.

十五 .
低坐可調節式靠背
竹和柞榴木／柞針木　十八世紀／十九世紀　江蘇地區
51公分 寬 x 34.5公分 深 x 44公分 高

多個世紀以來，低靠背和憑几是坐在地上或榻上時使用，而靠背亦曾被用作增添性情趣的工具。此類家具存世極少，目前已知的不到五件。北京故宮收藏的一件黑漆靠背與此件靠背做法極類似，是雍正時期在江南地區購得，宮廷營造機構的檔案中存有此購置記錄。〔朱：110；朱和王：117〕

這件罕有的椅座由三個既獨立又互有關聯的邊框組成。椅盤兩邊內側和靠背兩框的內側皆有凹槽，用來安裝竹條，使坐者感涼快和舒適。椅盤邊框延至靠背後成底座，椅背可作三段式調節。

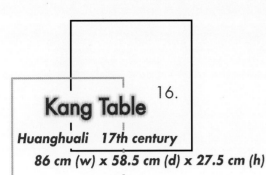

Low tables reflect the early mat level culture which existed in ancient China, although not entirely displaced by the later development of high seats and tables. During the Ming and Qing periods, low tables were still used on the ground or mats, as well as being placed upon raised platforms where they were used for dining, as a small reading table, or as a stand for flowers or a censer. These low tables exist in many sizes. In the colder northern regions of China such low tables were commonly placed upon raised brick platforms called *kang*, and as a result, came to be known as *kang* tables. The *kang* themselves ranged in size and combined to serve both as a heated bed and sitting space upon which various types of low furniture were placed.

This *kang* table has a choice single panel of finely figured *huanghuali* which is supported with three transverse braces below. The apron/waist sections are of one piece and carved at their midpoints with a decorative cloud motif, or perhaps, a stylised "sacred fungus of immortality" (*lingzhi*). Clouds, the source of rain and symbolic of good fortune and happiness, appear in many C-curved or scrolling amorphous forms, the latter of which often meld indistinguishably into stylised *ruyi* or *lingzhi* motifs. *Lingzhi*, traditionally rendered as a budding plant form, or developed with stem and leaves, offers the promise of longevity; its lobed head with handle-like stem is also closely associated to the *ruyi* as a wish-fulfilling device. The shoulders of the legs are carved in relief with a smoothly shaped lappet profiled with a *ruyi* cloud motif, which also appears as an abstracted *taotie* mask when viewed diagonally. The short cabriole legs terminate in scrolled feet, appearing like a coiled trunk sprouting leafy foliage.

炕桌 十六.

黃花梨 十七世紀

86公分 寬 x 58.5公分 深 x 27.5公分 高

矮桌反映了中國古代席地而坐的文化，後來發展的垂足坐椅和桌子沒法完全取代它。明、清年間，席地而坐或坐在蓆子上時仍使用矮桌，並且將之置於榻上作用膳、閱讀、花几、擺放香爐。這些矮桌或炕桌有許多不同尺寸。在中國較寒冷的北方，將此類型的桌子放在磚造的炕上，故稱炕桌。炕的面積也有大小，它是暖烘烘的床，也是坐的工具，上面放置不同的矮小的家具。

此炕桌的獨板面心以特選黃花梨製，花紋極美，下有三條穿帶。牙條和束腰部分一木連做，在牙條中間有大浪形如意雲紋或靈芝浮雕。雲是雨之源，也是好運和幸福的象徵，其形態有對稱的祥雲、蜿蜒舒卷的或毫無定狀的流雲，後者常常和如意及靈芝紋混合。靈芝傳統上是以含苞帶放的形式出現，或帶有枝葉，是長壽的象徵。其圓形突出的頭部和像手柄的枝幹，令人聯想到代表心想事成的如意。此桌腿足的肩部有緩慢下垂的輪廓，並有如意雲紋浮雕，從側面看像抽象的饕餮獸面紋。三彎腿至足部向內成卷書，上有卷葉浮雕。

17.
Square Kang Table

Huanghuali   late 16th/early 17th century

86.5 cm (w) x 86.2 cm (d) x 30.3 cm (h)

Low square tables were likely used much the same way that the square table of standard height was, and again reflect the early mat level culture of ancient China. A few extant square tables have detachable legs which may be used alternately as high or low tables; with legs removed, each appears as a low square table of similar height. (Ellsworth: 121, 123; Handler Sum 92: 43; Handler Aut 94: 21)

This unusually large square *kang* table is of waisted corner-leg form. The top frame is shaped with drip moulding around its outside edge and is fit with a three board panel plus a narrow strip that was likely a later addition. Each apron is carved in relief with entwined scrolling grass which rises from the beaded cusp along its midpoint. The rounded beading traces the curvilinear edge and flows around to the short cabriole leg where it terminates within the scrolled foot. The underside of the table is neatly finished with rounded-over edges on the transverse braces and frame members.

十七·
方型炕桌

黃花梨　十六世紀晚期／十七世紀初期

86.5公分 寬 x 86.2公分 深 x 30.3公分 高

矮方桌的使用和一般高度的方桌一樣，反映了中國古代席地而坐的文化。少數傳世的方桌有折腳，可以當高或矮方桌交替使用；把腳拆掉後，可成為高度相若的矮桌。〔Ellsworth：121，123；Handler Sum 92：43；Handler Aut 94：21〕

這件獨特的大方炕桌屬有束腰桌形結構，桌面邊框起冰盤沿，中納三塊面心板和一像是後加的直條。牙條的線腳在壺門中心升起成卷草紋浮雕，線腳沿著牙條的曲線與三彎腿足的線腳相接至足端，向內卷轉成珠而止。桌面底的邊框和穿帶皆精巧地倒稜成渾圓結構。

18.
Folding Low Table

72.5 cm (w) x 48 cm (d) x 28 cm (h)

Huanghuali   late 16th/early 17th century

Remnants of a low folding table were excavated from the Western Han (206 BC–23 AD) tomb of Prince Liu Sheng (Mancheng: 145). Evidence that such tables were once more common than the rarefied extant examples would suggest, can be found amongst the miscellaneous jottings of Ming scholars under the heading "Folding Tables" (*diezhuo*):

Of two, one measures 1 *chi*, 6 *cun* high, 3 *chi*, 2 *cun* long, 2 *chi*, 4 *cun* wide. The two sides have folding legs. When open it becomes a table; when folded, a case. It is rather convenient to carry along and use with a mat for drinking wine. The other, of similar folding style, measures 1 *chi*, 4 *cun* high, 1 *chi*, 2 *cun* high, 8 *cun* wide. Use water-polished (*shuimo*) *nanmu*. This table can be set up outside and arranged with a censer and a vase. [Tu 1: 241, Gao *juan* 8: 37b]

Here is direct reference to the use of a low table on a mat, presumably on the ground while on an outing. Perhaps because of the fragility of its moving parts, however, only a few folding *kang* tables have survived intact (cf. Bruce 1995: 26, Ellsworth: 112, Handler Sum 92: 40, Zhu and Wang: 140–1, Tian: 146, 158). According to Tian Jiaqing, "of all the folding and collapsible types of furniture that survive today, this *kang* table in the collection of Kai-Yin Lo is probably one of the most refined in design, material, and construction. The exceptional state of preservation makes it even more valuable to scholars and connoisseurs alike." (see this book's foreword: page 13)

This rare and ingeniously constructed low table has a waisted corner-leg form which folds. The top is constructed of two framed panels and joined with inset *paktong* hinges on top. The hinged *paktong* hasps mounted opposite on the underside permit the top to be locked into an open position. The top is vibrantly figured with narrow panels of small growth *huanghuali*. The segmented aprons along the long side meet at the cusped mid-point with splined tongue-and-groove joints where the end of each apron is also pinned to the frame with a wedge-shaped tenon dovetailed into its back. The short cabriole legs are shaped with a socket hinge configuration which permits the leg to be pulled out and folded diagonally into the underside of the table.

Previously published:

Bruce, Grace Wu. "Examples of Classic Chinese Furniture: 1. A Folding Table." *Oriental Art*. Winter 1990/91: 178, 233–5

National Heritage Board. *Asian Civilisations Museum; The Chinese Collections*: Singapore, 1997: No. 116

Piccus, Robert P. "Review of 'Best of the Best – An Exhibition of Ming Furniture from Private Collections.'" *Orientations*. February, 1995: 70

Wang Shixiang. "A Supplement to the Examples of Ming-Style Furniture" *Palace Museum Journal*. No. 1, 1993: 46–7

ibid. "Additional Examples of Classical Chinese Furniture." *Orientations*. January, 1992: 43

十八·

折疊桌

黃花梨　十六世紀晚期／十七世紀初期
72.5公分 寬 x 48公分 深 x 28公分高

西漢〔西元前206年至西元23年〕劉勝墓曾出土殘缺的折疊桌。〔滿城，145〕這類桌子曾經是非常普遍的家具，在明代學者的雜記中有記載，題為「疊桌」：

二張。一張高一尺六寸。長三尺二寸。闊二尺四寸。作二面折腳活法。展則成卓。疊則成匣。以便攜帶。席地用此。抬合以供?酤其小几一張。同上疊式。高一尺四寸。長一尺二寸。闊八寸。以水磨楠木為之。置之坐外。列爐焚香。置瓶插花。以供清賞。〔屠1：241，高卷8：37b〕

以上是出遊時席地而坐時使用矮桌的直接例證。大概是因為折疊桌可活動的部份較脆弱，只有極少數完整的作品能存留下來。〔比較 Bruce 1995：26，Ellsworth：112，Handler Sum 92：40，朱和王：140-1，田：146，158〕正如田家青指出：「在為數眾多的各式可折疊家具中，羅女士珍藏的這件炕桌無論在造型、用料還是結構的機巧上都相當精彩，而且保存完好，頗具研究價值。」〔見本書前言：頁13〕

這件少見的有束腰短桌，有可以折疊的束腰腿。桌面的硬板心由兩套邊框組成，上有白銅合頁將其聯成一體。相對於此合頁的桌底面安有白銅扣，在桌面展開後可牢牢鎖住。桌面是由小材黃花梨板拼成，大邊牙條在壹門中間尖端處分段，靠近分段處各開剔槽口，用一長銷像穿帶似的穿過去，上端出榫，納入大邊底面的榫眼中，使牙條固定貼緊。短三彎腿足的插座式合頁造型，可將腿足朝桌下對角臥倒或拉出。

曾經刊載於：

《亞洲文明博物館：中國文物收藏》，新加坡，1997：No.116

王世襄：〈明式家具實例增補〉，《故宮博物院院刊》，第1期，1993：46-7

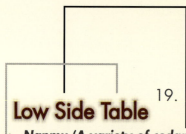

Low Side Table 19.

Nanmu (A variety of cedar)   17th/18th century   Jiangnan Region

168.5 cm (w) x 27 cm (d) x 36 cm (h)   The refined craftsmanship and style of this low table is typical of the fine furniture produced in the Jiangnan region during the seventeenth and eighteenth centuries. Although the masonry *kang* was not commonly used in the southern regions, southern-style furniture was shipped to the North along inland waterways. Long narrow low tables were used on platform beds, and were also placed upon large side tables or altar tables.

This long, narrow low table has a top panel of solid *nanmu*. Blind tenons secure the rounded-over everted flanges, of which each end is lightly carved with a scrolled volute. Each long apron is pinned at its midpoint with a wedged-shaped tenon housed in a dovetail groove. The aprons and spandrel heads are finely beaded, and the legs are moulded with "double incense stick" beading. The panel between the legs is pierced with a traditional opening, leaving a roundly modelled standing *ruyi*; a narrow panel above is cut out with a "begonia-shaped" opening. Along with other minor repairs, the feet and end aprons have been replaced.

十九 ·
炕案

楠木　十七世紀／十八世紀　江南地區

168.5公分 寬 x 27公分 深 x 36公分 高

此案的精湛手工和風格，代表了十七、十八世紀江南地區製造的精美家具。炕在南方並不普遍，但具有南方風格的家具可經內陸水運到北方。狹長的炕桌放在榻床上使用，也擺在大的條案或供桌上。

這件狹長炕案的案面以獨板楠木做成，翹頭以半榫相接，頂部淺浮雕捲曲的渦旋紋。長牙條的中段處有長銷以悶榫和大邊相接。牙板和牙頭皆起優美的陽線，案足起兩炷香線。擋板透雕向上翻出的如意雲頭成一傳統的花紋；其上有透雕海棠式紋樣小板。全案有少許修繕，案足和側牙板為新作取代。

20a.
Occasional Table

Yumu (Northern Elm) and Lacquer   18th/19th century   Shanxi
109 cm (w) x 46 cm (d) x 84 cm (h)

20b.
Occasional Table

Yumu (Northern Elm) and Lacquer   17th century   Shanxi
102.5 cm (w) x 64.5 cm (d) x 85 cm (h)

Tables of this style are called *zhuo*, instead of *an*, by the cabinet makers in Beijing's carpenter district and in most of northern China even though they bear characteristics of the latter. *Xiaozhuo* (food tables), *jiuzhou* (wine tables), *qinzhuo* (lute tables), and *gongzhuo* (altar tables) which are laden with sacrificial offerings and are placed in front of shrines, religious statues and ancestral tablets, are further examples. The style of these tables, with inserted shoulder joint construction, was developed by the Five Dynasties period (907–23) (Chen: 24–8), and survived as a traditional style through the Ming period. Numerous examples of vernacular softwood furniture of this form dating from the eighteenth and nineteenth centuries have been found in the conservative Shanxi region.

The Shanxi table of northern elm and lacquer (Plate 20a) has through tenons visible on the longer side of the top framework. Enclosed in the framework are three floating panels supported by three transverse stretchers. Iron nails have been used to reinforce the joint between the apron and the longer sides of the top framework. Relief-carved motifs are found where the two beaded-edge side stretchers meet the legs. The top stretcher is hidden-tenoned to the legs while the lower one has tenons exposed. A single raised beading runs down the centre of the legs and passes through the exposed tenons. The legs have been shortened by 1–3 cm due to their tips being slightly worn out.

The 17th century table (Plate 20b), of a sturdy yet elegant design derived from Jin and Yuan styles, has many distinctive features. The legs are joined to the apron with mitred bridle joints. The top frame is surrounded by an "ice-plate" edge. Two scroll carvings decorate each of the front and back stretchers. The cusped "horse-belly" shaped apron has a scrolled edge that flows smoothly down the legs with two lines of raised beading in the centre, ending in a leaf pattern resting on a pedestal shaped like an inverted lotus leaf. The legs of this table, both in design and execution, are unusual and refined. Despite its age, the ends of the legs are in relatively good condition as the low humidity of Shanxi province has prevented rotting.

插肩榫平頭桌　　二十a.

北方榆〔榆木〕　十八世紀／十九世紀　山西
109公分 寬 x 46公分 深 x 84公分 高

插肩榫花腿平頭桌　　二十b.

榆木髹漆　十七世紀　山西
102.5公分 寬 x 64.5公分 深 x 85公分 高

在北京魯班館及北方廣大地區，稱這種具有案型結構的家具為「桌」，已經是約定俗成。例如肴桌（油桌）、酒桌、琴桌及供桌。這種稱謂在家具分類學上是比較特殊。

這類型的小桌常靠牆而放，上置香爐或花瓶。類似尺寸的桌案也用來彈琴，因為便於移動，也可以放在床邊或移到花園用來吃飯或飲酒。插肩榫結構最早出現於五代（公元907–23）〔陳：24–8〕，一直流傳至明代成為了傳統的營造法。在落後的山西地區，就發現了多件此類型的柴木家具，屬於十八至十九世紀之製作。

"插肩榫法"一詞通常指腿足上截有斜肩榫與牙條相接合。此件小平頭案的腿足皆為透榫在大邊出透眼（圖版20a）。三板面心由三穿帶支撐。牙板與大邊接合處安有鍛鐵釘。腿足與兩根起線橫棖相接處雕有突狀紋樣；上面的橫棖以半榫相接；下面橫棖以透榫相接，腿足起延續不斷的一炷香線，貫穿橫棖的透眼斷面木紋。腿足底部有少許因風化造成的毫損，令整張案的高度減少了一至三公分。

供桌是放在神龕、佛像、祖先牌位前，用來擺放祭品和供物的。此供桌通體髹飾黑漆，造型穩健質樸，粗獷中帶幾分秀美，與金、元時期的家具風格一脈相承（圖版20b），是榆木供桌中的皎皎者。這件案型結構的供桌用插肩榫做法，桌面四攢邊，裝芯板，有欄水線，四面是冰盤沿線腳。牙板為彎曲有力的壺門陽線，與桌腿所起的陽線相連。腿下部份由迴轉曲線組成葉狀輪廓，並內翻為一片花葉。套住葉頸部的線上揚成兩炷香線腳。桌腿踩珠，珠下有一俯置荷葉小托，構思清新，大大豐富了桌腿的造型。由於此桌地處山西中部，氣候乾燥，雖然經過幾百年，腿端未有腐朽，保存原有桌腿全貌。前後桌腿，間連以起委角線的羅鍋棖。拱起的內側雕有一支婉約的草卷，造型生動而有神韻。

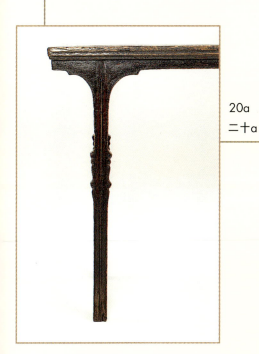

20a
二十a

20b
二十b

21.
Occasional Table

Jichimu (Chicken-wing wood)   18th century   Beijing

128 cm (w) x 42.5 cm (d) x 85.5 cm (h)

This table shows attributes of Imperial Workshop quality. Notes from the Yongzheng period record numerous food and wine tables made of precious hardwoods such as *huanghuali*, *jichimu*, *zitan* and *nanmu*. The exceptionally refined workmanship also reflects the early to mid-Qing *fanggu* tradition, led by the Imperial Court itself, of imitating antique forms and decorative motifs. The refined detailing of the legs with cloud-shaped flanges can be compared to those rendered in early paintings and in furniture of the Five Dynasties and Jin periods. (Chen : 24-8)   This table is similar in construction and style to other mid-Qing tables executed by the Palace Workshops. (Tian: 182) Tian Jiaqing comments that the craftsmen capable of the superlative 'zitan finishing' required by the Qing court were most probably recruited from Suzhou. (see this book's foreword: page 17)

This table, of inserted shoulder joint form, has several distinguishing technical merits of note: 1) the underside of the frame and its three transverse braces are unusually moulded with beaded edges; 2) the fine lines of raised beading – which accent the deeply curved and cusped line of the apron, decorate the top of each leg with a compound *ruyi* cloud design, and continue down the leg with additional *ruyi* clouds at the flange and again at the foot – has been produced by removing material from the remainder of the entire surface; 3) each leg, including spandrels and flanges, is shaped from one piece of wood; and 4) a clear indication of Imperial workmanship is demonstrated by each end panel, of joined construction with a standing *ruyi*, which is framed by a table top transverse brace intentionally aligned with the stretcher below.

二十一.
平頭案

128公分 寬 x 42.5公分 深 x 85.5公分 高

雞翅木　十八世紀　北京

此案有宮廷營造機構的特點。雍正年間的記錄載有多款飯桌和酒桌,是用珍貴的硬木如黃花梨、雞翅、紫檀和楠木做成。清初、中葉仿古形制和花紋的風格,亦反映了工匠精湛的技藝。在早期的繪畫和五代出土文物及家具,可找到類似腿足細緻的雲頭雕飾〔陳:24-28〕。此案的結構與風格,跟清中葉宮廷作坊的近似〔田:182〕,田家青認為清宮廷裡那些懂得"紫檀作工"的工匠,應是從蘇州徵聘而來的。(見本書前言:頁17)

這件插肩榫結構的平頭案有下列幾項特點:〔一〕案面裡的邊框和三條穿帶皆破格地起線腳。〔二〕沿著具有大弧度曲線的牙條起陽線和腿足上端的如意雲頭浮雕交圈,陽線延續不斷和腿足中間以及腿足底的突出如意雲頭紋相交。〔三〕每根腿足,包括突出的飾物,皆為一木連做。〔四〕橫板安有向上翻出如意雲頭,向上和穿帶、向下和橫棖分別對齊。這些皆是宮廷之製作特色。

22. Table with Detachable Legs

Jichimu (Chicken-wing wood) **18th/19th century** *Fujian*
110.5 cm (w) x 58 cm (d) x 83.5 cm (h)

Tables with detachable legs were constructed for ease of storage and portability. The upper part is generally made to a height corresponding to that of the traditional *kang* table, and was thus also suitable for use as a low table. (cf. Ellsworth: 121,123; Wang and Evarts: 106) In light of this table's design and construction, the entry in the *Lu Ban jing* for "folding tables" (*zhezhuo*), which has previously been difficult to interpret (Ruitenbeek: 238; Evarts Win 93: 39), seems now to be clarified. After some nominal measurements are given regarding the top frame and leg members, the entry continues:

The leopard legs (short cabriole, or curvilinear legs) are *5 cun, 7 fen* long, *1 cun, 1 fen* thick, and *2 cun, 3 fen* wide [and] are curved with a double line of raised beading. Each leg [unit] must be joined with two tenons to the leopard legs, only then are they secured firmly without movement. (trans. after Ruitenbeck II: 49)

The inclusion of this type of table in the *Lu Ban jing* also suggests that it was once a common vernacular form.

The upper part of this table appears like a low table of inserted shoulder joint construction. The top frame is typically constructed and houses a wide single panel; however, the aprons below deviate from the traditional shape with a radiused upper edge. Also uncommon is the half floral-button carved in relief at the top of each short leg, from which more traditional parallel lines of "double incense stick" beading extend downward to the foot pad. The back of each leg is shaped with a groove into which the leg frames are easily slid. The double stretchers of the leg frames are each firmly attached to the legs with through tenons to create solid detachable leg unit; leg and stretcher members are all shaped with indented corner mouldings. A sliding tenon near the top of each leg provides a locking mechanism.

折桌

二十二.

雞翅木　十八世紀／十九世紀　福建
110.5公分 寬 x 58公分 深 x 83.5公分 高

折桌便於收藏和攜帶。上面部分的桌面高度通常和炕桌一樣，因此也適合拿來當矮桌使用。〔比較 Ellsworth：121，123；Wang 和 Evarts：106〕透過此桌子的設計和營造，過去在解釋《魯班經》的「折桌」時所遇到難解之處〔Ruitenbeek：238；Evart Win 93：39〕，現在可迎刃而解。在量過框和腳足之後，文章續道：「... 豹腳五寸七分長，一寸一分厚，二寸三分大，雕雙線趕雙均〔鉤〕。每腳上要二榫鬥，豹腳上要二榫鬥，豹腳上方欞，不會動。」《魯班經》中的收錄和介紹，顯示出這類桌子曾在民間普遍使用。

此桌的上半部為插肩榫結構的炕几。桌面邊框為典型的營造法以裝納獨板面心；之下的牙條和牙頭則脫離傳統形式，雕成幅射弧形。短腿足上端浮雕半個如花扭扣紋，由此紋起兩炷香線紋至腿足底部之上。每根腿足背面剔榫槽便於安裝、拆卸。腿足側面的雙橫棖以透榫與腿足堅固地相接，用以營造可分離穩當的足部構件。腿足上端的滑動榫具鎖定功能。

23. Side Table

Tieli and Huamu (Burl)   18th century   Shanxi

96 cm (w) x 48.5 cm (d) x 85.5 cm (h)

The form of this table appears in a painting attributed to the Yuan dynasty where, on a garden terrace, scholarly gentlemen are gathered about enjoying paintings, and a square table, appearing like a waisted *kang* table raised to chair height with separate leg extensions, is set out with precious objects. (Suzhou 1981: 2, Nan Song: 60) A number of similarly styled tables with detachable legs have also survived in hardwoods. (cf. Plate 22; Ellsworth: 121, 123; Handler Sum 92: 43; Handler Aut 94: 21; Min Chiu: 279) However, that there is also a significant group which is only imitative in style with regard to actual detachable legs suggests a rather curious fashion for functionless form. (cf. Berliner: 135; Clunas: 47; Wang: 139, Min Chiu: 276) Such fashion may point to the Yongzheng and Qianlong periods when the artifice of materials and finishes was practised throughout the decorative arts and reached the height of technical achievement.

The frame and legs of this table are made from *tieli* wood, and the top features a decorative panel of burl with a clustered-grape figure – perhaps the burl of camphor. The single piece apron/waist sections are each pinned to the frame with long dovetail wedges. Each short cabriole leg, along with its longer round-leg extension, is shaped from one piece of wood.

二十三·　展腿式半桌

鐵力木和樺木　十八世紀　山西

96公分 寬 x 48.5公分 深 x 85.5公分 高

在一幅元朝的繪畫中可見此桌的樣式，畫中文人雅士聚集在花園繪畫，在一件似乎是有束腰、齊椅高度方炕桌上置放珍貴的物品，桌腳是另外加長。〔蘇州1981：2，南宋：60〕另外也有幾件類似式樣，且具有展腿的硬木作品留傳下來。〔比較圖版21；Ellsworth：121, 123；Handler Sum 92：43；Handler Aut 94：21，敏求精舍：279〕此外，有另一組重要的作品專仿其風格，展足部分並不實用，只著重奇特的造型。〔比較 Berliner：135；Clunas：47；王：139, 敏求精舍：276〕此風格跟雍正、乾隆時期，各種裝飾紋樣的模仿技術達到爐火純青的地步有關。

此桌邊框和腿足由鐵力做成，面心板為裝飾性的癭木板，上有成串成串的葡萄紋樣，似是樟木癭。一木連做的束腰和牙板中段裡側以穿銷和大邊相接，三彎腿和圓腿足亦是一木連做。

24a. Square Table with Corner Spandrels

Jumu (Southern Elm)   18th century   Beijing   108 cm (w) x 108 cm (d) x 84 cm (h)

24b. Square Table with Corner Spandrels

Baimu (Cypress)   18th/19th century   Suzhou   95.2 cm (w) x 81.5 cm (d) x 81.5 cm (h)

These square tables are traditional example of the "one leg, three spandrels" (*yitui sanya*) category. Their dynamic architectural form reflects the bracketed post-and-beam construction of ancient Chinese wood structures whose corner columns are slightly canted inward – a feature which both pleases the eye and adds stability to the structure. The similar architectural terminology "one bracket, three lifts" (*yidou sansheng*), describing the cantilever system under the traditional Chinese roof, may further extend the relationship. Pottery models of the "one leg, three spandrel" table excavated from Ming dynasty grave sites in Shanxi province (Keppel: 17) as well as its depiction in late Ming book illustrations confirm a style clearly associated with the Ming dynasty. The tradition of producing similar forms of furniture in both carved and plain styles can be traced to the *Lu Ban jing*. (Ruitenbeek II: 55–6, 75). Similar square tables of corresponding "decoratively carved" and "plain" styles are also found in *huanghuali* wood. (cf. Wang 1986: 142–3)

Of *jumu*, the top of the large square table from Beijing (Plate 24a) has a raised "drip-edge" moulding around it. Other than the beaded edges along the aprons and corner spandrels, the table is plainly styled. (cf. Wang and Evarts: 46) The top panel is unusually supported; four rather large transverse braces run perpendicular to the grain direction, and two secondary supports run parallel to the grain direction. The two-piece humpback stretchers are joined at their midpoints and pinned to the underside of the apron.

The top frame of the *baimu* table from Suzhou (Plate 24b) is shaped with a wide drip-edge moulding around the top outside edge; below, an additional moulding is typically pinned to the lower edge. The five-piece panel is cradled with two transverse stretchers spanning both directions, each with tenons exposed through its wide frame. The three beaded spandrels form three dimensional *ruyi* around each leg. The two-piece beaded humpback stretchers – deeply arched and pinned against the horizontal apron as well as to the legs – lend triangular reinforcement to the legs, as well as visual support to the table top. The legs are shaped with indented corner mouldings.

二十四a.
一腿三牙方桌

櫸木　十八世紀　北京
108公分 寬 x 108公分 深 x 84公分 高

二十四b.
一腿三牙方桌

柏木　十八世紀／十九世紀　蘇州
95.2公分 寬 x 81.5公分 深 x 81.5公分 高

此桌屬於傳統的「一腿三牙」造型。勻稱的建築式樣比例反映中國古代木結構中的樑柱營造，既悦目又可增加穩定性。中國建築術語中的「一斗三升」，是形容傳統的屋簷斗拱，這也或可用來解釋「一腿三牙」。山西省明墓出土的一腿三牙桌子陶器〔Keppel：17〕和晚明書中的插畫皆證明此為明朝的形式。製造此一家具的傳統，不論是雕刻或是光素，均見於《魯班經》。〔Ruitenbeek II：55、56、75〕具有裝飾性雕刻或光素的相類似的方桌，也有用黃花梨做成。〔比較王1986：142-3〕

這件來自北京的櫸木特大方桌（圖版24a），上部裝飾有升高的水滴狀邊緣，除了桌角和遮板處的珠狀邊緣外，造型極光素，（比較 Wang 和 Evarts：46）。桌子上部通常是有支撐的，四條相當大的交叉根子垂直於重心方向，而另外兩件則平行於地面，在這些根子中間又有兩件弓背根子，插入遮板的下部。

產於蘇州的柏木桌子（圖版24b）上部有凸線沿邊，下部再加一凸線，桌面由五條小木板拼成，其下有縱橫兩條交叉的根子，每一件都有榫頭和桌體相連，每一桌腿裝飾有三個由珠狀牙子所構成的如意。兩件弧度甚大的弓背根子，在沿水平方向插入遮板和桌腿后，形成了三角狀的支架，加固了桌腿的承受力，同時也有效地支撐了桌子的上部，四條桌腿則有齒狀邊沿。

25.
Bamboo-Style Table

Longyanmu (Longan)   18th/19th century   Fujian

119 cm (w) x 78 cm (d) x 84 cm (h)

The versatility and practicality of common bamboo as a material of ten thousand uses, along with other essential characteristic qualities, has earned it the exalted position as a symbol of virtue. Lacking permanence, however, bamboo was frequently reproduced in more durable materials. The popularisation of stylised forms of bamboo furniture produced in precious hardwoods is particularly evident during the eighteenth century. However, Wen Zhenheng's early seventeenth century notation regarding beds of recent manufacture that were "carved like bamboo from cypress" offers perhaps the earliest evidence of this newly emerging furniture style. (Wen *juan* 6: 4b)

The individual members of this small desk-like table are shaped from *longyanmu* to appear as bamboo, a material which further replicates its soft warm colour and fine texture. Wide frame members (12 x 5 cm) house a two-piece panel featuring prized material with rippling grain figure. Mouldings attached to the frame mimic the stacked construction of real bamboo furniture; most of the small bracket-like spandrels have been replaced. The humpback stretchers are steadied with short pillared struts, and their ends are neatly shaped so as to appear to wrap around the legs. Each leg, shaped from single piece of wood, appears as a four-piece bundle of bamboo.

二十五．
竹式桌

龍眼木　十八世紀／十九世紀　福建

119公分 寬 x 78公分 深 x 84公分 高

一般竹子的用途千變萬化。由於竹不能長久保存，故很多時候會以其它耐用的材料仿製。十八世紀時，流行以耐用、珍貴的硬木仿造竹製家具。十七世紀早期，文震亨對當時「以柏木刻出竹紋」營造家具的記錄，可能是此種新家具風格最早的文字記載。〔文 卷6：4b〕

此張桌式家具是以福建楓木，〔又稱龍眼木〕製成，其和暖的色系和質感看似竹。寬邊抹〔12 x 5公分〕內安有極優質的兩板合拼面心，上有波浪紋。邊框的起線模仿竹家具的結構，牙板皆為新做。桌面和羅鍋棖之間有矮老，兩根在腿足相交處也雕成渾圓狀，像是將腿足包裹起來一樣。每根腿足為一木雕成，外觀狀似四根一捆的竹子。

26.
High Waisted Table
Huanghuali late 16th/early 17th century
167.2 cm (w) x 62.5 cm (d) x 81.5 cm (h)

Although of manifold use, large tables are most frequently associated as the centre-piece of the scholar's studio. There it was used for painting, calligraphy, and reading, and may have been set out with a few carefully placed utensils such as an inkstone, a brushpot, a brush, a water vessel, and perhaps, a small table screen. Similar to this table's high waisted form and overall proportion is a miniature wood table excavated from the late Ming tomb of Pan Yunzheng. (Berliner: 76) The structural dynamics of the high waist provided additional lateral support to early tables that were otherwise without braces. Later developments with the vertical dovetail wedge concealed within the corner-leg joint provided the lateral reinforcement which permitted lighter, more elegant, open forms. (Evarts Win 90: 22)

The narrow frame (4.3 cm wide) of this table houses a relatively wide single panel of beautifully figured *huanghuali* (54.4 cm wide). The panel is supported below with five transverse braces. Large dovetail wedges pin the two piece apron/waist sections to the underside of the frame. The entire underside retains much of its original lacquer undercoating. Concave beading accents the edge of the apron and continues down the leg where it terminates at the hoof foot.

二十六．
高束腰條案

黃花梨 十六世紀晚期 ／ 十七世紀初期

167.2公分 寬 x 62.5公分 深 x 81.5公分 高

儘管大桌有許多不同的用法，它通常是文人書房裡重要的家具，常用來繪畫、寫字、閱讀，桌上精心擺設文房四寶和桌屏。晚明潘允徵墓出土一件相同高束腰形式但整體比例縮小的袖珍木桌〔Berliner：76〕。高束腰型式的結構，為早期無棖桌提供額外的側面支撐，後來發展出來隱藏在腿足的垂直穿銷，提供側面補強作用，讓桌子看起來輕便、高雅和開揚。〔Evarts Win 90：22〕

這張案邊框較長〔4.3公分寬〕，安一紋理極美的黃花梨獨板〔54.4公分寬〕面心。面心由五根穿帶支撐。兩木分做的束腰和牙子由一大穿銷與邊底部相接。整個裡皮仍保留大部分原來的底漆。牙子大挖作法的線腳在與腿足的線腳相接後延續至馬蹄足而止。

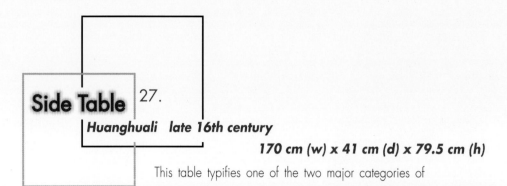

Side Table 27.

Huanghuali   late 16th century

170 cm (w) x 41 cm (d) x 79.5 cm (h)

This table typifies one of the two major categories of Chinese furniture construction techniques termed "recessed-leg construction" which is closely related to traditional post-and-beam architectural construction. Reduced to a smaller scale in furniture-making, the basic technique revolves around a horizontal panel (be it for a seat, table top or cabinet top), and four legs, joined at points inset (or "recessed") from the corners of the top frame. The legs splay outward toward the base, and are connected by various configurations of stretchers and/or aprons. The universal style of tables, bench, and stools which follow this basic pattern was well developed by the Song dynasty. While this table is of common form, its aesthetic merit lies in its excellent material and overall proportions, such a balanced, elegant stance recalls the Chinese proverb, "When the root is firm, the branches will flourish" (*bengu zhirong*).

This side table is of standard recessed-leg form and construction. The top features a single panel contained within a neatly moulded frame. The aprons are shaped with a beaded edge; the apron spandrel-heads are joined with half-lap mitres; one end apron has been replaced. The underside of the table retains much of Its original lacquer undercoating.

條案　二十七.

黃花梨　十六世紀晚期

170公分 寬 x 41公分 深 x 79.5公分 高

此條案屬中國傳統家具兩大分類之一的案型結構營造，與傳統建築式樑柱營造有密切關係。在一水平板面下〔例如座面、桌面或是櫃頂〕向內縮進安上四腿，且四腿為側腳，以橫根、牙條的結構聯接四腿。宋代此種營造桌子、條凳和凳子的基本方法已十分發達。雖然這件桌子設計普通，它的優點在於卓越的用料、整體的均衡比例，讓人連想到「本固枝榮」的成語。

這件條案屬標準夾頭榫營造。桌面為獨板面心，安在整齊起線的冰盤沿邊框中。牙條起線，牙頭以夾頭榫結構相接；一牙頭為新做。裏皮仍留有原來漆裏。

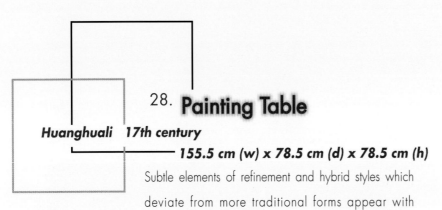

28. Painting Table

Huanghuali 17th century

155.5 cm (w) x 78.5 cm (d) x 78.5 cm (h)

Subtle elements of refinement and hybrid styles which deviate from more traditional forms appear with increased frequency during the early Qing period. These are due in part to the atmosphere of innovation at the Imperial Workshops as well as to the advancement of new ideas for furniture design by Li Yu and other avant-garde individuals who were challenging traditional conventions.

This table is of standard recessed-leg form and construction; however, it is also detailed with several notable, yet subtle, refinements: 1) the surrounding edge of the frame is moulded with a band of raised double beading; 2) the aprons are outlined with wide concave beading; 3) the legs are moulded to a "melon-shaped" profile raised with double beading on four sides, and 4) single humpback stretchers of similarly moulded profile join each pair of legs.

二十八 · 畫案

黃花梨 十七世紀

155.5公分 寬 x 78.5公分 深 x 78.5公分 高

清初宮廷營造機構改革創新的潮流，以及李漁和一些前衛人士對傳統形式作出質疑，提倡新的家具設計，導致愈來愈多的傳統設計衍生出精緻且多樣的變化，結合了多種不同的風格。

這是一件標準的案型結構營造，其中也有幾點值得注意：〔一〕邊抹四周起雙線腳；〔二〕牙條和牙頭起線腳有窪面；〔三〕每瓣起雙線類似甜瓜稜腿足；〔四〕腿足側面為樸素但起相同線腳的羅鍋根。

29.
Formal Side Table with Everted Flanges
Baimu (Cypress)   *18th/19th century*   *Shanxi*
219 cm (w) x 47 cm (d) x 91.5 cm (h)

In households throughout China, long side tables were commonly placed against the back wall of the main room as an altar where ancestral tablets, images of Buddhist and Daoist deities, and/or various ceremonial vessels and utensils were arranged; a scroll painting was usually hung directly above. Depending on the degree of devotion amongst family members, periodic to regular offerings of food and incense were set out to acknowledge patrilineal descent and communal links. Relative to the one-piece leg construction of this table, an interesting passage is found in the Wanli period publication *Zhangwu zhi* [Treatise on Superfluous Things], where the construction of such tables with solid wood tops and gently rounded everted flanges is praised along with the following comments:

do not use four legs such as painting tables have...... use pieces of thick wide timber like that of the top, hollow them out and carve them lightly with designs such as cloud scrolls and *ruyi* heads. They must not be carved with such vulgar patterns as dragons, phoenixes, flowers, and grass. The long, narrow ones made recently are abominable. (Wen *juan* 6: 2a)

This long narrow side table also has a sold one-piece top which is fit with gently rounded everted ends. Each leg panel is also shaped from a solid single panel which has been pierced with a decorative opening and standing *ruyi*-like *lingzhi* motif.

二十九 ·
翹頭案
柏木　十八世紀／十九世紀　山西
219公分 寬 x 47公分 深 x 91.5公分 高

在中國的家庭裡，常在廳堂內的正面靠牆處擺放一長的條案當成神桌使用，並在上面安放祖先靈位、佛教或是道教神位以及一些儀式用器皿和香燭；往往在牆上懸掛畫軸，並且定時供奉食物和點香來祭祀祖先。萬曆年間刊行的《長物志》裡，有一段描述與此一木連做的腿足營造法有關，文中讚美一木連做腿足的獨板翹頭案做法，並有以下的論述：「......不可用四足如書桌式。或以古樹根承之不則。用木如臺面闊厚者空其中略雕雲頭如意之類。不可雕龍鳳花艸諸俗式。近時所製近狹而長者最可厭」。〔文 卷 6：2a〕

這件狹長的條案有一獨立面板，兩端加翹頭。兩腿足之間的擋板一木連做，透雕了傳統的靈芝紋。

Double Cabinet

30.

Yumu (Northern Elm)   19th Century   Suzhou

227 cm (w) x 51 cm (d) x 214 cm (h)

Cabinets were used in the study to store books, paintings, and treasured objects – bedrooms were furnished with clothing cupboards, and shops of every kind imaginable also had cabinets, shelves and chests laden with goods. Traditionally, there are two types of Chinese cabinets: tapered cabinets, which follow the recessed-leg construction pattern, and square-cornered cabinets, which are constructed with a mitred, mortise-and-tenon box frame. This rare and unusual double-cabinet appears as a hybridised version of a tapered cabinet.

Elm of excellent, uniform quality has been used throughout the main body of this cabinet. The four doors and two side frames are each fit with finely figured single-board panels featuring "layered mountain" grain patterning. Although the construction pattern generally adheres to the recessed-leg techniques, no splay has been imported to the legs. Two rows of shelves span the interior space, and shallow drawers are fitted at the bottom. Otherwise, the interior space is undivided. The shelves at the back of the cabinet are made from pine. This cabinet was found in excellent condition, with little apparent use.

三十.

連體櫃

榆木　十九世紀　蘇州

227公分 寬 x 51公分 深 x 214公分 高

櫃子置於書房用來擺放書籍、畫軸和珍貴物品；也放在臥房儲存衣物；各店家也有各式各樣的櫃子擺放貨品。傳統上，櫃分為兩大類：一是圓角櫃，以案型結構營造；另一為方角櫃，以格角榫攢邊營造箱形邊框。這件罕有獨特的連體櫃為混合的圓角櫃。

櫃的整體以木紋精美的榆木製成。四扇門和兩側櫃幫皆為有「層山木紋」的獨板，雖然是依案型結構營造，但沒有側腳。櫃內有兩格板分隔空間，下安淺的抽屜，背板為松木製成。櫃的狀況極佳，過去似乎不常用。

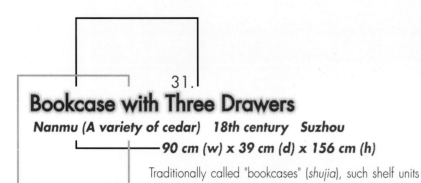

31.
Bookcase with Three Drawers
Nanmu (A variety of cedar)   18th century   Suzhou
90 cm (w) x 39 cm (d) x 156 cm (h)

Traditionally called "bookcases" (*shujia*), such shelf units also served to display precious objects. In regions with perpetual or seasonal high humidity, bookcases and cabinets were often constructed with high legs, or placed upon short stands to distance the bottom of the cabinet from fungus and mould which were destructive to paper and fabric.

This slim-styled bookcase is constructed in two parts: the upper bookcase, and the lower stand with drawers. The frame of the upper bookcase is constructed with mitred, mortise-and-tenon joinery. The shelf frames are constructed from two-piece panels. The top shelf is also fit with a flush panel above and a slightly recessed panel to its underside, with its two cross stretchers invisibly sandwiched in between. The stretchers on the lower shelves, being somewhat less visible, are not concealed. The top of the bookcase stand is fit with four shallow sockets which receive the square legs of the bookcase; below, three drawers provide additional storage.

三十一 ·
三抽屜書櫥
楠木　十八世紀　蘇州
90公分 寬 x 39公分 深 x 156公分 高

書架除了用來放書本，也用來擺放珍貴的物品。在終年或季節性潮濕的地區，通常將書架或櫃子做成高腳，或在櫃下放一矮座，避免長霉損壞紙和紡織物。

這件窄長的書架由兩部分組成：上面是書架，下面是有抽屜的底座。上半部書架的邊框是以格角榫攢邊法營造。書架的頂層以兩塊面心板合成。上面是平鑲面心板，兩個面心板之間有兩根穿帶。下面的兩格板皆為兩拼的單層面心板。下面底座的面板四角有略為下凹的方眼用來放上面書架的腿足；底座有三個抽屜增加儲存空間。

32.
Compound Cabinets (Pair)

Yumu (Northern Elm) and Huamu (Burl) 19th century Beijing
100.5 cm (w) x 45.5 cm (d) x 225.5 cm (h)

The traditional Chinese house was not constructed with built-in closets. Thus, storage was accomplished by cabinets and chests of various sizes and configurations. Compound wardrobes are comprised of upper and lower units. The doors of each are generally fitted with a removable central stile, so that long scrolls, folded garments, or bolts of fabric could conveniently be placed across the entire width of the shelves. A concealed space for storage of valuables is located behind the panel below the doors, and is accessed through removable lids inside the cabinet. Seldom used items or out-of-season garments were presumably placed in the upper cabinet, which required a small ladder or stool for access.

These cabinets are predominantly constructed with elm, and the door panels all feature bookmatched panels of elm burl rich with embryonic abstraction. Wide aprons at the base of the lower units conceal the front, lower frame members, and each is carved in relief with mirrored decoration of auspicious motifs, including tea ware, a censer with a *lingzhi* branch, a plate on a stand with pomegranates, Buddha's hand fruit, a *ruyi* sceptre, and a vase with a sprig of flowering magnolias. The reflected decoration on the two aprons, along with the asymmetrical, yet mirrored construction techniques employed on each of the two cabinets suggests that they were originally made to be placed side by side.

三十二.
四件櫃〔一對〕

榆木和榆樺木　十九世紀　北京
100.5公分 寬 x 45.5公分 深 x 225.5公分 高

傳統的中國家庭沒有依牆而做的固定衣櫥，儲放衣物的櫃子、櫥子有不同的尺寸和造型。四件櫃由上、下兩個單元合成。櫃門有活動的閂杆，以便利用整個櫃子的寬度放置長軸、摺疊起來的衣物或是布匹卷。貴重的物品放在櫃門下的櫃膛裡，櫃子裡有一活動的蓋子蓋住櫃膛。因為要用小梯子或凳子才搆得著頂箱，所以不常用的物品或過了季節的衣物通常置放於此。

此櫃大體是榆木做成，櫃門用整板對開，榆木瘿抽象的紋理對稱。立櫃底下寬大的牙條取代蓋住前面下部的邊框。兩片牙條上浮雕對稱的吉祥紋樣，包括茶具、插有靈芝的香爐、放在几上的盤子內盛石榴、佛手、如意笏和內插木棉花枝花瓶。牙條上對稱的裝飾更進一步地看出這兩組頂箱立櫃原是擺在一起的。

33.

Small Cabinet

Longyanmu (Longan)   18th/19th Century   Fujian

40 cm (w) x 21.5 cm (d) x 55 cm (h)   This small table-top cabinet bears marked characteristics of Fujianese regional style. The long, narrow pulls, the bulging of the lower front frame member to house the door pivots, and the decorative profile of the aprons are all typical elements of Fujianese tapered cabinets. *Jichimu* and *longyanmu* are both native to Fujian, and were favourite woods of local furniture-makers.

Made from *longyanmu* with a flaming curly-grained figure, an exceptionally dramatic impression is created by the bookmatched door panels as they radiate outward from the centre. The top panel is a solid board fit with breadboard ends, and panels similarly figured to the doors are found on the back and sides. The aprons are beaded on the front, and plain on the sides. The inside is fit with a single shelf.

三十三·

小圓角櫃

龍眼木　十八世紀／十九世紀　福建

40公分 寬 x 21.5公分 深 x 55公分 高

這件桌上型小圓角櫃深具福建地方特色。窄長的拉手、噴出的前面底枨以納門軸和牙條、牙頭的裝飾紋樣皆為福建式縮小圓角櫃的要素。雞翅木和龍楊木原產於福建,曾是福建家具工匠最喜用的木料。

此櫃以有火焰木紋的中國楓木一類的龍眼木做成,用整板對開紋理對稱的面心,以極引人注目的火燄般紋理,由中心向外形成輻射狀紋樣。櫃帽面心為獨板以透榫拍抹頭法安上。後面及側面也用類似櫃門紋樣的面板。前面牙條和牙頭有起線,側面的則為素牙條,櫃內安一格板。

34. Large Tiered Box

Liumu (Willow)   18th/19th century   Shanxi
82 cm (w) x 54 cm (d) x 93.5 cm (h)

Descriptions of large and small carrying boxes are found in the Ming dynasty carpenter's manual *Lu Ban jing*. Although their use is commonly associated with carrying food, these handy portable units, with tiered trays and carrying racks, were used for organisation and transportation of an endless range of goods. Several episodes from the novel *Jin Ping Mei* are illustrative.

(1)   When Li Ping'er asks Ximen to bribe an official on her husband's behalf with sixty large bars of silver, Ximen sends his servants to carry away the silver in food boxes (*shihe*) so as not to arouse the suspicions of neighbours. (*JPM juan* 14)

(2)   After a sacrificial ceremony at the temple, delicacies and a set of miniature priest's apparel for Ximen's newly born son were delivered to his home in a large, tiered box. (see woodblock illustration *JPM juan* 39)

(3)   After Ximen's death and with the arrival of the Qingming Festival, his one remaining widow makes arrangements to visit his grave and make a sacrifice. She fills two large food boxes (*da shihe*) with incense, candles, paper money, the sacrificial foods of fish, pork and fowl, as well as wine and delicacies, all of which were shouldered on poles by servants. (*JPM juan* 89)

Tiered carrying boxes, similar to that illustrated here, are still in use in Shanxi province today. However, the use of willow should be specially noted. Because of its association with disruptive *yang* energies, the placement of the willow tree in the courtyard or the use of willow as a material is traditionally avoided in Shanxi. Nevertheless, because the activating *yang* principle has positive associations with funerary traditions, willow was used for various burial accessories. The willow carrying box illustrated here may well have been reserved for funerary rites such as the Qingming festival.

This large tiered box consists of a carrying frame and four tiered trays with a lid. The boxes rest upon two stretchers which span across the base frame and are contained within a gallery-like balustrade constructed on top of the frame. Vertical beaded pillars with lotus head finials form the corner posts for a series of framed and open-carved panels decorated with auspicious designs including peaches, pomegranates, flowers and other fruit. The long vertical side posts are tenoned to the base and are supported with standing spandrels carved as scrolling grass, as well as iron supports twisted like rope. The side posts are joined above with two horizontal stretchers which frame decorative struts and carved spandrels. A wrought iron ring for use with a carrying pole is attached to the midpoint of the upper stretcher with iron mounts; the mounted ring is additionally secured with an iron band that wraps around to the base where it is attached to the bottom of the frame. Twisted iron rings on each side also provide alternate lifting points. The corners of the trays are wrapped with protective iron attached with large boss head nails. The corners of the base are also protected with iron mounts.

三十四 · 大扛箱

柳木　十八世紀／十九世紀　山西
82公分 寬 x 54公分 深 x 93.5公分 高

明朝《魯班經》有類似的扛箱和提盒的記錄。雖然這些用具通常是用來提食物，可是其提梁及盒也可作不同的組合和用來運送不同的東西。在《金瓶梅》的幾個章回，展示了它多種用途：

1. 當李瓶兒請西門慶用以六十錠大元寶為她丈夫去賄賂一官員時，西門慶差遣小廝將六十錠大元寶裝在兩架食盒先抬到他家，避免引起鄰舍街坊的懷疑。〔見木版插圖，《金瓶梅》第十四章〕

2. 西門慶在玉皇廟為小兒打醮，到了午朝拜表結束之後，吳道官差小童將齋菜佳餚羹果插卓禮和一套給西門慶小兒的小道冠髻、道衣、小襯衣、小襪和小履鞋裝入八抬盒擔，送去西門慶家。〔見木版插圖，《金瓶梅》第三十九章〕

3. 西門慶死後的清明節，寡婦吳月娘準備了香燭金錢冥幣，三牲祭物酒肴之類裝了兩大食盒，由兩小廝以一扁擔挑了去掃墓。〔《金瓶梅》第八十九章〕

今天，山西省仍使用如上所述之扛箱。

然而，有關柳木的用途在這裡還有必要着重提一下，因為柳樹被認為是會破壞陽氣，所以在山西地區習慣上是避免在庭院栽柳樹，或者使用柳木質器具。但另一方面，柳木的這種特性和傳統的喪葬習俗相適應，因此，它經常被用作喪葬用具。如圖所示的這件柳木箱，就很可能是用來保存那些在清明節時所使用的器具。

這件大扛箱包括一個提梁及盒四撞外加盒蓋。盒落在邊框中有兩根的底座槽內，底座的周圍安有圍欄式裝飾。圍欄的蓮花頭形柱立在四周，欄圍安有透雕包括桃子、石榴、花、果實等等的吉祥紋樣板。立柱以榫與底座攢接有刻成卷草紋的站牙抵夾，並有扭繩狀的鐵條支撐。立柱上端安有橫梁和橫根，梁根之間有矮老，兩端安有雕刻的端牙板。橫梁的中間有鐵托架上安鍛鐵環以穿扛箱的棍子；鐵環由一圍在四周直達底座與底座邊框相接的鐵條加固。兩根立柱的扭繩狀鐵環提供了又一扛箱點。盒的四角有釘上大圓釘的鐵護片保護。底座四角也有鐵護片保護。

35.
Window Lattice Panel with Stylised Floral Pattern (Pair)

Baimu (Cypress) Frame and Hetaomu (Walnut) Lattice   17th/18th Century   Suzhou
75 cm (w) x 141 cm (h)

Lattice window panels are often moulded and/or carved on one side, and left flat without carving on the back to facilitate the attachment of semi-transparent protective paper or cloth. Similar panels of wood or glazed porcelain tile decorated on both sides were often used as ornamental openings alone, walls within garden walkways.

These relatively large lattice panels – decorated with a wave and flower motif are composed of exceptionally thick members. The lattice work is composed of a repeating pattern with four S-shaped members tenoned to a central four-petal persimmon. Both sides of the lattice work are shaped with carving. The S-shaped wave sections are convexly shaped with beading raised along the edges, while the large petals are concavely shaped and highlighted with incised beading; the centre of each is carved in relief emphasising the calyx, and interpreted in different ways.

三十五.
花格窗〔一對〕

柏樹框和核桃木花格　十七世紀／十八世紀　蘇州

75公分 寬 x 141公分 高

通常櫺格窗板只在一面起線或雕刻，背面則不雕刻，以便糊上具保護作用的棉紙或布。花園的廊經常使用兩面皆有裝飾的木製或上釉瓷磚格板。

這些有波浪和花朵雕飾較大的櫺格板是由厚的邊框組成。櫺格是由重複四根S型短材攢接一朵四瓣柿子之紋樣做成。格板的兩面皆有雕刻。沿著S型短材起有線腳，大的四片柿子瓣沿也起線腳，但是花瓣稍具立體。四片瓣中刻有浮雕，以不同的方式特出了花萼的樣式。

36

18th/19th century   *Left: Huamu (Burl)   12.5 cm (diameter) x 19.2 cm (h)*
Centre: Baimu (Cypress)   20.6 cm (diameter) x 21 cm (h)
Right: Huanghuali   21.5 cm (diameter) x 19.2 cm (h)

Three Brush Pots

Brush pots were a desk top accessory in which brushes, fly whisks, *ruyi* sceptres and other miscellaneous items were placed. They were produced in various sizes, shapes and decorative styles ranging from plain cylindrical surfaces to elaborate carved detail. Because some woods reveal highly figured imagery in their smooth-polished tangential surfaces, it was generally considered unnecessary to further embellish them with carving. Those with less interesting imagery were sometimes carved with lines of calligraphy, or more finely carved with landscapes and figures, or carved to imitate a gnarled branch.

The foliate shape of the *huanghuali* brush pot is more difficult to achieve than the simple cylindrical forms which were turned on a wood lathe; the undulating surface also further enhances the dramatic imagery of the heavily striated material. While cypress is a wood with little grain, here the unusual light colour of the wood gives it special appeal; the strongly waisted form of the one illustrated also adds further visual interest. Burls, one of nature's unexplained curiosities, have fascinated man since ancient times; the burl brush pot here is patterned with the many small bud formations and clusters of round curls that are typical of its aberrant growth and irregular cell division.

三十六．

筆筒〔三件〕

十八世紀／十九世紀
左：樺木　直徑12.5公分，高19.2公分
中：柏木　直徑20.6公分，高21公分
右：黃花梨　直徑21.5公分，高19.2公分

筆筒屬案頭擺設，供插放毛筆、塵拂、如意和其他雜物用。筆筒大小、造型及紋飾豐富多姿，由光素無紋的圓筒形以至精雕細琢的設計，式式俱備。有些素面的木製筆筒打磨光滑，斜切面令紋理瑰麗如畫，無須添加雕飾已優美動人。紋理較遜者或刻有題字，或細雕山水人物，或仿雕成癭木模樣。

黃花梨筆筒形如花瓣，製作過程較複雜，並非如圓筒形般在車床上旋製。起伏的花瓣，令密佈的條絲狀紋理更富變化。柏木紋理不顯，此柏木筆筒色澤雅淡，另有一番韻味，束腰造型更覺別緻。花木來自樹木的癭瘤，自古以來，人們都被這難以解釋的自然界現象深深地吸引著。此花木筆筒滿佈芽粒和叢狀螺旋紋，是樹木細胞不規則畸變造成的特有型態。

Stationary Tray with Drawers

37.

Hongmu (Redwood/Blackwood) and Huamu (Burl)   *18th/19th century*

38 cm (w) x 29 (cm) d x 6.5 cm (h)

Trays have existed since antiquity in a variety of forms and materials. Both rectangular and octagonal "serving trays" (*tuopan*) and "tea trays" (*chapan*) are recorded in the late Ming carpenter's manual *Lu Ban jing*. (Ruitenbeek II: 87) Those with inlaid panels decorated as "double six" game boards may well have served multiple functions. (cf. Wang and Evarts: 190) "Stationary trays" are associated with the literati brush-and-ink tradition. They were used on the painting table to contain neatly brushes, small scrolls, ink sticks, water droppers, inkstones and so on. Serving as small portable desks, they could also be easily carried around for convenience. Such trays were often produced in refined materials including those of inlaid lacquer and fine hardwoods with decorative stone (cf. Ellsworth: 228) and burl panels.

This stationary tray is constructed with a panel of decorative burlwood set in a smoothly rounded frame of *hongmu*. A compartment below houses two shallow drawers whose faces are inlaid with burlwood veneer, and whose size is suitable for holding small brushes and ink sticks. Rather ingeniously hidden behind the two "pull-less" drawers is a hinged pivot arm; as either drawer is pressed slightly inward, the pivot arm correspondingly pushes the other outward so that it may be pulled fully open. This clever internal mechanism works admirably to preserve the overall sleek exterior impression of the tray.

三十七·

雙屜都承盤

紅木、樺木　十八世紀／十九世紀

38公分 寬 x 29公分 深 x 6.5公分 高

盤子有極悠久的歷史，造型和物料豐富多姿。據明末木工手冊《魯班經》（Ruitenbeek II：87）所載，有方形和八角形的托盤和茶盤。嵌有雙陸棋盤的盤子既可盛物，亦可作奕棋之用。（比較 Wang 和 Evarts：190）都承盤屬文房用品，可置於畫桌上，盤內放著毛筆、手卷、墨條、水滴、墨硯等。興之所至，亦可攜帶到他處或戶外作小几用。這類盤子大多用料考究，有嵌花漆盤，亦有用優質硬木製造，內嵌花紋石片（比較 Ellsworth：228）或花木片。

這件都承盤以紅木為框，線條圓暢流麗，盤心嵌花木片，底下有一雙淺屜，屜面鑲花木片作飾。從盤子的大小看來，適合擺放小支的毛筆及墨條等物。抽屜無拉手，但後方卻暗藏支臂，設計非常巧妙，將其中一個抽屜向內輕推時，支臂會將另一抽屜稍微彈出，以便拉開抽屜。裝置了這個機關，可省卻拉手，令都承盤更具線條美。

List of Woods
木料詞彙

Chinese Precious Hardwoods
中國貴重木材

Pinyin Name 拼音名稱	English name or nearest approximation 英文名稱／近似名稱	Chinese Name 中文名稱
huanghuali	yellow flower pear wood	黃花梨
huali	flower pear wood	花梨
hongmu	redwood (blackwood)	紅木
jichimu	chicken wing wood	雞翅木
tielimu		鐵力木
wumu	ebony	烏木
zitan	purple sandalwood	紫檀

Other Chinese Woods
中國雜木材

baimu	cypress	柏木
qiumu	similar to catalpa	楸木
duanmu	linden	椴木
fengmu	maple	楓木
hetaomu	walnut	合桃木
huamu	burlwood	樺木
huaimu	similar to locust	槐木
huangyanmu	boxwood	黃楊木
jumu	southern elm wood	櫸木
liumu	willow	柳木
longyanmu	longan	龍眼木
nanmu	similar to cedarwood	楠木
sangmu	mulberry	桑木
shanmu	spruce	杉木
songmu	pine	松木
yumu	northern elm wood	榆木
zhajingmu/zhazhenmu		柞榅木／柞針木
zhangmu	camphor	樟木
ziyumu	purple elm wood	紫榆木
zuomu/xiangmu	oak	柞木／橡木

Map of Sites
相關地方位置圖

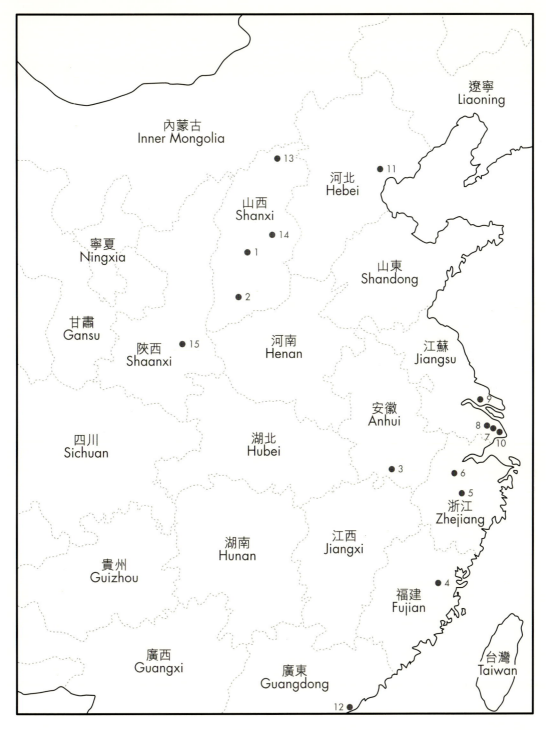

遼寧
Liaoning

內蒙古
Inner Mongolia

河北
Hebei

●13

●11

山西
Shanxi

●14

●1

山東
Shandong

寧夏
Ningxia

●2

甘肅
Gansu

陝西
Shaanxi
●15

河南
Henan

江蘇
Jiangsu

●9

●8
●7 ●10

四川
Sichuan

湖北
Hubei

安徽
Anhui

●3

●6
●5

浙江
Zhejiang

湖南
Hunan

江西
Jiangxi

貴州
Guizhou

福建
Fujian
●4

廣西
Guangxi

廣東
Guangdong
●12

台灣
Taiwan

1. Qixian 祁縣	5. Dongyang 東陽	9. Nantong 南通	13. Datong 大同
2. Dingcun 丁村	6. Longmen 龍門	10. Shanghai 上海	14. Wutaishan 五台山
3. Mingqingxian 黟縣	7. Zhouzhuang 周莊	11. Beijing 北京	15. Xian 西安
4. Yixian 闈清	8. Suzhou 蘇州	12. Guangzhou 廣州	

Chronology
年代簡表

舊石器時代	Paleolithic Period	約公元前170萬年前 – 約公元前1萬5千年前	c. 1700000 – 15000 years ago BC
新石器時代	Neolithic Period	約公元前1萬4千年前 – 約公元前21世紀	c. 14000 years ago – 21st c. BC
夏	Xia	約公元前21世紀 – 約公元前16世紀	c. 21st c. – 16th c. BC
商	Shang	約公元前16世紀 – 約公元前11世紀	c. 16st c. – 11th c. BC
周	Zhou	約公元前11世紀 – 約公元前256	c. 11st c. – 256 BC
	西周 Western Zhou	約公元前11世紀 – 約公元前771	c. 11st c. – 771 BC
	東周 Eastern Zhou	公元前770 – 256	770 – 256 BC
	春秋 Spring and Autumn period	公元前770 – 476	770 – 476 BC
	戰國 Warring States period	公元前475 – 221	475 – 221 BC
秦	Qin	公元前221 – 206	221 – 206 BC
漢	Han	公元前206 – 公元220	206 BC – AD 220
	西漢 Western Han	公元前206 – 公元25	206 BC – AD 25
	東漢 Eastern Han	公元25 – 220	AD 25 – 220
三國	The Three Kingdoms	公元220 – 265	AD 220 – 265
	魏 Wei	公元220 – 265	AD 220 – 265
	蜀 Shu	公元221 – 263	AD 221 – 263
	吳 Wu	公元222 – 280	AD 222 – 280
西晉	Western Jin	公元265 – 316	AD 265 – 316
東晉	Eastern Jin	公元317 – 420	AD 317 – 420
南北朝	Northern and Southern Dynasties	公元420 – 589	AD 420 – 589
	南朝 Southern Dynasties	公元420 – 589	AD 420 – 589
	〔劉〕宋 (Liu) Song	公元420 – 479	AD 420 – 479
	齊 Qi	公元479 – 502	AD 25 – 502
	梁 Liang	公元502 – 557	AD 502 – 557
	陳 Chen	公元557 – 589	AD 557 – 589
	北朝 Northern Dynasties	公元386 – 581	AD 386 – 581
	北魏 Northern Wei	公元386 – 534	AD 386 – 534
	東魏 Eastern Wei	公元534 – 550	AD 534 – 550
	西魏 Western Wei	公元535 – 556	AD 535 – 556
	北齊 Northern Qi	公元550 – 577	AD 550 – 577
	北周 Northern Zhou	公元557 – 581	AD 557 – 581
隋	Sui	公元581 – 618	AD 557 – 581
唐	Tang	公元618 – 907	AD 557 – 581
五代	Five Dynasties	公元907 – 960	AD 557 – 581
遼	Liao	公元916 – 1125	AD 557 – 581

宋	Song	公元960 – 1279	AD 960 – 1279
	北宋 Northern Song	公元960 – 1127	AD 960 – 1127
	南宋 Southern Song	公元1127 – 1279	AD 1127 – 1279
金	Jin	公元1115 – 1279	AD 1115 – 1279
元	Yuan	公元1279 – 1368	AD 1279 – 1368
明	Ming	公元1368 – 1644	AD 1368 – 1644
	洪武 Hongwu	公元1368 – 98	AD 1368 – 98
	建文 Jianwen	公元1399 – 1402	AD 1399 – 1402
	永樂 Yongle	公元1403 – 24	AD 1403 – 24
	洪熙 Hongxi	公元1425	AD 1425
	宣德 Xuande	公元1426 – 35	AD 1426 – 35
	正統 Zhengtong	公元1436 – 49	AD 1436 – 49
	景泰 Jingtai	公元1450 – 57	AD 1450 – 57
	天順 Tianshun	公元1457 – 64	AD 1457 – 64
	成化 Chenghua	公元1465 – 87	AD 1465 – 87
	弘治 Hongzhi	公元1488 – 1505	AD 1488 – 1505
	正德 Zhengde	公元1506 – 21	AD 1506 – 21
	嘉靖 Jiajing	公元1522 – 66	AD 1522 – 66
	隆慶 Longqing	公元1567 – 72	AD 1567 – 72
	萬歷 Wanli	公元1573 – 1620	AD 1573 – 1620
	泰昌 Taichang	公元1620	AD 1620
	天啟 Tianqi	公元1621 – 27	AD 1621 – 27
	崇禎 Chongzhen	公元1628 – 44	AD 1628 – 44
清	Qing	公元1644 – 1911	AD 1644 – 1911
	順治 Shunzhi	公元1644 – 61	AD 1644 – 61
	康熙 Kangxi	公元1662 – 1722	AD 1662 – 1722
	雍正 Yongzheng	公元1723 – 35	AD 1723 – 35
	乾隆 Qianlong	公元1736 – 95	AD 1736 – 95
	嘉慶 Jiaqing	公元1796 – 1820	AD 1796 – 1820
	道光 Daoguang	公元1821 – 50	AD 1821 – 50
	咸豐 Xianfeng	公元1851 – 61	AD 1851 – 61
	同治 Tongzhi	公元1862 – 74	AD 1862 – 74
	光緒 Guangxu	公元1875 – 1908	AD 1875 – 1908
	宣統 Xuantong	公元1909 – 1911	AD 1909 – 1911

Biographies

作者簡介

JOHN KWANG-MING ANG

John Kwang-Ming Ang, the Director of Artasia, Fine Asian Antiques and Art Consultancy in Taipei, received his M.A. in Chinese art history at the University of Michigan. In the last few years, he has researched regional styles of Chinese furniture and has given well-received lectures on the subject in Hong Kong, Southeast Asia, and New York. In addition to his book *The Beauty of Huanghuali* and several articles on Chinese vernacular furniture, he has published numerous articles on other Chinese art topics.

CHEN ZENGBI

Chen Zengbi graduated from the Architecture Faculty of Tsinghua University, and was later a student of Ming furniture under Professor Yang Yaoxian. Formerly a Professor at the Central Academy of Arts and Handicrafts in Beijing, he is now Head of the China Ming Dynasty Furniture Society. A recognised authority on Chinese furniture, his major writings include studies of Song dynasty chairs, a discussion of a Five Dynasties *ta*, and the classifications and characteristics of Ming furniture. In addition to his academic pursuits, Professor Chen has designed furniture for such prestigious establishments as Beijing's Diaoyutai and Zhongnanhai.

CURTIS EVARTS

Curtis Evarts is a Chinese furniture consultant and freelance research scholar who has written widely on the subject of Chinese furniture. He previously held positions as curator of the Museum of Classical Chinese Furniture and was president of its Classical Chinese Furniture society. He now lives in Taipei, where he publishes and maintains the web-site "Classical Chinese Furniture" at http://www.chinese-furniture.com which serves as an informational resource centre for scholars, collectors, and general enthusiasts.

洪光明

台北亞世亞佳古美術與藝術顧問公司總監，美國密西根大學中國藝術史碩士。洪氏過去數年從事有關中國家具區域風格的研究，曾在香港、東南亞及美國等地作專題演講，反應熱烈。除出版《黃花梨家具之美》一書外，他還發表多篇有關中國民間家具與中國藝術的專論

陳增弼

肄業於清華大學建築系，後隨楊耀先教授研習明式家具。曾任北京中央工藝美術學院教授，現任中國明式家具學會會長，是中國家具研究方面的權威。陳氏主要著述包括《寧波宋椅研究》、《千年古榻》、《明式家具類型與特徵》等。除從事學術研究外，他還為北京釣魚台及中南海等設計家具。

柯愓思

中國家具顧問，以自由身從事學術研究，有關中國家具的著述甚豐。曾任中國古典家具博物館館長及該館中國古典家具學會會長。伊氏現居台北從事有關中國古典家具出版事務，設有網址：http://www.chinese-furniture.com，為學者、藏家及喜愛中國家具的人士提供有關資訊。

PUAY-PENG HO

Puay-peng Ho joined the Department of Architecture, The Chinese University of Hong Kong, in 1992. Now an Associate Professor and Head of the Graduate School's Division of Architecture, Dr. Ho received his degree in architecture at the University of Edinburgh. He later obtained a Ph.D. in art history from the school of Oriental and African Studies, University of London. His research interests focus on the history of Chinese architecture, sacred architecture, vernacular culture and the architectural environment. Puay-peng Ho has published several articles in international art journals, and has contributed entries on Chinese architectural history and bronzes to the *Macmillan Dictionary of Art*.

RONALD G. KNAPP

Ronald G. Knapp is now Professor and Chairman of the Department of Geography at the State University of New York at New Platz. An authority on rural architecture and cultural geography, he received his Ph.D. in geography from the University of Pittsburgh. Professor Knapp is the author or editor of nine books, including *China's Living Houses – Folk Beliefs, Symbols and Household Ornamentation* and *China's Old Dwellings*, to be published in 1998-99.

KENSON KWOK

Kenson Kwok is currently Director of the Asian Civilisations Museum in Singapore which opened its first wing in April 1997. He graduated from the University of Sydney with a Bachelor of Architecture (Hons) degree, and completed his Ph.D. in Environmental Psychology from University College, London. Dr. Kwok joined the National Heritage Board in 1992, and contributed to the success of exhibitions such as "Gilding the Phoenix: The Straits Chinese and their Jewellery" and "Alamkara: 5000 Years of India. Dr. Kwok is keenly interested in Chinese and South East Asian ceramics, and is a past President of the South East Asian Ceramic Society.

何培斌

一九九二年加入香港中文大學建築學系,現任該系副教授及研究院建築學部主任。何氏早年於愛丁堡大學修讀建築專業學位,後獲倫敦大學亞非學院藝術史博士學位。專事研究中國建築史、宗教建築、民俗文化及建築環境等。他曾於國際藝術雜誌發表多篇論文,並為《麥美倫藝術辭典》撰寫有關中國歷史建築及青銅器的條目。

那仲良

紐約州立大學地理學系教授及主席,是研究鄉土建築及文化地理的專家。納氏為匹茲堡大學地理學博士,共撰寫及編纂書籍九本,其中《中國居室-民間信仰、寓意及居室裝飾》和《中國的老房子》將於一九九八至九九年出版。

郭勤遜

新加坡亞洲文明博物館館長,該館第一期於一九九七年四月對外開放。郭氏獲澳洲悉尼大學建築學士學位,繼而負笈倫敦大學學院,獲環境心理學博士學位。一九九二年加入新加坡國家文物局,曾籌辦不少出色的展覽,展覽主題包括海峽華人及其首飾、印度文化藝術等。他對中國及東南亞陶瓷尤感興趣,曾任東南亞陶瓷學會會長。

TIAN JIAQING

Tian Jiaqing was born in Beijing, and graduated from Tianjin University in 1976. A dedicated scholar of Chinese culture, he is particularly interested in Ming and Qing furniture and has been active with the Association of Chinese Classical Furniture in Beijing since its inception in 1991. Tian Jiaqing has published widely in the field, with articles appearing in publications based in China, Hong Kong and the USA. His *Classic Chinese Furniture of the Qing Dynasty*, published in Chinese in 1995 and followed by an English edition in 1996, is the most authoritative and comprehensive book on the subject to date.

WANG SHIXIANG

Wang Shixiang is widely acknowledged as the foremost figure in the classical Chinese furniture field. Professor Wang received his undergraduate and graduate degrees from Yenching University before serving with The Society for Research in Chinese Architecture in the mid-1940s. Throughout his long and productive career he has served with distinction whether at the Palace Museum, Central Academy of Arts and Crafts, Institute of Research on Cultural Relics and Museums, or the Cultural Relics Bureau of the Ministry of Culture. Wang Shixiang's seminal study *Classic Chinese Furniture* and his masterful two-volume *Connoisseurship of Chinese Furniture*, in addition to his other publications and studies, have introduced the subject to a world-wide audience. Professor Wang is now retired and lives in Beijing.

WANG QIJUN

Wang Qijun studied art history at Nanjing's Art Academy and architecture at Chongqing's School of Architecture before receiving his Ph.D. in architectural history from Tsinghua University. Keenly interested in vernacular furniture in the living environment, he has contributed – the series Traditional Chinese Dwellings of Shanxi, *Traditional Chinese Dwellings of Sichuan*; and *Traditional Chinese Dwellings – Courtyards of Beijing*. Wang Qijun currently lives in Canada where is he is affiliated with the University of Toronto.

田家青

生於北京，一九七六年肄業於天津大學，酷愛研究中國文化，對明清家具興趣尤其濃厚。一九九一年北京中國古典家具研究會成立至今，他積極參與該會事務。田氏著作豐富，文章在中國、香港、美國等地多次發表。一九九五年出版《清代家具》一書，翌年英文版面世，是目前研究清代家具最權威和周詳的書籍。

王世襄

肄業於燕京大學，先後獲文學學士及碩士學位。四十年代中期加入中國營造學社為研究員，從事家具研究達半個世紀，是公認的中國古典家具研究先驅。王氏曾任職故宮博物館、中央工藝美術學院、文物博物館研究所，文化部文物局古文獻研究室等，成績斐然。著作不下數十萬言，其中《明式家具珍賞》一書及鉅著《明式家具研究》兩冊最為人稱譽，其著作與學術研究大大提高了中外人士對中國家具的興趣和認識。王氏現已退休，居於北京。

王其鈞

先後肄業於南京藝術學院及重慶建築工程學院，其後於清華大學攻讀建築歷史及理論，獲工學博士學位。王氏對民間家具與居室擺設興趣濃厚。著作包括《老房子 - 山西民居》、《老房子 - 四川民居》、《老房子 - 北京四合院》等一系列有關傳統民居的書籍。現旅居加拿大，在多倫多大學繼續其研究工作。

Caption Bibliography
參考書目

Berliner, Nancy. *Beyond the Screen: Chinese Furniture of the Sixteenth and Seventeenth Centuries.* Boston: Museum of Fine Arts, Boston, 1996.

Bruce, Grace Wu. "Examples of Classic Chinese Furniture: 1. A Folding Table." *Oriental Art*, Vol. XXVI: 4, Winter 1990/91: 178, 233–5.

Bruce, Grace Wu. (1991) *Dreams of the Chu Tan Chamber and the Romance with Huanghuali Wood: The Dr. S.Y. Yip Collection of Classic Chinese Furniture.* Hong Kong: New Island Printing Co. Ltd., 1991.

Bruce, Grace Wu. (1995) *Ming Furniture.* Hong Kong: Grace Wu Bruce, Co. Ltd., 1995.

Chen Zengbi. "A One-Thousand-Year-Old Daybed." *Journal of the Classical Chinese Furniture Society* Autumn, 1994: 24–8.
【陳增弼：＜一件一千年歷史的榻＞，《中國古典家具協會會刊》，4：4（1994年秋季號）：24-8】

China Art. *Antiques in the Raw.* Hong Kong: China Art, 1997.
【《歲月中的家具》，香港：華藝，1997年】

Clunas, Craig. *Chinese Furniture.* London: Bamboo Publishing Ltd., 1988.

Christie's. *The Mr. and Mrs. Robert P. Piccus Collection of Fine Classical Chinese Furniture.* September 18, 1997 New York: Christie's, 1997.

Cui Yongxue. *Zhongguo jiaju shi – zuoju bian* [The History of Chinese Furniture – Seating Furniture]. Taipei: Ming Wen shuju, 1987.
【崔詠雪：《中國家具史‧坐具篇》，臺北：明文書局，1997年】

Ellsworth, Robert Hatfield. *Chinese Furniture: One Hundred Examples from the Mimi and Raymond Hung Collection.* New York, 1996.

Evarts, Curtis. (Win 90) "Integrity and Joinery in Chinese Furniture." *Journal of the Classical Chinese Furniture Society* Winter, 1990: 11–13.

Evarts, Curtis. (Win 93) "The 'Classic of Lu Ban' and Classical Chinese Furniture." *Journal of the Classical Chinese Furniture Society* Winter, 1993: 33–44.

Gao Lian. *Zunsheng bajian* [Eight Discourses on the Art of Living]. Ming text, National Central Library, Taipei.
【明‧高廉：《遵生八牋》，臺北：國家圖書館】

Guo Xi. *Linquan gaozhi* [The Lofty Message of Forests and Streams]. Yishu congbian ed., vol. 10, no. 67. Taipei: World Publishing Co., 1967.
【郭熙：《林泉高致》，《藝術叢編》10卷，67期，臺北：世界出版社，1967年】

Handler, Sarah. (Sum 92) "On a New World Arose the Kang Table." *Journal of the Classical Chinese Furniture Society* Summer, 1992: 22–47.

Handler, Sarah. (Spr 93) "A Yokeback Chair for Sitting Tall." *Journal of the Classical Chinese Furniture Society* Spring, 1993: 4-23.

Handler, Sarah. (Aut 94) "Square Tables Where Immortals Dine." *Journal of the Classical Chinese Furniture Society* Autumn, 1994: 4–23.

Jin Ping Mei. Beijing: Wenxue guji kanxingshe, 1957.
【《金瓶梅》，北京：文學古蹟刊行社，1957年】

Keppel, Sheila. "The Well-Furnished Tomb, Part 1." *Journal of the Classical Chinese Furniture Society* Summer, 1992: 13–21.

Excavation Report of Han tombs at Mancheng, 2 volumes, Beijing: Wenwu chubanshe, 1980.
【《滿城漢墓發掘報告》，2卷，北京：文物出版社，1980年】

Min Chiu. *In Pursuit of Antiquities.* Hong Kong: Hong Kong Museum of Art, 1995.
【《好古敏求—敏求精舍35週年紀念展》，香港：香港藝術館，1995年】

Nan Song ming huace. Beijing: Wenwu chubanshe, 1981.
【《南宋名畫冊》，北京：文物出版社，1979】

National Heritage Board. *Asian Civilisations Museum; The Chinese Collections.* Singapore, 1997.

Piccus, Robert P. "Review of 'Best of the Best' – An Exhibition of Ming Furniture from Private Collections'" *Orientations* February, 1995: 70.

Ruitenbeek, Klaas. *Carpentry and Building in Late Imperial China; A Study of the Fifteenth-Century Carpenters Manual Lu Ban jing.* Leiden: E.J. Brill, 1993.

Suzhou bowuguan huaji. Beijing: Wenwu chubanshe, 1981.
【《蘇州博物館畫集》，北京：文物出版社，1981】

Suzhou shi bowuguan. "Suzhou huqiu Wang Xijie mu qinli jilue." *Wenwu* 1975,3: 51–6.
【《蘇州虎丘王錫爵墓清理紀略》，第三期，蘇州：蘇州博物館，1975年，頁51–56】

Tian Jiaqing. *Classical Chinese Furniture of the Qing Dynasty.* London and Hong Kong: Philip Wilson Publishers and Joint Publishing Co. Ltd., 1996.
【田家青：《清代家具》，香港：三聯書店，1996年】

Tu Long. *Qiju qiwu jian.* Meishu congshu 2:9. Jiangsu, 1986.
【屠隆：《起居器服箋》，《美術叢書》，二集，第九輯，江蘇：1986年】

Wang Shixiang. (1986) *Classic Chinese Furniture: Ming and Early Qing Dynasties.* Translated by Sarah Handler and the author. Hong Kong: Joint Publishing Company, 1986.
【王世襄：《明式家具珍賞》，香港：三聯書店、文物出版社】

Wang Shixiang. (1990) *Connoisseurship of Chinese Furniture.* 2 vols. Hong Kong: Joint Publishing Co. Ltd., 1990.
【王世襄：《明式家具研究》，兩冊，香港：三聯書店，1990年】

Wang Shixiang. (1992) "Additional Examples of Classical Chinese Furniture." *Orientations* January, 1992: 40–50.

Wang Shixiang. (1993) "A Supplement to the Examples of Ming Style Furniture." *Palace Museum Journal* 1, 1993: 46–7
【王世襄：〈明式家具實例增補〉，《故宮博物院院刊》，第1期，1993：46–47】

Wang Shixiang and Curtis Evarts. *Masterpieces from the Museum of Classical Chinese Furniture.* San Francisco: Tenth Union, 1995.

Wen Zhenheng. *Zhangwu zhi* [The Treatise on Superfluous Things] compiled 1615–20. Yishu congbian 29. 257.
【文震亨：《長物志》，《藝術叢編》，廿九卷，頁257】

Zhu Jiajin and Wang Shixiang. *Zhongguo meishu guanji. Gongyi meishu bian.*
【朱家溍、王世襄：《中國美術全集·工藝美術編》，北京：中國建築工業出版社】

Zhu Jiajn 1. "Yongzheng nian de jiaju zhizuo kao" [A Study of the Yongzheng Imperial Furniture Workshops, part 1] *Gugong bowuyaun yuankan* [Palace Museum Journal] 1985, 3: 104–11.
【朱家溍：〈雍正年代家具製造考〉，《故宮博物院院刊》，第三期，1985年，頁104–111】

Index
索引

Numbers in bold type refer to plate captions.